AUDIO DRAMA

Alain Baczkowski
Aus/78

Neville Teller was born in London, read Modern History at Oxford University, and then had a varied career in advertising, marketing, general management, publishing, the Civil Service and a national cancer charity. At the same time he was consistently writing for BBC radio as dramatist and abridger. He has more than 50 BBC radio dramatizations to his credit. Latterly, as guest playwright for an American independent radio production company, Shoestring Radio Theatre, his work is being heard by radio and on-line across the United States. In the Queen's Birthday Honours in 2006 he was awarded an MBE "for services to broadcasting and to drama".

AUDIO DRAMA

10 PLAYS FOR
RADIO AND PODCAST

Neville Teller

Matador
9 Priory Business Park,
Wistow Road, Kibworth Beauchamp,
Leicestershire. LE8 0RX
Tel: 0116 279 2299
Email: books@troubador.co.uk
Web: www.troubador.co.uk/matador
Twitter: @matadorbooks

ISBN 978 1789017 878

British Library Cataloguing in Publication Data.
A catalogue record for this book is available from the British Library.

Printed and bound by CPI Group (UK) Ltd, Croydon, CR0 4YY
Typeset in 11pt Adobe Jenson Pro by Troubador Publishing Ltd, Leicester, UK

Matador is an imprint of Troubador Publishing Ltd

*For Sheila
and the family*

CONTENTS

FOREWORD

Britain leads the world in radio drama. The most cursory glance at *Radio Times* reveals the extensive range and vast quantity of drama broadcast by BBC Radios 3, 4 and 4 Extra – an output totalling scores of thousands of hours each year. The radio drama output of the BBC reflects its popularity with the listening audience – a popularity that, despite every sort of alternative media distraction, continues to grow.

Not so many years ago, in order to catch a radio play you had to switch on your radio when the programme was actually scheduled for broadcast, and select the right channel. These days almost the whole of the BBC's radio output, as well as more than 80,000 hours of its radio archive, is available to stream or download from the new BBC Sounds at any time convenient to the listener, to be heard on a mobile, a tablet, a PC or a digital receiver.

In fact, the internet, by way of WiFi and 3 or 4G, provides access to a vast range of podcasts, including audio drama, from across the world. Increasing numbers of specialist radio drama providers are making available downloads and podcasts for a mushrooming audience eager to listen. That audience is growing so fast that the BBC itself is busily engaged in carving out its own chunk of the expanding market. The BBC iPlayer is turning itself into a great download and podcast engine, while separately BBC Archive on 4 allows listeners to wander through a treasure house of past radio programmes and listen to them on-line.

Audio culture is booming world-wide. Johanna Zorn, executive director of Third Coast, a Chicago-based audio podcast hub, has said that audio storytelling in the US "is in a wild west moment", expanding beyond all measure. "There were these once-dead hours," she said, "where you were driving or in the kitchen, and now people are filling them, listening to audio stories, fiction or non-fiction."

To feed these rapidly increasing audiences, US producers have been building up podcast networks like Radiotopia and Serendipidity, which advertises itself as "radio drama for the 21st century". It operates through the Acast platform, which connects listeners, podcast creators and advertisers in an integrated, one-stop shop. Serendipity, launched a few years back by New York radio producer, Ann Heppermann, is linked to The Sarah Awards, a US audio award scheme which celebrates and rewards the best audio fiction from around the world.

In Britain too there is a podcast competition. Established in 2017, the British Podcast Awards (BPA) welcomes all podcast makers, big and small, to enter their productions. BPA asserts that it exists to highlight the work of podcast producers, promote podcasts and expand audiences for them, and provide space for producers, presenters, sponsors, platforms, writers and performers "to have fun."

This book has been conceived with the idea of providing any podcast producers especially interested in audio drama with material to use in creating audio productions. It has an equally important purpose, namely to give those many thousands of keen listeners to radio drama the opportunity of creating audio dramas for themselves, by reading well-loved stories dramatized and adapted for radio.

I have spent more than 35 years as a radio dramatist and abridger, both for BBC radio and for Shoestring Radio Theatre, an American radio production company whose output is syndicated and broadcast across the States. Although I have certainly written a fair number of original scripts in my time, my specialty has been adapting the literary works of others for performance at the microphone.

What is so special, and so different, about audio drama? Its unique quality is that it builds a private and exclusive picture in the mind of each separate member of its audience. Through a combination of aural elements – dialogue, sound effects, music, technical devices – radio drama becomes a personal experience, individual and different, for each person listening. How you envisage the heroine will certainly not be as someone else envisages her. Where you place characters in a confrontation, and how you picture them in your mind's eye, will be your vision. Someone else's will be different. This is its fascination.

These characteristics mean that a radio drama script looks nothing like a play, film or TV script. An audio production has nothing visual to show you, and the script reflects this. A stage play is more-or-less restricted to the time and place of what is being enacted. Film and TV productions put before you what the director wants you to see. Radio faces no such restrictions. It is free of time, place, persons. In a radio play you can have animals or even inanimate objects converse, you can be whisked from England to Spain, from earth to Mars, from the top of mount Everest to the deepest coal mine, in an instant. All the action takes place in the mind.

It is perhaps an unfortunate fact that, except for one or two basic rules, there is no universally agreed methodology for crafting a radio drama script, or even an agreed format in which to present it. Examine the scores of sample scripts on the BBC's Writer's Room website, and you will find a host of different presentations. Search "audio drama" on the internet, and dozens of suggested templates are thrown up.

Writers trying their hand at a radio play for the first time often find it difficult to think aurally. They will include directions such as "SFX: *John gets off the train, folding bicycle in one hand and suitcase lugged behind,*" or "SFX: *John gets out of the car and gets his stuff from the boot*" (SFX, or FX is short for sound effects). To be meaningful on the air, such actions would need to be conveyed by the dialogue and interpreted aurally by the studio manager. Sometimes radio drama scripts are peppered with technical directions to the actors or to the studio manager such as "off MIC" (MIC is short for microphone) or "SFX gunshot". I avoid technical directions like the plague.

Over the many years that I have been writing radio dramas I have evolved my own philosophy on these matters, which the reader will find exemplified in the following pages. Quite simply, I write my scripts from the standpoint of the listener. What I put down on paper is what I envisage emerging from the loudspeaker. All my scripts are written with the sole intention of conveying to the producer, the actors and the studio technicians what I want the listener to hear.

In an indented paragraph set in the script I provide the non-verbal audio material which is for the studio manager to provide, such as sound effects, music, electronic effects like the telephone, fading in and out, etc. Adjacent to, or within, each character's speech appear, when necessary, simple directions about positioning or moving in respect of the microphone (such as "remote, advancing" or "close"). How to carry out these directions will usually be conveyed to the actor by the producer or the studio manager.

As for directions on character interpretation or speech delivery, I keep those to the barest minimum. I provide character notes at the front of each script, usually concentrating on the age and accent of the character concerned – ie how they should sound. I elaborate on these notes only in cases of complex characterization or plot (such as "The Turn of the Screw" by Henry James, which is included in this collection). In general I regard characterization and interpretation as matters for the producer, not the writer. It is only rarely, and for a very good reason, that I indicate how I think a line should be delivered.

To write radio drama, therefore, it is necessary to be fully aware of how to paint a sound picture through the audio medium, and then how to express it on the page. Take a very simple example. When John enters a large drawing-room in a stately home, the directions provided would depend on whether the drama requires the listener to be with John, or with Jane who is already in the room.

In the former case, the technical paragraph would read: "Door opens (this is for the studio manager or his assistant to do)." John is on-microphone. Jane would be "remote". Like this:

(DOOR OPENS)

JOHN: Hullo, Jane. I made it.

JANE: *(remote, calling)* Hi, there. Good to see you.

Jane should be positioned to the side of the microphone, or "off-mike", so that the correct sound picture is conveyed to the listener.

If the drama has placed us with Jane, though, the technical instruction would be quite different, to allow a different sound picture to emerge. Like this:

(REMOTE – DOOR OPENS)

JOHN: *(remote, advancing, calls)* Hullo, Jane. I made it.

JANE: Hi there. Good to see you.

In short, my rule of thumb is "Think loudspeaker, think headphones."

A radio play goes through a number of stages before copies of the final production script are handed out to the cast for the first read-through. Here is where the few basic rules do apply. That script will have been broken down into separate scenes. Each page of the script will be numbered, and on each page the speeches will also be individually numbered, starting with 1. Thus during rehearsal, and later during post-production, it is simple to identify any part of the script as "page 47, speech 5" or whatever. ("The Archers" producers, for their own reasons, have devised a version of this with every single line on each page individually numbered).

But much earlier in the dramatization process I will have produced a script that reads seamlessly, creating in the mind's ear precisely how the final product, the radio play, should sound as it emerges from the loudspeaker or though the headphones. And it is in that version that I present the ten radio dramas contained in this book. The scripts in this form will, I trust, offer individual readers the best opportunity of creating their own audio drama in the mind. At the same time, I believe that in this form they best provide podcast producers with material on which to exercise their audio skills and talents.

I hope these audio dramas provide consumers and producers alike with as much pleasure as I have had in writing them.

NOTES FOR AUDIO PRODUCERS

The ten audio dramas in this collection offer rich fare for modern audio- and podcast-seasoned listeners. They were selected with the idea of providing producers with the widest range of opportunities to deploy imaginative audio techniques in recreating the plays in new productions. Here are a few thoughts on each.

ALADDIN AND THE WONDERFUL LAMP

This is a tale full of sorcerers, black magic and genies. Characters, and even palaces, are whisked from place to place. All of this needs to be created aurally, so that the mind is left dazzled. Realizing an audio version of this tale of wonder offers the chance of using the sound palette to the full.

THE LOOKING GLASS

Edith Wharton, a towering literary figure in America over the turn of the twentieth century, had a special feeling for ghost stories. Her supernatural was never explicit. She hinted at it – which makes her tales all the more intriguing. "The Looking Glass" needs to capture that eeriness. At the end, we need to be left wondering. Has there been communication with the dead? Or not?

THE MAN THAT CORRUPTED HADLEYBURG

This tale by Mark Twain is a tilt at hypocrisy. It shows moral rectitude being undermined by greed. The audio drama interweaves narration with action in a series of fast-moving scenes which allow the producer to build tension to an unexpected climax.

OZMA OF OZ

This is one of Frank Baum's sequels to his "The Wizard of Oz" and, like the original, is full of talking animals, bizarre characters and extraordinary adventures. The opportunities for imaginative audio invention and innovation are enormous. Dorothy and her faithful companion, the hen Billina, endure a storm at sea, a shipwreck, a long journey full of hazards, an encounter with a monarch who lives underground, and much else.

THE PROBLEM OF CELL 13

This tale by Jacques Futrelle is considered among the dozen best detective stories ever written. It features his iconic character, the Thinking Machine, who maintains that nothing is impossible if one only applies one's mind properly. So he undertakes to escape from a prison cell within one week. Keep the listener guessing, and ratchet up the tension. There's a good denouement.

BOX AND COX

This is a real piece of fun – basically a swiftly-moving two-hander, with the speeches shunted to and fro like a tennis ball in a fast-moving match. The original play by J M Morton was used by Sir Arthur Sullivan for his comic opera, which he renamed "Cox and Box".

THE TURN OF THE SCREW

The novel by Henry James presents the reader with one of the great enigmas of modern literature, and the basic situation is ideal for the audio medium to explore and optimize. Do the ghosts that the main protagonist, the unnamed governess, sees and describes really exist – or is everything she perceives a mere figment of her over-heated imagination? An imaginative audio production can draw the listener into the horror story as fully as the written word – and perhaps even more vividly.

THE GHOST SHIP

This audio drama is based on a short story by Sir Arthur Conan Doyle about the *Mary Celeste*, a sailing vessel discovered floating on an empty sea without a person on board. Set in the 1870s, this drama offers ample opportunity for a colourful interpretation of a rattling good adventure yarn, while also providing a reflection of the causes of the American civil war, and the then-hot topic of the abolition of slavery in the United States.

THE FOUR JUST MEN

This was Edgar Wallace's first crime thriller, and what a debut! It was a huge popular success in its day, not least because the newspaper that Wallace was working for agreed to offer a cash prize to anyone guessing how the murder of a Cabinet Minister was carried out in a locked room. This is the only script in this collection in which I provide a list of internet-available music and sound effects – in particular the chimes of Big Ben as the deadline set by the Four Just Men draws to a close.

THE DAMNED THING

An early science fiction story by American author, Ambrose Bierce. The audio dramatization gives ample opportunity for weird and wonderful evocations of an invisible, but deadly, beast which stalks one of the characters and eventually mauls him and tears his arm from his body. How the chief coroner of the town knows about it, and why he hushes it up, provide the background.

ALADDIN AND THE WONDERFUL LAMP

A PLAY FOR RADIO
BY NEVILLE TELLER

Running time: 45'

FIRST BROADCAST IN THE
BBC WORLD SERVICE ON 17 MAY 2003

CHARACTERS IN
ORDER OF APPEARANCE

RASHID   *Young Arab male – about mid-20s. Trace of accent only.*

SAVITA   *Young Indian woman – mid-20s. Trace of accent only.*

SORCERER   *Middle-aged. Smarmy, oily, oozing evil intent.*

SATAN   *(One speech). The voice of the devil – some echo, hoarse, fiendish*

GENIE 1   *'The Genie Of The Ring' – Mid-50s. School-masterish. Rather pedantic.*

ALADDIN   *Late teens. He matures as the play progresses. 'One of the boys' at the start, immature, rather foolish. A romantic lead by the end.*

MOTHER   *Late-50s/early-60s. Care-worn hard-working decent respectable widow woman.*

GENIE 2   *'The Genie Of The Lamp' – Deep brown vibrating voice, portraying a huge African spirit. Genial enough, though.*

SULTAN   *Mid-50s. Supreme ruler of the land. His every word is law. Aware of his powers, but human as well. A loving father, and not unreasonable.*

GRAND VIZIER   *60s. The politician personified, and not a little corrupt as well. Always ready with the smooth explanation, but plotting like fury beneath it all for his own ends.*

PRINCESS   *18, no more. A sweet girl who, like Juliet, finds her true lover. But she's no dishcloth – the girl has character.*

HERALD   *(One speech).*

(MUSIC. DOWN FOR OPENING ANNOUNCEMENT. UP MUSIC. FADE BENEATH FOLLOWING. SAVITA AND RASHID ARE SPRAWLED ON A CLOUD. THEIR ACCOUSTIC MUST BE QUITE DISTINCT)

RASHID: Rather nice, perched up here on a cloud. What do you say, Savita?

SAVITA: You can certainly see something of the world.

RASHID: Like astronauts will be able to, one day…

SAVITA: …only much less traumatic. This cloud's like a feather mattress. I suppose *you'd* prefer to go hurtling round the globe every ninety minutes, Rashid?

RASHID: Only to know what it's like. No, I quite like lazing on all this fluff. What's that, down there? – you're the great one for geography.

SAVITA: Persia – at least, that's what it's called at present.

RASHID: H'mm. Everywhere looks peaceful enough.

SAVITA: Oh, no it isn't! Over there. To the west. Something nasty's brewing.

RASHID: You're right, Savita. Bad magic. I can almost smell it. Where *is* that?

SAVITA: Morocco, perhaps? Somewhere in Africa. And Rashid, you're not wrong. That Dervish is up to no good.

RASHID: He's a sorcerer. It's the black arts he's practising…

(MUSIC. FADE IN OPEN AIR. WIND RISES BENEATH SORCERER TO HOWLING GALE)

SORCERER: Show me, Master, where it is hidden. See, I have sacrificed a black ram. I have poured out the blood on your altar. I have burned the gizzard and the spleen. I have eaten the heart and the brains. I have fulfilled the ancient rites and obligations. Now, O Master, come forth! Come forth and tell me where it is hidden…

(GALE WHISTLES, CLAP OF THUNDER)

SATAN: Slave! You have presumed to call me forth to fulfil not my purposes, but your own. Since you have correctly undertaken the rituals, I am obliged to tell you what you ask. But you must pay for your presumption. You yourself may not take the great prize from its hiding place. That must be undertaken by another, and he must hand it to you of his own free will. If you lay hands on it yourself, in that instant you will surely perish. This chart will direct you to what you seek. And never dare summon me forth on such a frivolous errand again!

(CLAP OF THUNDER. WIND DIES DOWN. RUSTLE OF PARCHMENT AS SCROLL IS UNROLLED)

SORCERER: Let me see, let me see! Samarkand – the Golden Road. A journey of many weeks from Africa. But I think we can do better than that. (*chuckles*) Oh yes! Oh yes!

(ELECTRONIC WHOOSH! EFFECT)

GENIE 1: The Genie of the Ring is at your service, O master. Ask and it shall be done.

SORCERER: Transport me now, at once, to the place on this chart. Here, in Samarkand. By the Bibi Khanum mosque.

GENIE 1: Your wish is my command.

(WHOOSH EFFECT. CROSSFADE TO MUSIC. HOLD TO END. FULL UP CLOUD)

SAVITA: And there he is, Rashid! In the twinkling of an eye, right in the centre of the city…

RASHID: … in the middle of the bazaar. Market stalls lining both sides of the street, donkeys laden with silks and carpets…

SAVITA: …and boys playing in the gutter. But Rashid – our sorcerer's up to no good. Why would he draw one of the urchins away…

7

RASHID: …and give him gold? He's after information. Look how long he's talking to the boy. He's pumping him.

SAVITA: But what about?

RASHID: I can guess. Look who they're pointing to – young Aladdin. I think he's questioning the boy about Aladdin.

SAVITA: Poor Aladdin. So innocent. So unsuspecting. So gullible…

(FADE IN BUSY ARAB MARKET)

SORCERER: *(approaching)* Excuse me, young man.

ALADDIN: Eh? What?

SORCERER: I've no wish to interrupt your game of knuckles with your friends. But I must say – the family resemblance is remarkable. Remarkable!

ALADDIN: The family resemblance to who, sir?

SORCERER: To my brother, of course – your father.

ALADDIN: I don't quite…

SORCERER: Your name *is Aladdin*, isn't it?

ALADDIN: It is, sir.

SORCERER: I could have sworn it. Nephew! My dear departed brother's son! My brother, the tailor. Your father was a tailor, wasn't he?

ALADDIN: That's right. So you are…?

SORCERER: Your long lost uncle! And now that my brother's dead, I've come to find comfort in his only son. My dear boy!

ALADDIN: But my father never told me about you.

SORCERER: Too proud. You see, though my brother worked hard for his living, he remained poor all his life. Whereas I – I became a wealthy man, wealthy beyond your wildest dreams. Your father was too proud to ask me for help. He didn't want charity. And I respected him for that. But now that he's dead, and you and your mother are in need – well, that's a different story.

ALADDIN: Is it?

SORCERER: Oh, yes! See these gold coins.

(CHINK OF COINS)

ALADDIN: I do!

SORCERER: They're yours.

ALADDIN: What – all of them?

SORCERER:	Every one. Take them as a token of my good intentions. If you'll let me, Aladdin, I'll make a great man of you. Now, go home to your mother, and tell her I'll have the great honour of calling on her this very evening, when we can discuss your future.
ALADDIN:	*(retreating)* Oh, I will, uncle, I will. And thank you…

(EDGE OUT MARKET. FULL UP CLOUD)

SAVITA:	Not a suspicion in the world! Can't we warn him in some way?
RASHID:	You know we can't, Savita. We're allowed to observe – we must not interfere.
SAVITA:	And that poor woman – she's turning the house inside out. Scrubbing, cleaning, cooking – all for a wicked sorcerer who's out to deceive her and her son. I can scarcely bear to look.
RASHID:	Two, three hours – and here he comes, picking his way down the narrow alley, knocking at the modest door…

(DOOR OPENS. EXTERIOR)

MOTHER:	Welcome, my lord, welcome to our humble home.
SORCERER:	Not "my lord", sister-in-law. Call me brother.
MOTHER:	Brother!

SORCERER: It grieves me that I've returned too late to look upon the face of my own dear brother in this life. But I shall redeem my obligations to him. This I swear.

MOTHER: Enter, enter...

(DOOR CLOSES. INTERIOR)

Will you be seated? Will you share our modest meal with us?

SORCERER: Gladly. But first, let me tell you why I'm here. I've never known the comforts of a wife and family. But when I heard that my brother had died leaving a son, I thought 'let his boy be the son I never had'. I want to treat Aladdin as if he were my own. Tell me, Aladdin, do you know any art or trade?

MOTHER: Alas, my son knows nothing. He spends all his time as you found him – playing with riff-raff in the streets.

ALADDIN: Mother!

MOTHER: By now, he should be supporting me – but the boot's on the other foot.

SORCERER: Aladdin, would you like to be a merchant?

ALADDIN: Indeed I would, uncle.

SORCERER: Then I'll give you a shop and fill it with goods. You'll sell your merchandise, and buy more things with the money, and you'll make profits and grow wealthy.

MOTHER: Oh, brother, if you'd truly do this for my son, I could wish for nothing more for him. What a happy, happy chance brought you to Samarkand…

(CLOUD)

SAVITA: Poor, foolish woman.

RASHID: Doesn't she know that nothing is for nothing in this life?

SAVITA: And poor, innocent, gullible Aladdin. How delighted he is with all the clothes his new uncle is buying him.

RASHID: You see how the sorcerer pays without a moment's bargaining, no matter how outrageous the price? The gold coins pour from his pocket as if there were no end to them.

SAVITA: As indeed there isn't – for as you know, Rashid, the whole lot have been conjured into existence through black magic.

(ARAB MARKETPLACE)

ALADDIN: Oh, uncle, how can I thank you enough? You've dressed me like a wealthy merchant. When I open my shop for business, everyone will respect me. The customers will see that they're dealing with a man of substance. How can I ever repay you?

SORCERER: There *is* one small thing you can do for me, my dear boy.

(CLOUD)

RASHID: Here it comes!

SAVITA: Now we're getting at the truth…

(MARKETPLACE)

ALADDIN: Anything, dear uncle. Ask anything of me.

SORCERER: It's a small thing. If you come with me a little way out of the city, I'll show you. Come, Aladdin. *(retreating)* This is the road we must take…

(MUSIC – TO END. FADE IN COUNTRY)

SORCERER: This is the place. Let's rest here a while, and make a fire. Would you just gather those few sticks together…

ALADDIN: Willingly, uncle.

(STICKS)

SORCERER: And now, I have a way to make a fire which may surprise you. It's a method I learned some years ago, during my travels. Just watch. One, two…

(DULL BOOM! AND INSTANT CRACKLING OF WOOD)

And now, I sprinkle just a little of this powder on the flames… And… *(incantation)*
Abra-cadabra – flame and fire
Tear apart the funeral pyre!

(EXPLOSION. RUMBLE AS EARTH OPENS)

ALADDIN: Uncle! Save me! The earth – it's opening beneath our feet. *(running, retreating)* Save me!

SORCERER: *(running – striking Aladdin)* Stay! Stay where you are!

ALADDIN: Ow! Uncle, what have I done? Why hit me?

SORCERER: My dear boy, I'm so sorry. Please forgive me. I got carried away by the wonders I'm about to reveal to you. You see – there – where the earth has split asunder… that marble slab with the brass ring in its centre?

ALADDIN: Indeed I do, uncle.

SORCERER: Then do as I tell you, Aladdin, and you'll become richer than all the kings on this earth.

ALADDIN: What must I do?

SORCERER: Beyond that marble slab lies vast treasure – and only you can obtain it and live. So go forward, my son, take hold of the brass ring, lift up the slab.

ALADDIN: But I'll never be able to pull up that huge chunk of solid marble – never!

SORCERER: Grasp the ring, and repeat the names of as many of your ancestors as you can remember. Start with your father and mother and work backwards. Now, grab hold of the ring. Go on!

(MUSIC. FADE BENEATH FOLLOWING – HOLD UNDER. CLOUD)

RASHID: And up it comes! Out of the way – this cloud's blocking my view. What's under the slab, Savita?

SAVITA: Stone steps leading down, down, down into the earth.

RASHID: And the Dervish wants Aladdin to go down…?

SAVITA: He's none too keen, is he?

(CROSSFADE MUSIC TO EXTERIOR)

ALADDIN: No, uncle, no! Not down there – not into the bowels of the earth. I'm too young to go to my grave. Anything but that!

SORCERER: Don't be frightened, my son. See, I take this ring from my finger. Put it on. It'll protect you against all dangers – as it has always protected me. But I only lend it to you. You must return it when you come back with the treasure.

ALADDIN: Thank you, uncle. Yes, I feel different already. Now what do you want me to do?

SORCERER: Listen carefully, and obey my instructions to the letter – to the letter! Go down the stone steps that lie before you. A short passage will lead you to a cavern divided into four parts, each containing four gold vessels. Do not touch these under any circumstances – for if even the fringe of your robe comes into contact with them, you'll be turned instantly into stone. Go through the cavern, and you'll come to a door. Open this, and a beautiful garden will stretch before you. A pathway leads through the garden. Walk along it until you come to an alcove, above which a lamp is hanging. Take this lamp from its fastening, pour out the oil it contains, and place it in your robe above your heart. Then bring it to me. Is all this quite clear, Aladdin?

ALADDIN: Quite clear, uncle.

SORCERER: Then start your journey.

(MUSIC. DOWN AND HOLD UNDER FOLLOWING. CLOUD)

RASHID: Well, he's got as far as the garden. Why's he stopping?

SAVITA: He's looking up at the trees. Ah, I see. It's not fruit they bear, but jewels. Sparkling, glittering jewels.

RASHID: And he can't resist them. He's plucking them off as fast as he can. He's filling his pockets.

(ECHOING INTERIOR – MUSIC UNDER)

ALADDIN: These'll be great for playing knuckles with.

(CLOUD – MUSIC STILL UNDER)

RASHID: Now he's caught sight of the lamp. Yes, he's doing just as the sorcerer told him…

SAVITA: …and he's on his way back. But he's going slower and slower.

RASHID: It's all those jewels. He's weighed right down. Do you think he'll make it up the stairs?

SAVITA: He's starting up them. One… two… It's a bit of a struggle…

(UP MUSIC TO END. SORCERER IN OPEN AIR; ALADDIN IN ECHOING INTERIOR. WE'RE WITH ALADDIN)

SORCERER: *(calling)* What's keeping you, boy?

ALADDIN: *(panting – calling)* It's this stairway, uncle. It's so steep. I can't … get up it…

SORCERER: But the lamp. Do you have it?

ALADDIN: Oh yes. But these stairs… Give me your hand, uncle. Help me up the last bit.

(CLOUD)

SAVITA: Ah – but the wizard daren't do that. Remember, Rashid? Aladdin must hand the lamp to him *of his own free will.* If the sorcerer once helps the boy, he'll perish on the spot.

(AS BEFORE)

SORCERER: No, no. You can make it, Aladdin. It's the lamp that's weighing you down. Why don't you reach up and place it on this ledge? Come, you want to help me, don't you? You want to give me the lamp?

ALADDIN: *(obstinate)* You want that lamp more than you want me. If you won't give me a helping hand, then I won't give you the lamp.

SORCERER: *(enraged)* Then the devil take you, you ungrateful fool. If I'm not to get the lamp, then let it perish along with you. *(incantation)*
Abra-cadabra – death and doom
Close once more the magic tomb!

(SLAB CRASHES INTO PLACE – RUMBLE AS EARTH CLOSES. MUSIC. DOWN FOR:)

ALADDIN: *(over music)* Help! Help! Let me out! Don't leave me down here to die! He-elp!

(UP MUSIC TO END. CLOUD)

SAVITA: That poor boy! Sealed under ground with no hope of escape. How frightened he must be.

RASHID: But at least he knows the truth now. That sorcerer was no uncle, but a wicked wizard. He'd just used Aladdin to acquire something he couldn't get in any other way.

SAVITA: A lot of comfort that is to Aladdin! What can he do? What hope is there for him?

RASHID: Not much.

SAVITA: Oh, I don't know – I've had an idea. *(whispers)* Aladdin!… Aladdin!…

RASHID: You're interfering. You're breaking the rules.

SAVITA: I'm not – I'm just … thinking. If Aladdin happens to think the same thing, that's not my doing. *(whispers)* Aladdin – the ring! Think of the ring!

(THE CAVERN)

ALADDIN:	The ring! He said it would protect me from all harm, as it had protected him. I wonder. If I rub it like this…

(ELECTRONIC WHOOSH! EFFECT)

GENIE 1:	Hail master!
ALADDIN:	Good heavens! Who are you?
GENIE 1:	I am the genie of the Ring. Command, and I shall obey – for I am the servant of whoever bears the ring on his finger.
ALADDIN:	And can you give me whatever I ask for?
GENIE 1:	Anything within the circle of my powers – and that is very wide, I can assure you. Try me. What is it you want?
ALADDIN:	I want to be removed from this dungeon and returned to the open air.
GENIE 1:	Nothing simpler. Your word is my command!

(MAGIC EFFECT. OPEN AIR)

ALADDIN:	Genie – you're a genius! Now to make my way home.
GENIE 1:	And I'll return to *my* home – in the ring.

(WHOOSH EFFECT. MUSIC – TO END. FADE IN INTERIOR)

MOTHER: That man was always a bit too good to be true. You've had a lucky escape, Aladdin.

ALADDIN: Don't I know it! But all these adventures have made me hungry, mother. In fact I'm starving. What's for supper?

MOTHER: My poor boy – there isn't a bite of food in the house. But don't worry – I've got some spinning which is ready to be sold. I'll just take it quickly to the bazaar, and buy our supper with what I get for it.

ALADDIN: Just a minute, mother. Why not take this old lamp with you? I can't see any use for it, but someone's sure to want it.

MOTHER: Good idea. But it's a bit grubby. I'd better polish it up, if I want a quick sale. Hand me that duster, will you?

(DEEPER LONGER WHOOSH EFFECT)

MOTHER: *(terrified scream)*

GENIE 2: You have summoned forth the Genie of the Lamp. What is your desire?

MOTHER: Mercy on me! I meant no harm! What have I done!

21

ALADDIN:	Don't worry, mother. I told you all about the genie of the ring. Now I see why that wizard wanted me to get this lamp for him. Give the lamp to me – for the genie will obey only the person who has it in his hand.
MOTHER:	Here – take it. I don't want anything to do with the thing.
ALADDIN:	Genie, I desire food – the finest food that ever was set before a king.
GENIE 2:	You have but to say the word, O master!

(MAGIC EFFECT. MUSIC. FADE IN CLOUD)

RASHID:	And now Aladdin's fortune is surely made. He has only to wish for gold, and it's his…
SAVITA:	And of course, that's what he does.
RASHID:	…so he sets himself up as a merchant, and soon he's highly respected in business circles – and very wealthy.
SAVITA:	Rashid, do you think that Aladdin and his mother will live happily ever after?
RASHID:	Well, they may – but not yet. For events of great moment are brewing.
SAVITA:	Where are they brewing?

RASHID: Look over there, Savita…

SAVITA: What, the Sultan's palace?

RASHID: Where else for events of great moment…?

        (MUSIC. FADE IN PALACE. LARGE INTERIOR SPACE)

SULTAN: I agree with you, Grand Vizier. A young woman's opinions are quite irrelevant when a marriage is being arranged. All the same, a father does have a heart – even if he happens to be Sultan. And, to put it bluntly, the Princess Bedr-el-Budur doesn't want to marry your son.

GRAND VIZIER: But politically, Highness, this marriage would be highly beneficial. As you know, royal blood runs in my family's veins. A union between my son and your daughter would end for ever the threat of civil disturbance. No faction would again attempt to install any member of my family on the throne – for the families will have been united.

SULTAN: All very true, my dear Vizier. But at the end of the day it'll be your son who'll succeed me – your family who'll take over the throne.

GRAND VIZIER: Alas, Highness, by our ancient custom women may not succeed to the Sultanate. The succession must pass to a male.

SULTAN: Indeed – though this doesn't alter the facts of the case. I would wish my daughter to be happy. But have no fear – I do see the political necessity of this marriage. And of course my daughter will do as I tell her. Ah, here she is. May I ask you to withdraw, Grand Vizier?

GRAND VIZIER: *(retreating)* As you request, Highness…

PRINCESS: *(approaching - distressed)* My Lord, my father. A truly terrible thing has happened.

SULTAN: Tell me, my daughter.

PRINCESS: My Lord, my father, this morning I went as usual with my ladies to the Hammam, to take my bath. As I passed through the market, the herald preceded us as usual…

(MARKETPLACE – EXTERIOR)

HERALD: Beware! Beware! By command of the Sultan, King of the Age and Lord of the Earth. Close every door. No person may come forth from any shop, on pain of instant death! The Sultan's daughter, the high and mighty Princess Bedr-el-Budur, comes to the bath. Beware!

(PALACE INTERIOR)

PRINCESS: My royal father, I arrived at the Hammam, and my ladies started to disrobe me. They'd just lifted my veil, and my features were open to the world, when…

24

SULTAN: When what, my daughter? Tell me.

PRINCESS: I'm so ashamed. At the moment my veil was cast aside, the guards discovered ... a man!

SULTAN: A man! In the name of the Almighty! Where? Where was he? Where is he?

PRINCESS: He was hidden behind the open door. As soon as he was discovered, the guards gave chase, but he was young and very active, and he made his escape.

SULTAN: In heaven's name I swear this – if his identity is ever revealed, in that hour he'll be put to death.

> **(MUSIC. FADE BENEATH FOLLOWING. INTERIOR)**

ALADDIN: Mother, she was the most beautiful creature on earth. Never have I beheld a woman as lovely as the Princess. The very instant my eyes saw her, my heart melted. I couldn't help loving her. Love? That's too poor a word. Adore! Desire! I tell you this, Mother, I shan't rest – I'll let nothing stand in my way – until I win the Lady Bedr-el-Budur and make her my wife.

MOTHER: Have you gone totally mad? The Sultan's daughter!

ALADDIN: No, Mother, I'm not mad – except with passion. But I risked my life to see her, so I'll risk it again to win her. Because, quite frankly, now that I've seen her, life wouldn't be worth living without her in any case.

(CLOUD)

SAVITA: A pretty kettle of fish!

RASHID: That's love for you.

SAVITA: He doesn't stand much chance, Aladdin, does he?

RASHID: Oh, I don't know. You mustn't forget he's got a couple of Genies at his beck and call. Magic might be able to work miracles.

SAVITA: This is going to be interesting. I wonder what scheme Aladdin will concoct to help him win the Princess – she is, after all, about to be married to the Grand Vizier's son.

RASHID: The plot thickens…

(INTERIOR)

ALADDIN: Mother, I need your help.

MOTHER: I'll do what I can.

ALADDIN: You must go to the Sultan, and ask him for his daughter's hand in marriage for your son.

MOTHER: For heaven's sake, Aladdin. Think straight. Me – a common widow woman, approach the ruler of this realm, and with a daft request like that? I'm likely to be flung into jail – if not beheaded on the spot.

ALADDIN: Ah, but mother dear, you wouldn't go to the palace empty-handed. You'll be bringing the Sultan greater riches than any king in the world could offer. He couldn't possibly ignore such gifts. But we must proceed step by step.

MOTHER: What do you mean?

ALADDIN: First, you'll present yourself tomorrow morning at the Sultan's levée, and you'll be carrying a bowl – that one over there – filled to the brim with the jewels I brought back with me from the magic garden. Now, once you've been noticed – and noticed you'll certainly be – this is what you say…

(FADE OUT. FULL UP. SULTAN'S PALACE. LARGE INTERIOR. CROWD MURMUR)

SULTAN: Approach, woman. My chamberlain informed me that you were bearing a large and unusual burden – and now I can see it for myself. If you have a wish that I can grant, then ask.

MOTHER: O king of all the ages, peace be upon you. I do have a request, but it's so strange that I beg for mercy before I say what it is.

SULTAN: Now you've aroused my curiosity. I must hear what it is you seek. You certainly have my word that no harm will come to you, whatever it may be. *(calls)* Everybody will withdraw! At once! *(speaks)* Except, of course, for you, Grand Vizier.

(MURMURING FADES)

And now, woman, you may speak.

MOTHER: O king of all the earth, my son, the merchant Aladdin, has in his heart a very great love for the Princess Bedr-el-Budur. It is a love so great that he can neither eat nor sleep because of it. Life has lost all meaning for him – except how he might win the Princess for his wife. If this is not possible, he's quite content to die – either of grief, or because he has aroused your anger, mighty Sultan. Since his life is in the balance in any case, I've come to beg you to bestow your daughter on my son.

SULTAN: Incredible! Unbelievable! Never in the course of my life did I expect to hear so extraordinary a request. Well, Grand Vizier. You've heard what is asked. What do you say?

GRAND VIZIER: Highness, King of the Age, you surely have no need of my opinion. You know how to deal with such a request.

SULTAN: *(laughs)* That great parcel under your arm, woman. That intrigues me. What do you have there?

MOTHER: A small – a very small – token of my son's regard for your Majesty.

SULTAN: Unwrap it Grand Vizier.

(CLOTH WRAPPINGS)

GRAND VIZIER: *(astounded)* Dear heaven!

SULTAN: Upon my word! This is beyond belief. What wonderful jewels. Tell me, Vizier, have I in my treasury a single gem that can compare with even the smallest of these?

GRAND VIZIER: Your majesty, I've never seen anything like these jewels in the whole course of my life.

SULTAN: Another question, Vizier. Isn't the man who can send me this kingly gift worthy of my daughter? I am the Sultan, King of the Age, I have supreme power – and I withdraw my former promise to bestow my daughter on your son. The Princess Bedr-el-Budur, the one beautiful jewel in the treasury of my heart, is my gift in return to the man who has sent me these priceless jewels.

GRAND VIZIER: Supreme Highness – I bow to your will. I make but one request. Allow a period of three months to elapse. It may well be that in that time a gift of even greater value will be offered to your majesty. Three months, O Sultan!

SULTAN: Three months let it be. Woman, return to your son. You may inform him that he has my royal assent to his marriage with my daughter. He may present himself to me in three months' time for the wedding.

(MUSIC. FADE UNDER FOLLOWING. CLOUD)

SAVITA: Oh, I don't trust that Grand Vizier.

RASHID: He's hiding something up his sleeve. Let us – as they're going to say in a few centuries' time – fast forward.

SAVITA: Yes – about two months from the present. What's the situation now?

(ALADDIN'S HOUSE. INTERIOR. DOOR OPENS)

MOTHER: *(approaching)* Oh, Aladdin! Have you heard the news?

ALADDIN: I've heard nothing, mother. What's happened?

MOTHER: Oh Aladdin – my dear son. The whole city's in a ferment. The Grand Vizier's son is to marry the Princess Bedr-el-Budur this very evening.

ALADDIN: Betrayed! Fool that I was to trust the word of a great man. You must put your faith in no one – not even the Sultan. So the wedding's this evening… I must call on the Genie for his help. Mother, hand me down the lamp. And, now…

(LAMP WHOOSH)

GENIE 2:	Master, here I am. Command me, and I will obey. What is your will?
ALADDIN:	Genie, my friend. The Sultan promised me that I should marry his daughter, but he's broken his word. She's to be united with the Grand Vizier's son this very day. That marriage must remain unconsummated. As soon as they retire for the night, I want you to bring them, and the couch on which they lie, here to this house. Then transport the young man to the woodshed.
GENIE 2:	I hear, Master, and I will obey.

(WHOOSH. CLOUD)

SAVITA:	A fine thing to happen to a girl on her wedding night! Though, on second thoughts, Rashid, she might regard it as a blessing in disguise.
RASHID:	Not very fair on the Vizier's son.
SAVITA:	If he's anything like his father, it probably serves him right.

(WHOOSH. ALADDIN'S HOUSE)

PRINCESS:	*(scream)* Where am I? What's happened?
ALADDIN:	My lady, don't be frightened. No harm will come to you, I swear it.

PRINCESS: But who are you?

ALADDIN: My lady Bedr-el-Budur, my name is Aladdin. I am the man to whom your father has promised you in marriage. Princess, I fell in love with you the moment I beheld your face…

PRINCESS: You saw my face…? It was you! You were the man in the Hammam!

ALADDIN: I was. Can you forgive me? I yearned to look upon your beauty. And the very instant I saw you, my heart was yours and I longed for you. My princess – surely you don't love this man you've been joined to?

PRINCESS: I admit it. But my father decreed it, and I had to obey.

ALADDIN: Ah, but your father the Sultan promised you to me. He's broken his word, but I'm determined that no-one else shall have you as his wife. My lady, you may sleep in peace on this couch. I won't lay a finger on you. I'm not your husband, and neither will I steal your husband's honour. No harm has come to him, and he's got the logs in the woodshed to lie on. He may be a bit cold, though.

(EDGE OUT. FULL UP CLOUD)

RASHID: Rather him than me. In fact, poor fellow, the whole incident made such an impression on him that, as soon as the Genie restored the couple to the palace, he went straight to his father and implored him to obtain a release from the marriage.

(PALACE INTERIOR)

GRAND VIZIER: He was thoroughly browbeaten, Highness, by this huge fellow who locked him into the woodshed. The man told him that he'd be transported to the shed every night until the marriage was annulled. And, King of the Earth, as my son says, it's better to be without a bride and sleep in peace, than to have one and perish with cold in a woodshed. But if your majesty would set a guard tonight...

SULTAN: Certainly not! This isn't a happy marriage, as we know. You persuaded me that my promise to that woman about her son wasn't binding – but this business makes me think you were wrong. Grand Vizier, proclaim the marriage annulled. The people must cease rejoicing, and go about their business as if it had never been. Then send for the woman.

GRAND VIZIER: O King of the Age, I hasten to do your bidding. One thing, before I leave. The woman's son may have acquired that bowl of gems by chance. You should be assured that the man, Aladdin, is indeed a man of substance. Ask him to provide you with forty gold bowls filled with jewels of the same quality, to be carried by forty female servants with a further retinue of forty. Let this be the dowry for your daughter's hand.

SULTAN: So let it be ordered!

(CLOUD)

RASHID: No problem – not when you're Aladdin, and you have the Genie of the Lamp to fulfil your every wish.

SAVITA: So there goes the procession from Aladdin's house, magically wished into existence. Eighty strong!

RASHID: Every one of the female servants is a ravishing beauty…

SAVITA: …and heading them all is Aladdin's mother.

(MUSIC – TO END. PALACE INTERIOR)

SULTAN: This is indeed a most wonderful sight. Woman, your son must be one of the great ones of the earth. Assure him that this time I shall keep my promise. Let him have no doubts about that. But tell him to come here as quickly as possible, so that I may accept him as my son-in-law. For the marriage takes place tomorrow night.

(CLOUD)

RASHID: And now Aladdin summons the Genie, and prepares himself for his meeting with the Sultan. He orders the Genie to bring him a Chief of Memluks with forty-eight warriors – twenty-four to precede him, and twenty-four to go after.

(ALADDIN'S HOUSE. INTERIOR)

ALADDIN: See that they have splendid horses and equipment, as good as the best in the world. And for myself, Genie, I want an Arab stallion that can't be equalled by anyone – not even the Sultan himself. To each Memluk give a thousand gold pieces, and to the Chief Memluk ten thousand – for along the way to the Sultan's palace we'll be scattering largesse to the crowd. Wait! Also twelve maidens of unequalled grace and loveliness must accompany my mother.

GENIE 2:   O master – it is all already done.

ALADDIN: Then I'm ready to meet the Sultan!

(MUSIC TO END. MAIN HALL IN PALACE. CROWD IN BACKGROUND)

SULTAN: Aladdin, your wealth and generosity overwhelm me. I'm delighted to greet you as my future son-in-law. Come up and sit here, on my right hand.

ALADDIN: O my lord the Sultan – King of the Earth and Heaven's Dispenser of all Good! Truly you've honoured and blessed me in granting me your daughter's hand in marriage. Please don't think me ungrateful if I make one further request of you.

SULTAN: Ask, Aladdin – and anything within my power shall be granted.

ALADDIN: Most noble majesty, I ask for a site on which to build a palace for the comfort and happiness of your daughter. I assure your Highness that it will be completed so quickly that it will amaze you.

SULTAN: Come with me Aladdin. *(moving)* From this embrasure, you can see how far the gardens stretch into the distance. Do you see the lake over there, about a league away?

ALADDIN: I do, your majesty.

SULTAN: Build your palace on the side of the lake. Take all the ground you need – and you may consider the lake itself as part of your estate. And now, my dear Aladdin, go home and prepare yourself – for tomorrow is your wedding day.

(MUSIC. FADE IN PALACE INTERIOR)

SULTAN: Look! Look! I cannot believe my eyes. Grand Vizier, am I dreaming? Do you see what I see? Is it real?

GRAND VIZIER: I … I …

SULTAN: Lost for words? Then you *do* see it. How is this possible? How can Aladdin have had this wondrous, this magnificent, palace constructed during the course of a single night? How? Tell me that, Grand Vizier.

GRAND VIZIER: O King of the Earth, there is only one explanation. Aladdin is in league with the devil. He has access to the black arts. He can conjure up evil spirits to do his bidding. This is no husband for the divine Bedr-el-Budur.

SULTAN: Spite and envy, Vizier. Watch what you say. To a man with the wealth of Aladdin, nothing is impossible. I've grown very fond of that young man. He'll make my daughter an excellent – and very suitable – husband.

GRAND VIZIER: Majesty…

(CLOUD)

RASHID: Such a wise head Aladdin has acquired, for such young shoulders. Did you notice, Savita, how he scattered ten thousand gold coins to the crowd as he made his way to the Sultan's palace for the wedding…?

SAVITA: … and another ten thousand on his way back to his own brand new palace, with his brand new bride? As a result, the entire population of Samarkand adore their new prince as much as they revere Tamburlaine.

RASHID: I think, in their present mood, they'd defend Aladdin to the death.

(FADE IN BEDROOM. ALADDIN AND THE PRINCESS ARE IN BED, POST-COITAL)

PRINCESS:	*(intimate)* The people love you, Aladdin.
ALADDIN:	*(intimate)* And you, heart of my heart?
PRINCESS:	I, my husband? I adore you. I'm scorched with the heat of your passion. I shiver with desire for you.
ALADDIN:	Light of my life – the power of my love consumes me, I'm weak with yearning for you.
PRINCESS:	My angel… *(kiss)*

(MUSIC TO END. CLOUD)

SAVITA:	Oh, Rashid! Such love. Surely nothing can touch two people who share such a love.
RASHID:	If only. But look over there, Savita – to the west, to Africa. There, in the land of the dervishes, can't you feel the black magic?
SAVITA:	It's the sorcerer! He's casting some sort of spell.
RASHID:	The fame of this new prince has spread all the way from Samarkand to this far edge of Arabia. The sorcerer thought Aladdin had been entombed along with the lamp. Now he's not so sure. Now he thinks this new prince may indeed be Aladdin, raised high through the magic of the Genie. So he's casting his divinations…
SAVITA:	Then it won't be long, Rashid, will it? Aladdin and the princess are in great danger. As soon as

the sorcerer knows where they are, he'll surely travel back along the Golden Road to Samarkand.

RASHID: Of course he will. And he'll do his utmost to get the lamp – which, of course, must still be handed to him willingly, if he's to escape death.

SAVITA: What will he do? What evil plan will he hatch?

RASHID: Time will tell.

(MUSIC. DOWN FOR AND FADE UNDER FOLLOWING. EXTERIOR. RATTLE OF METAL LAMPS)

SORCERER: *(calling)* New lamps for old! New lamps for old!

PRINCESS: *(high up – calling)* Hey, pedlar! You there!

SORCERER: *(moving)* Me, my lady? Were you calling me?

PRINCESS: Yes, pedlar. What are you selling?

SORCERER: I'm not selling anything, my lady. I'm providing a service.

PRINCESS: What sort of service?

SORCERER: Well, my lady, I collect people's old and worn out lamps, and I replace them with new ones.

PRINCESS: I don't believe you. Now if you were offering new *wine* in exchange for old, there'd be some sense in it. But who wants old lamps?

SORCERER: Oh my lady, I know a worker in metals who greatly values old copper and brass and iron. The more worn and battered it is, the better he likes it.

PRINCESS: Really? Well, we do have one very battered old lamp which is totally out of place with the décor. Will you exchange that?

SORCERER: Certainly, my lady.

PRINCESS: Wait down there. I'll send my maid out with it.

(EDGE OUT. CLOUD)

SAVITA: The poor girl! She hasn't an inkling of the damage she's done.

RASHID: And there's the sorcerer running like a madman out of the city, clutching the wonderful lamp to his bosom.

(WHOOSH EFFECT. EXTERIOR)

GENIE 2: Master, I am the genie of the lamp you hold in your hands. What is your bidding? Ask, and it shall be done.

SORCERER: This is my will. Take the palace of Aladdin with all it contains, and transport it to the heart of India – to... to... Jabalpur!

(MAGIC EFFECT. CLOUD)

RASHID: He's done it! It's done!

SAVITA: Right on the banks of the Narmada.

RASHID: Those huge cliffs on the other side – what are they?

SAVITA: Oh, I know them well. They're called the Marbal Rocks. And a little further down the river, you come to the Dhuandar waterfall. It's awesome.

RASHID: This isn't the time to go all gooey about the Indian landscape, Savita. Do you realise that the Princess is inside the palace, and that Aladdin is still in Samarkand?

SAVITA: Good grief, no! I didn't know. What shall we do?

RASHID: *We* will do nothing, Savita. We're just not allowed to. You know the rules. Oh, but trouble's brewing all right.

(EDGE OUT. FULL UP PALACE INTERIOR)

SULTAN: Where's the palace? Grand Vizier, come and look. Where's the palace? Do my eyes deceive me? What's happened to the palace?

GRAND VIZIER: *(approaching)* Gone! Oh, your majesty – it's vanished.

SULTAN: And my daughter? Where is she? Where is the jewel of my life?

GRAND VIZIER: It pains me to say it, O King of the Earth, but she has disappeared along with the palace. Most High, does this not confirm what I said? Aladdin, his wealth and all his works are but things conjured up by sorcery.

SULTAN: Where's Aladdin? Has he vanished as well?

GRAND VIZIER: No, most high. He went hunting very early this morning.

SULTAN: Then fetch him. Bind him and shackle him. Bring him before me. For this day he'll die! I swear it!

(MUSIC. CLOUD)

SAVITA: It's horrible. I can't bear to watch.

RASHID: Poor Aladdin. They've manacled his hands and his feet – they've forced him to his knees. The executioner is raising his scimitar. See, he looks up to the Sultan, standing on the balcony. He waits for the signal.

SAVITA: No... no...

RASHID: No! The crowd's crying out in anger. People are grabbing the iron gates of the palace. Some are trying to climb over. Look Savita...

THE LOOKING GLASS

BY EDITH WHARTON
DRAMATIZED FOR RADIO
BY NEVILLE TELLER

Running time: 30'

FIRST BROADCAST ACROSS THE USA
ON 30 MAY 2018 IN A PRODUCTION BY
SHOESTRING RADIO THEATRE, SAN FRANCISCO

CHARACTERS IN
ORDER OF APPEARANCE

MRS ATTLEE *Mid-60s. Distinct Irish accent. Homely, pleasant, not highly educated, but worldly wise.*

FATHER DIVOTT *Mid-50s, Distinct Irish accent. Typical churchman.*

MOYRA *25. American, with a touch of the Irish about her.*

MRS CLINGSLAND *Early 60s. Woman from the upper class American elite. Spoilt through money and too much admiration. Canny but vulnerable.*

HARRY *21. English accent. Handsome, debonair.*

MRS BENTLEY *(One speech). 40s. American. Kindly.*

SEONAC *30. Irish-American. Dying of consumption. Weak.*

(MUSIC. DOWN FOR OPENING
ANNOUNCEMENT. UP MUSIC. FADE SLOWLY
BENEATH FIRST SPEECH. INSIDE CHURCH.
SLIGHT ECHO)

MRS ATTLEE: Sure, I don't find it easy to make my way to church these days. Father. It's becoming a bit of a struggle.

FATHER DIVOTT: All the more credit to you, Mrs Attlee. You're one of my regulars. I depend on you.

MRS ATTLEE: That's kind of you to say so, Father. It's the rheumatism, you see.

FATHER DIVOTT: But I'd say you were quite mobile.

MRS ATTLEE: No, no. Not my legs. My hands. Just look at my hands. It's all those years of massaging the rich and famous. If it weren't for the tablets, I'd be in constant pain.

FATHER DIVOTT: My dear Mrs Attlee. I'm so sorry.

MRS ATTLEE: Father Divott, tell me now – am I a good Catholic?

FATHER DIVOTT: I would say so.

MRS ATTLEE: Would you? Would you really?

FATHER DIVOTT: I would.

MRS ATTLEE: I hope so, and I'd like to be at peace with heaven, if ever I was took suddenly.

FATHER DIVOTT: And why should you not be?

(EDGE OUT. FULL UP. MRS ATTLEE'S LIVING ROOM)

MRS ATTLEE: But you see, Moyra, there was no point telling Father Davitt about it, because I've never repented.

MOYRA: Repented? About what, Gran?

MRS ATTLEE: No, I've got to risk my punishment.

MOYRA: But what have you done, Gran?

MRS ATTLEE: I did a great wrong to Mrs Clingsland.

MOYRA: Mrs Clingsland? I can scarcely believe it. Mrs Clingsland, of all people. You did her a wrong? Mrs Clingsland was your favourite client – so wealthy, so generous. I remember you talking about Mrs Clingsland when I was a tiny tot. And yes, what about that big doll you gave me on one of my birthdays – was I five, six? – and telling me it came from Mrs Clingsland with her love? How on earth could you ever have wronged her?

MRS ATTLEE: Generous? Yes indeed, that she was.

MOYRA: And wasn't it through her help that you were able to buy this house?

MRS ATTLEE: It was, Moyra – and more than that. It was only because of her that I lasted through the worst of the Great Depression. What saw me through were the careful, safe investments that she passed on to me from her great banker friend.

MOYRA: Well, thank goodness things are looking better now.

MRS ATTLEE: Oh, that's all due to Franklin Delano Roosevelt. Did you know that Mrs Clingsland was a great friend of our President?

MOYRA: I did not, Gran. Did you ever meet him? You were always going out to the houses of the grandest people.

MRS ATTLEE: No, no. I never met the Roosevelts. But Mrs Clingsland had so many friends, and they were all high-up people. Many's the time she'd say to me: "Cora" (think of the loveliness of her calling me Cora), "Cora, I'm going to buy some Golden Flyer shares on Mr Stoner's advice – Mr Stoner of the National Bank, you know. He's getting me in on the ground floor, as they say, and if you want to step in with me, why – come along. There's nothing too good for you, in my opinion." And, as it happens, Moyra, those shares kept their head above water all through the bad years. And now, I think, they'll see me through, and be there when I'm gone, to help out you children.

MOYRA: Gran, that's all well and good, but you're wandering off the track. You said: "The great wrong I did to Mrs Clingsland." I simply cannot believe that you could ever have injured your great benefactor and protector. How can you say that you did harm to a friend like Mrs Clingsland?

MRS ATTLEE: Harm? Oh no, I don't say that. I never harmed her. I could never have done that. But I did her a great wrong. I wronged her, when all I wanted was to help.

MOYRA: All right, then. You did her a wrong. Tell me, Gran. Tell me about it.

(SOFT MUSIC. HOLD UNDER)

MRS ATTLEE: What would you have done, I wonder, if you'd ha' come in on her that morning and seen her laying in her lovely great bed? With the lace a yard deep on the sheets, and her face buried in the pillows.

MRS CLINGSLAND: *(sobbing)*

MRS ATTLEE: Would you have opened your bag same as usual, and got out your coconut cream and talcum powder, and the nail polishers, and all the rest of it, and waited there like a statue till she turned over to you? Or would you have gone up to her, and turned her softly around, like you would a baby...

(FADE MUSIC BENEATH FOLLOWING)

MRS ATTLEE: There, there, my dear. What's the trouble, eh? You can tell Cora Attlee. Tell me what it's all about, and I'll help you.

MRS CLINGSLAND: *(sobbing)* Help me? Nothing can help me, now I've lost it.

MRS ATTLEE: What have you lost? Come on, you can tell Cora.

MRS CLINGSLAND: My beauty, Cora, my beauty. This morning, just before you arrived, it suddenly came to me. My beauty – it's gone. It's been slipping away, day by day, and now there's nothing I can do about it.

MRS ATTLEE: Your beauty? Is that all? And there was me thinking it was your husband, or your son – or your fortune, even. If it's only your beauty, can't I give it back to you with these hands of mine? But what nonsense all this is, with that seraph's face looking up at me – tear-stained though it is. Now what brought this on?

MRS CLINGSLAND: The looking glass. This morning, for the very first time, I saw these wrinkles round my eyes. Do you see? There – and there. Wrinkles. Tiny lines. I've never seen them before.

MRS ATTLEE: One late night. I'll have those disappear within minutes. You just see. Let me get at them.

(FADE OUT. FULL UP)

MOYRA: Well, was it true?

MRS ATTLEE: That she'd lost her beauty? No, no, things like that don't happen in an instant. But youth and beauty are living things, Moyra. Like flowers, they bud, then they blossom, then they fade. Yours, too, *macushla*. Remember that. Oh we can hold back the passage of time – but only briefly. What my dear Mrs Clingsland had glimpsed was the first signs of the inevitable process. Poor lady.

MOYRA: So what did she do, Gran?

MRS ATTLEE: Well, we started a new routine. Every morning she'd demand her looking glass and then make me tell her that it wasn't true. And every morning she believed me a little less. She'd ask her husband, poor man, and him never noticing any difference in her looks since the day he'd led her home as his bride, twenty years before maybe.

MOYRA: Life must have become very difficult.

MRS ATTLEE: It did, because nothing that he, or anyone else, could have said would have made any difference. From the day she saw those first little lines around her eyes she thought of herself as an old woman.

MOYRA: Did the thought never leave her?

MRS ATTLEE: Not for more than a few minutes at a time. Oh, when she was dressed up and laughing and receiving company, then the faith in her beauty would come back to her and go to her head like champagne. But it wore off more quickly than champagne ever did. I've seen her run upstairs like a giddy young girl – and then toss off her finery and sit in a heap in front of one of her big looking glasses. It was looking glasses everywhere in her rooms. She'd look and look, and the tears would run down over the powder.

MOYRA: Oh well, I suppose it's always hateful growing old.

MRS ATTLEE: Ah now, *macushla*, how can I say that, when my own old age has been so peaceful – and only because of all her goodness to me?

MOYRA: And yet you tell me you acted wrong to her. How am I to know what you mean? What do you mean, Gran? What terrible wrong did you do to Mrs Clingsland? Tell me,

(SOFT MUSIC STARTS BENEATH FOLLOWING. HOLD)

MRS ATTLEE: You know, Moyra my love, that I've always had a touch of the second sight. It runs in the family. I believe you have it too.

MOYRA: I certainly sometimes have feelings about people and places. I sometimes seem to know that trouble is looming for someone. I walk into a place for the first time, and I can know it was the scene of some awful tragedy.

MRS ATTLEE: It's a gift, *macushla*, passed on from generation to generation of Irish folk, going back to the mists of time.

MOYRA: A gift? Yes, sometimes. And sometimes a curse.

MRS ATTLEE: You're right, my darling.

(FADE MUSIC)

Well, you know what happened in the Great War – I mean the way women of all classes took to running to the mediums and the clairvoyants.

MOYRA: Oh you mean those long lists each day in the papers of the young men killed. Day after day. It was awful.

MRS ATTLEE: It was – and the wives and mothers had to have news of their menfolk. They were made to pay high enough for it. And the price wasn't only money, either. There was a fair lot of swindlers and blackmailers in the business. Oh, the stories I used to hear. I'd have sooner trusted a gipsy at a fair. But the women just *had* to go to them. Well, when I was going from one grand house after another to give my massage and face treatment, I got more and more sorry for the poor wretches. Those soothsaying swindlers were dragging the money out of them all for a pack of lies. One day I couldn't stand it any longer. I knew I could help some of them – but I also knew that the Church did not look kindly on such things. So I went to Father Davitt.

(EDGE OUT. FULL UP. SLIGHT ECHO)

FATHER DIVOTT: The poor creatures. Your heart goes out to them, does it not? When we lose a loved one, the powerful bond of love remains, and many folk – perhaps most – seek some sort of continued connection. You can't but feel for these grieving people looking for assurances from their dead loved ones. But what are they really getting when they seek the services of a medium? The Church teaches us to reject all forms of divination – conjuring up the dead. consulting horoscopes, clairvoyance, all such practices conceal an unhealthy desire for power. They contradict the honor, respect and love that we owe to God alone.

(EDGE OUT. FULL UP)

MRS ATTLEE: But what Father Davitt said didn't touch me. Yes, I was with him in rejecting all this fake clairvoyance, but what he never mentioned was what those of us gifted with the second sight might do to help those poor distracted women. So one day, when I saw a lady half out of her mind because for ages she'd had no news of her boy at the front, I said to her: "If you'll come over to my place tomorrow, I might have a word for you."

MOYRA: But wasn't that rather dangerous? Suppose… *[you'd not been able to tell her…]*

MRS ATTLEE: I know – but the wonder of it was that I really did have something to tell her. For that night I dreamt that a message came saying there was good news for her. So next morning I told her that good news was on the way. The very next day, sure enough, she had a cable telling her that her son had escaped from a German camp and had found his way back to Allied lines.

MOYRA: Good heavens, Gran. I don't suppose she kept quiet about that!

MRS ATTLEE: She did not. And you can guess the result. The ladies started coming in flocks, in flocks. You're too young to remember, child, for the same thing once happened to your mother, back in Connemara – until the priest got to hear of it. Then it had to stop. Now she won't talk of it, so there's no need asking her.

MOYRA: I've never heard a word about that.

MRS ATTLEE: I'm not surprised. Perhaps I shouldn't have told you.

MOYRA: No, I'm pleased to know. And when these women came to you…?

MRS ATTLEE: How could I help it? For I *did* see things – and hear things – at that time. Of course, the ladies were supposed to come just for the face treatment – but was I to blame if I kept hearing those messages for them, poor souls, or seeing things they wanted me to see?

MOYRA: No, of course not, Gran. But had you been quite honest with Father Davitt? Would he have said it was all right to pass on what you saw and heard?

MRS ATTLEE: No, and he said as much years later, when I told him

(EDGE OUT. FULL UP. CHURCH. SLIGHT ECHO)

FATHER DIVOTT: It's a terrible thing that you did, Cora. Whether you have the second sight or not, it was not for you to put yourself up as knowing what the good Lord was keeping from those poor women. That is seeking to exercise a forbidden power over others. God's ways are not our ways, Cora. We may see needless suffering; God, in his infinite wisdom, may see everything quite differently.

MRS ATTLEE: Oh Father Davitt, will I ever be forgiven? I've put myself on the same level as a woman like that Mrs Mallinger.

FATHER DIVOTT: Mrs Mallinger? I don' think I [know anyone of that name...]

MRS ATTLEE: The devil incarnate, Father.

FATHER DIVOTT: Oh, surely...

MRS ATTLEE: She's a tout – one of the most notorious in New York. She controls five or six so-called mediums. They find vulnerable people, and fasten on them. It's not difficult to find out information about lost relatives. I know cases where she's sucked people dry, selling them news they wanted to hear. It's just the same as peddling drugs.

FATHER DIVOTT: No, no, calm yourself, Cora. Your case is quite different from this Mrs Mallinger. You aren't using your God-given gift to rob people. Nor are you knowingly telling them lies they want to hear. But all the same what you are doing is wrong, wrong. Cora, I am going to ask you to swear, by everything that is holy, with your hand on this Bible, that you will never commit such blasphemy again – not ever, in the whole of your life. Do you swear?

MRS ATTLEE: I do, Father. Indeed I do.

FATHER DIVOTT: Whatever may be revealed to you, you must keep to yourself. If you see things that others do not see, that is a personal gift to you from the Almighty. Do I make myself clear, Cora?

MRS ATTLEE: Indeed you do, Father Divott.

(EDGE OUT. FULL UP)

MOYRA: But at the time, Gran…

MRS ATTLEE: At the time I thought I was doing a good thing for those poor women – keeping them out of the clutches of fraudsters who were only after their money.

MOYRA: But Mrs Clingsland? What happened with her?

MRS ATTLEE:	Oh, with Mrs Clingsland it was a different story. From the day she saw those first wrinkles the thought that she was old never left her. Nor could she help herself asking people all the time – her husband, of course, but friends, visitors, even the servants...
MRS CLINGSLAND:	Tell me honestly now, don't you think I'm beginning to go off a little? I'm not what I was, am I? You can be quite honest with me. I need to know. Do say what you think.
MRS ATTLEE:	She wore everyone out. After a bit her friends fell away. Fewer and fewer came to the house. As for some of the newer ones who did visit, well I didn't much care for the likes of them. But no-one – the friends who clung on, the visitors who called – no-one could give her what she craved: the gaze of men struck dumb by her beauty.
MOYRA:	She could have paid for that. She had enough money.
MRS ATTLEE:	Oh, she was much too smart to be humbugged in that way. How she used to laugh at the elderly double-chinners trotting round to the nightclubs with their boy-friends. She laughed – yet she couldn't bear no longer having men around her, flattering, admiring, loving.
MOYRA:	I can understand that.

MRS ATTLEE: Can you? Can you really, Moyra? I don't believe that anyone can really know what a beautiful woman suffers when she loses her beauty. For you and me, and perhaps most women in the world, beginning to grow old is like going from a bright, warm room to one a little less bright, a little less warm. But to a beauty like Mrs Clingsland it's like being pushed out of a brilliant ballroom, all flowers and chandeliers, into the winter night and the snow.

MOYRA: Oh, Gran.

(FULL UP BALLROOM ORCHESTRA STRIKES UP POLKA, DOWN FOR FOLLOWING. HOLD UNDER)

MRS CLINGSLAND: What a season, Cora. A ball every night of the week. And a different partner each time. I'd no sooner shown my face in the ballroom than the young men were clustering round, each asking for a dance. My card was always filled in seconds. And the proposals. I could have married a hundred times over. Who gave a thought to the future? We were eternal – forever young, indestructibly beautiful. All of us – women and men alike. Day after day we'd glance into the looking glass and see no changes. Life itself was a dance. We were happy, carefree, young. Nothing could touch us.

(MUSIC FADES QUICKLY TO SILENCE)

(pause) But we were blinded by youth. Perhaps that's as it should be. Reality is too harsh for the young to bear. And the reality, Cora, is that human beings are not immortal, that youth passes away all too soon. *(starts to break down)* I have only to look in the mirror to see the truth of that. Time is inexorable. Time is cruel. *(sobs)*.

MRS ATTLEE: I think this was about the worst time of her life. She lost a tooth; she began to dye her hair; she went away to have her face lifted, but it wasn't a success. She came back looking different, but no better. That's when I really began to worry about her. She began to rely on me more and more, keeping me by her bedside for hours and paying me for the appointments she made me miss. And then there were the hangers-on…

MOYRA: Hangers-on? How do you mean, Gran?

MRS ATTLEE: People prowling about in the background – people I didn't like the look of. People who make a living from exploiting the weaknesses of old women.

(BEDROOM. PAPER RUSTLES)

MRS CLINGSLAND: Look at this letter, Cora. Did you ever see such a thing?

MRS ATTLEE: Who's it from?

MRS CLINGSLAND: That's just it. I've never met him, and he's asking me to marry him.

MRS ATTLEE:	Merciful heavens!

MRS CLINGSLAND: I don't know him, but I do know about him. He's a Count something or other – a foreigner. And he's in trouble in his own country.

MRS ATTLEE: And he has the effrontery...*[to write and ask you to marry him...]*

MRS CLINGSLAND: I know what he's after, of course. Those kind of men are always on the lookout for silly old women with money. Oh Cora, how different it was in the old days. Let me tell you about one special day. I remember it like yesterday. I'd gone into a flower shop to buy some violets. As I came in there was a young fellow at the counter talking to the florist. He turned – and the moment he saw me his face went so white I thought he was going to faint. He stopped short in what he was saying. He just couldn't go on. He gestured to me to go ahead. So I bought my violets, and as I went out one violet dropped from the bunch. I saw him stoop and pick it up and hide it away.

MRS ATTLEE: Now isn't that romantic?

MRS CLINGSLAND: It's not the end. A few days later...

(CROSSFADE INTO SMALL CROWD, CHATTER, LAUGHTER. GLASSES. DOWN FOR)

MRS CLINGSLAND: Good heavens! Aren't you the man in the flower shop?

HARRY: Er…er… indeed I am. And you bought violets.

MRS CLINGSLAND: I came away with one less than I paid for.

HARRY: You don't want it back?

MRS CLINGSLAND: No, no. Keep it. But tell me, why have we never met? Who are you?

HARRY: My name is Harry Buchanan.

MRS CLINGSLAND: Buchanan? You're not related to a Suzanne, by any chance?

HARRY: She's my mother.

MRS CLINGSLAND: Good heavens above. She used to look after me when I was little. Baby-sit – that kind of thing. My parents were always gallivanting about. I loved her. Very much. Then she went over to Europe, oh twenty-odd years ago, and I haven't seen her since. I did hear she'd married an Englishman, and I remember she became Suzanne Buchanan.

HARRY: He's Scottish, actually, my father. Something big in the Civil Service. I was brought up in England. I've come over here to take up a new job. A family friend on my mother's side is giving me a start in the banking business. I'll be working in New York.

MRS CLINGSLAND: That sounds just great. Do send my love to your mother when you next write.

HARRY: Of course. But I'll be seeing her before too long. I have to go back to England shortly, to settle everything up. Meanwhile, I'd love to get to know New York a little better. Do you think...*[you might be able to spare the time...]*

MRS CLINGSLAND: Why don't you let me show you around?

HARRY: Would you?

MRS CLINGSLAND: We'll make a start tomorrow. Where are you staying?

HARRY: The Waldorf-Astoria.

MRS CLINGSLAND: I'll pick you up at midday.

(CROSSFADE INTO CROWD, CHATTING. FADE OUT. BEDROOM. FULL UP)

MRS CLINGSLAND: I didn't know it then, Cora my dear, but I suppose that was the only time I've ever been in love. Really in love...

MRS ATTLEE: Mr Clingsland?

MRS CLINGSLAND: Oh yes, I love him. And he adores me, of course. But there's nothing like first love – is there, Cora?

MRS ATTLEE: Tell me about it.

MRS CLINGSLAND: There's so little to tell. I met Harry only four or five times. He was so handsome, so full of life, such fun. But nothing really serious passed between us before he had to travel back to England to tidy up his affairs, ahead of settling in New York. He booked his return to the States on the maiden voyage of the *Titanic*. On the night of April the 15th, 1912, he went down with the ship. He drowned, along with hundreds and hundreds of others. All that youth, all that life...

MRS ATTLEE: Mercy upon us. But that was twenty-four years ago.

MRS CLINGSLAND: The years make no difference, Cora. The way he would look at me, I know no one ever worshipped me as he did. If only he hadn't died, Cora. It's the sorrowing for him that's brought me to this pass. To grieve for someone for a quarter of a century. It's a terrible thing.

MRS ATTLEE: Well, a day or two after that I got a shock. Coming out of Mrs Clingsland's door, just as I was going in, I met a woman I'd know among a million, even if I was to meet her again in hell – which is exactly where I will, if I don't watch my steps. It was a woman called Mrs Mallinger – a pimp who controls a team of fake mediums across New York. And all of a sudden, pieces of a jigsaw came together. I'd heard it said that this Mrs Mallinger had fallen in with a foreign count who was costing her a fortune.

MOYRA: The count who'd written to Mrs Clingsland!

MRS ATTLEE: Exactly. And I saw well enough what could happen. She could persuade my poor lady that the count was mad over her beauty, and get a hold over her that way. Or else, and this was worse, she could make Mrs Clingsland talk, and get at the story of the poor young man called Harry Buchanan, who was drowned. Then she'd start bringing messages from him – and that could go on forever and bring in even more money.

MOYRA: You couldn't let that happen, Gran.

MRS ATTLEE: I could not. I was so sorry for my Mrs Clingsland. I could see she was sick and fading away. Her will was so much weaker than it used to be. If I was to save her from those gangsters, I had to do it straight away. The solemn oath I'd given to Father Davitt, and my conscience, would have to be sorted out later – if they could be.

(SLIGHT ECHO. REPEAT EARLIER EXCHANGE)

FATHER DIVOTT: What you are doing is wrong, wrong. Cora, I am going to ask you to swear, by everything that is holy, with your hand on this Bible, that you will never commit such blasphemy again – not ever, in the whole of your life. Do you swear?

MRS ATTLEE: I do, Father. Indeed I do.

(ECHO OFF)

MRS ATTLEE: Believe me, Moyra, I never did such hard thinking as I did that night. It seemed to me I was after doing something that was against the Church and against my own principles. But then, I told myself, what'll happen if that woman really gets her claws into Mrs Clingsland? She'll bleed her white, and then leave her without help or comfort. I'd seen it happen – and I wasn't about to let it happen to my lady. I spent most of the night in thought, and in the morning I was sure of what I had to do. I had to beat that Mrs Mallinger at her own game. I felt pretty sure that the Mallinger woman would soon realize that my lady would never fall for the Count – so she'd try to reach her through the young man who drowned. Harry. I had to get in ahead.

(EDGE OUT. FADE IN. BEDROOM)

MRS CLINGSLAND: Not so well, Cora, since you ask. I'm still finding it hard to get a night's sleep. I woke at about three in the morning, and couldn't get to sleep again.

MRS ATTLEE: Well now, I find that very peculiar.

MRS CLINGSLAND: Why?

MRS ATTLEE: Because exactly the same thing happened to me last night.

MRS CLINGSLAND: Really?

MRS ATTLEE: Yes, and something very strange as well. I don't know why – perhaps it was the way you spoke

71

about that young man on the *Titanic*. But at just about three o'clock I suddenly felt as though he was in the room with me...

MRS CLINGSLAND: Oh, Cora! Perhaps he was! Quick – tell me – what happened?

MRS ATTLEE: There was nothing to see. But out of the darkness something came to me – in my mind. I never told you I have the second sight.

MRS CLINGSLAND: Cora!

MRS ATTLEE: I never speak of it. All my life I've felt things, known things, that other people don't. I never use the gift these days. It's against the Church's teaching. But this happening last night – it was so clear that I just have to tell you. It was from Harry – it was a word he desperately wanted me to bring you.

MRS CLINGSLAND: *(highly emotional)* What? What was it?

MRS ATTLEE: He wanted me to tell you that he'd always loved you. From the very moment he first set eyes on you in that flower shop.

MRS CLINGSLAND: Then why, oh why, didn't he tell me so?

MRS ATTLEE: I'll have to try to reach him again, and ask him that.

MRS CLINGSLAND: Tonight, Cora. Tonight. I just know he'll come. And you must be ready for him. You must write down everything he says. I want every single word written down the moment he says it.

(EDGE OUT. FULL UP)

MRS ATTLEE: Well, here was a real difficulty. Writing wasn't ever my strong suit. As for finding the words a young gentleman in love who'd gone down on the *Titanic* might use – well you might as well have asked me to write a Chinese dictionary. But it's wonderful, as Father Divott says, how Providence sometimes seems to be listening behind the door. That night, when I got home, I found a letter waiting for me from one of my patients...

(CROSSFADE)

MRS BENTLEY: My dear Mrs Attlee – May I appeal to your generosity of heart, which I know from personal experience is overflowing with love and compassion? Some years ago, before the financial disaster, when we were very well off, we employed a young Irishman as tutor to our three girls. We all grew to love him dearly, but of course when our fortune and our income were wiped out, we had to let him go. We are now living in very reduced circumstances. Now, I have just learned that Seonac *[pronounced Sho-nak]* is virtually down and out. But much worse, I was told that he is dying of consumption. He is living in some wretched rooming house in Montclair. I'll put the address at the foot of this letter. Mrs Attlee, could I ask you to visit him, and do whatever you can for the poor fellow? You are so good with your hands and your medications, to say nothing of the great comfort you bring to people in distress. I shall forever be grateful to you for how you supported me in the days of the Wall Street crash. I send you my best regards. Aurora Bentley.

(EDGE OUT. FULL UP)

SEONAC: *(coughs from time to time, always breathless. Weak. He's dying from consumption)* You're not the only one with the second sight, Mrs Attlee. It runs in my family, too.

MRS ATTLEE: Second sight doesn't come into it, at all, Seonac. This is simply to save that poor lady from falling into the hands of cheats and blackguards who'd rob her blind. And it will bring some comfort to the poor soul. Tell me, now, are you any good at all with the writing?

SEONAC: We'll soon find out what three years in Dublin university did for me. Now what's needed? Give me the story.

MRS ATTLEE: His name was Harry Buchanan. My lady – her first name is Dorothy, by the way – met him 25 years ago, before the Great War. They met in a flower shop as strangers, but she was astonished to see him at a dinner shortly afterwards, when she discovered he was the son of someone who'd looked after her when she was young. They spent only a short time together before he had to go back to England. Although nothing was said, she is as certain as she can be that he adored her. He booked to return to the States on the maiden voyage of the *Titanic*, which, as you know, was sunk with much loss of life in April 1912. Harry died in the disaster.

SEONAC: *(contemplative)* Yes… yes… Harry…

MRS ATTLEE: If I don't jump in first, my Mrs Clingsland will be at the mercy of a particularly ruthless fake medium. She is so vulnerable. All I could tell her was that Harry came to me last night to say he had always loved her. You should see the effect it had on her. But she immediately asked why he'd never told her – and so I was forced to say that I would ask him. That's when she demanded I write down every word he uttered. It's beyond me, Seonac.

SEONAC: Write this down, Mrs Attlee. *(Moody, as if actually receiving a message from the beyond. Dictating)* "My dearest Dorothy. You ask me why I didn't declare my love for you. In the florist, I was so struck by your beauty I could scarcely speak…

MRS ATTLEE: A little slower. "…could scarcely speak". Yes?

SEONAC: "But when I saw you next at that dinner, so elegant in that gown, I felt further away from you than ever." Got that?

MRS ATTLEE: "Further away from you than ever". Yes.

SEONAC: "I walked the streets all night – then I went home and wrote you a letter. But in the end I didn't dare send it.

MRS ATTLEE: Yes, yes. That's really very good. "Didn't dare sent it."

SEONAC: End like this. "We had so little time together, I could never get up the courage to speak. But I loved you then. And I love you still. Harry."

(EDGE OUT. FULL UP)

MOYRA: I bet that went down well, Gran.

MRS ATTLEE: It certainly did. Mrs Clingsland swallowed it like champagne. "Blinded by her beauty", "struck dumb by love of her". Exactly what she'd been thirsting and hungering for all those years.

MOYRA: I can guess what followed. She wanted more of the same.

MRS ATTLEE: Of course. How fortunate it was that I had young Seonac to help me. He was dying from consumption, fading away before my eyes. Yet I had only to sit down beside him, with my pencil and notebook to the ready, and he would seem to retreat into another world, and the words would flow. In the end I believe he actually felt the emotion he was dictating to me. He began to look forward to my visits. He would fret for me on the days I didn't come. But my, what questions she asked.

MRS CLINGSLAND: Tell him, if it's true that I took his breath away that first evening at dinner, to describe to you how I was dressed. They must remember things like that even in the other world, don't you think, Cora?

MOYRA: My, that must have been a poser, Gran.

MRS ATTLEE: Actually not. She'd described that dress to me so often that I was easily able to tell Seonac every detail. And so it went on and on – and every time, one way or another, I managed to find an answer that satisfied her. Until one day...

MRS CLINGSLAND: Oh, why did he never say things like that when we were together?

MRS ATTLEE: That floored me. Going back that night to Seonac's wretched room, I just couldn't imagine why he hadn't. But when I told Seonac what she'd asked, he went dreamy for a bit.

SEONAC: *(as if receiving a message)* An evil influence was at work. Yes, someone was jealous, and did all they could to come between us. Somehow I was prevented from saying what was in my heart. Here, Mrs Attlee, give me your notebook. I'll write it out myself.

MRS CLINGSLAND: I knew it! I always knew it! Oh, Cora! Tell me again – how he said I looked the first day he saw me.

MRS ATTLEE: Why, you must have looked just as you look now. For there's twenty years fallen from your face.

MOYRA: But Gran, how long did this go on? Surely Seonac isn't still helping you?

MRS ATTLEE: Seonac, my darling, is dead. He died quite a while back.

MOYRA: But Mrs Clingsland – didn't she come to rely on those messages? What happened to her?

MRS ATTLEE: Mrs Clingsland is happy and contented.

MOYRA: Really?

MRS ATTLEE: She has been, ever since Seonac passed away. Shall I tell you how it all happened?

MOYRA: Please, Gran.

MRS ATTLEE: You see, I didn't visit Mrs Clingsland every day. And even on the days I called, I spent only a few hours with her. I couldn't stop her seeking help and comfort from other people. And she did, of course. But she quickly saw through them.

MRS CLINGSLAND: Cora, I can't get on without the messages you bring me. The ones I get through other people don't sound like Harry. Yours do.

MRS ATTLEE: Mrs Clingsland, I've been going against my Church, and risking my immortal soul, to get those messages through to you. If you've found others that can help you, so much better for me, and I'll go and make my peace with Heaven this very evening.

MRS CLINGSLAND: But the other messages don't help me, Cora. And I don't want to disbelieve you. Only, lying awake all night and turning things over, I get so miserable. I shall die if you can't prove to me that it's really Harry speaking to you.

MRS ATTLEE: But it wasn't, of course. The messages came from Seonac. I really was the medium.

MOYRA: Granny, you don't mean... Do you think that Seonac...?

MRS ATTLEE: Let me go on. I went over to Mrs Clingsland and took her two hands in mine.

MRS ATTLEE: How can I prove it to you? It's not possible.

MRS CLINGSLAND: There's only one way.

MRS ATTLEE: And what's that?

MRS CLINGSLAND: You must ask him to repeat to you that letter he wrote and didn't dare send to me. I'll know instantly then if you're in communication with him, and if you are I'll never doubt you again.

(FADE OUT. FADE IN)

SEONAC: *(coughing and weak)* Ah, that's difficult, to be sure, Mrs Attlee. I couldn't produce that all at once. You must give me some time to think it over, to get into the spirit of the thing.

MRS ATTLEE: You'll do your best, I know. The poor lady has come to depend on you so much – well, on me, I suppose, for she doesn't know you exist. Yet nothing has satisfied her – she's kept asking for more and more. But this letter, if you can give it to her, I truly believe this will bring her peace of mind.

SEONAC: I understand that, Mrs Attlee. I'll need some time on my own. Come and see me tomorrow.

(EDGE OUT, FULL UP)

MRS ATTLEE: I went back to his room the next evening. You can understand this, Moyra *macushla*, but as I climbed the stairs I felt one of those sudden warnings – the sort that takes you by the throat.

MOYRA: Oh, Gran…

MRS ATTLEE: I could tell that something terrible was waiting for me. I pushed open the door and went in. He lay there in his bed, his eyes open – but he couldn't see me. I took hold of his hand, and it was icy cold. I held the cracked looking glass to his lips – and I knew he'd gone to his Maker. I closed his eyes, and fell on my knees beside the bed.

MRS ATTLEE: *(whisper)* You shan't go without a prayer, you poor fellow.

MRS ATTLEE: When I stood up I knew I would have to call the people in the house. But before doing so, I took a quick look around. I didn't want any of those bits he'd written down for me to be left lying about. Luckily I found no pieces of writing, and in the shock of finding him dead like that, I'd completely forgotten about the letter. But as I turned for a last look at him, there on the floor, half under the bed, was a sheet of paper scribbled all over in pencil in his weak writing. I picked it up and, holy Mother, it was the letter from Harry to his darling Dorothy.

MOYRA: But you had to copy it out.

MRS ATTLEE: And what a work that was! I was so intent on getting each word right that I hardly noticed what was in it. If I thought about it at all, it was only to wonder if it wasn't worded too plain-like. I missed some of the long words that Seonac had used in previous messages. Anyway, all this took me some time, and what with arranging for the poor fellow's funeral, it was a few days before I went back to Mrs Clingsland.

(EDGE OUT. FULL UP)

MRS CLINGSLAND: Well, Cora? Well? The letter? Have you brought me the letter?

MRS ATTLEE: I pulled it out of my bag, and handed it to her. And then I sat down and waited, my heart in my boots. I waited a long time.

(PAPER RUSTLING BENEATH FOLLOWING)

MRS CLINGSLAND: *(murmurs to herself from time to time)* Oh, no, Harry... you silly fellow ...Oh, how foolish... *(laughs out loud)* No need, no need... Oh, if only... *(to Mrs Attlee)* Oh, Cora, Cora!

MRS ATTLEE: Well?

MRS CLINGSLAND: *(emotional. sobbing)* Oh, Cora – now at last he's spoken to me, really spoken.

MRS ATTLEE: And now, my dear, you'll believe in me, I hope. Won't you?

MRS CLINGSLAND: I was mad ever to doubt you, Cora. But how on earth did you manage to get this, you darling, you?

MRS ATTLEE: It's not an easy thing, my dear, to coax a letter like that from the dead.

(EDGE OUT. FULL UP)

MOYRA: From the dead. Wasn't that the truth, though, Gran! But what I want to know is, which dead did it come from – Seonac or Harry?

MRS ATTLEE: Moyra!

MOYRA: Had the thought never crossed your mind? Oh, this might all have started as a trick – the two of you just as false as those fake mediums you hate so much. But Seonac – he was as Irish as you or me, and he did tell you he had the second sight. Did Harry Buchanan speak through him from time to time? And even if all the previous messages were invented by Seonac, didn't you say that final letter was somehow different, simpler? Was that the real Harry speaking? Did he come to Seonac some time during his last night on earth and use him to write that message?

(FADE OUT. FADE IN. SLIGHT ECHO)

FATHER DIVOTT: But this is most generous, Mrs Attlee. How can I ever thank you? .

MRS ATTLEE: As I explained, Father Divott, it doesn't come from me. This is an anonymous gift from a lady I know and work with. She wants part of her donation to pay for Seonac O'Flaherty's funeral, and for masses to be said for his soul.

FATHER DIVOTT: The poor young fellow. She knew him well?

MRS ATTLEE: She didn't know him at all. I was the one who knew him, and her kind, generous heart was touched when I told her how he had died,

FATHER DIVOTT: Well, the Church is most grateful. And of course this pays for masses for some years ahead.

Although she wants to remain anonymous, will you pass on our thanks for her generosity?

(FADE OUT. FULL UP)

MOYRA: So Father Divott was a sort of accomplice to the deception, though he never knew?

MRS ATTLEE: Well, the Church benefitted a little, I suppose.

MOYRA: And did you ever clear your conscience with Father Divott? That solemn oath you took before him, with your hand on the holy book…

MRS ATTLEE: Well, I thought about it a great deal, as you can imagine. And in the end, I realized that I hadn't broken my oath at all. Oh I may have done a little wrong, though with the best of motives, but my oath – oh, no, I'd stayed true to that.

MOYRA: How do you make that out, at all at all?

(CREEP MUSIC BENEATH FOLLOWING)

MRS ATTLEE: What I swore solemnly to Father Divott was that I'd never again use my second sight to pass on information to other people – to foretell the future, or bring messages from beyond the grave. And nor did I. I kept my oath to Father Divott. It wasn't my second sight I was using to help poor Mrs Clingsland. It was play acting, as far as I was concerned. Pure theatre. Second sight never came into it.

MOYRA: Not your second sight, perhaps. But that final letter from Seonac? What of that?

MRS ATTLEE: Ah that, *macushla*, is something we'll never know.

(UP MUSIC. DOWN FOR CLOSING ANNOUNCEMENT. UP MUSIC TO END)

THE MAN THAT CORRUPTED HADLEYBURG

BY MARK TWAIN
DRAMATIZED FOR RADIO
BY NEVILLE TELLER

Running time: 30'

FIRST BROADCAST ACROSS THE USA
IN 2019 IN A PRODUCTION BY SHOESTRING
RADIO THEATRE, SAN FRANCISCO

CHARACTERS IN
ORDER OF APPEARANCE

NARRATOR *One introductory speech only*

MARK TWAIN *Middle aged. Affable. A born story-teller.*

HARRIET *Harriet Beecher Stowe – the famous writer of "Uncle Tom's Cabin". Middle aged. Mark's friend.*

STRANGER *40s. Somewhat detached and mysterious.*

MARY *50s. Country woman. Good hearted but easily swayed.*

EDWARD *50s. Poor bank clerk. Basically a good type, but easily yields to temptation.*

COX *Mid-40s. Newspaper editor. Businesslike. Eye for main chance.*

MRS COX *Mid-40s – society dame. Quite a hard type.*

JOHNNY *18. Know-all journalist in the making. One short scene only – 3 speeches*

BURGESS   *60s. Preacher type. Fruity. Used to be in command – leading others.*

WILSON   *Mid-50s. Leading citizen. Thinks he's entitled to ride roughshod over everyone*

MAN#1 }
MAN#2 }   *Anonymous voices shouting from the crowd*
MAN#3 }

HARKNESS   *40s. Ruthless local politician type. One scene only – 4 short speeches*

(MUSIC. DOWN FOR OPENING ANNOUNCEMENT. MUSIC UP BRIEFLY. DOWN FOR FOLLOWING, THEN OUT)

ANNOUNCER: One wintry evening Mark Twain was sitting on one side of a blazing log fire, while his great friend, Harriet Beecher Stowe, sat on the other,

(EDGE OUT. FULL UP)

MARK TWAIN: Hadleyburg. What do you know about it, Harriet?

HARRIET: Well, as far as I recall, it was an agreeable little town in Lorrain County, Ohio. But didn't it change its name? I've been there once or twice. Much like any other mid-western parish.

MARK TWAIN: Yes, but now it does have one distinguishing feature.

HARRIET: You mean its reputation for honesty?

MARK TWAIN: Exactly. It's the most upright town in the whole region.

HARRIET: So they say, Mark. So they say..

MARK TWAIN: And so it is – now. And that's how it was way back in 1875, when it was still known as Hadleyburg.

HARRIET: But something happened in between?

MARK TWAIN: It certainly did. And that's what I want to tell you about.

HARRIET: Go on.

MARK TWAIN: Well, in 1875 every man, woman and child in Lorrain County would have sworn that the citizens of Hadleyburg were more upright, honest and decent than any you could find in the whole United States of America. What's more, the inhabitants of Hadleyburg were fiercely proud of their reputation. After all, it stretched back three generations.

HARRIET: Too proud?

MARK TWAIN: Maybe. Anyway, at some point – nobody knows quite how, or indeed why – someone in Hadleyburg managed to offend a passing stranger. Not just offend. Mortally offend.

HARRIET: Why, what did he do?

MARK TWAIN: You know, Harriet, that never did exactly come to light. But it was so hurtful, such a deeply wounding incident, that the stranger determined to make the town pay.

HARRIET: What, take his revenge on the whole town?

MARK TWAIN: Exactly. Of course, like everyone else in the region he knew of Hadleyburg's renowned reputation for honesty and straightforward dealing. So this was what he decided to attack. Hadleyburg thought itself incorruptible? Well, he was going to show them up for the hypocrites he believed them to be. He was going to corrupt them.

HARRIET: Goodness gracious. So how did he go about it?

MARK TWAIN: Well, in those days Hadleyburg wasn't a very large town. Taking the inhabitants as a whole, only six families stood out in terms of status and position. The heads of these households considered themselves the leading citizens of Hadleyburg.

HARRIET: So I suppose the stranger picked out one of these six?

MARK TWAIN: Not at all. To set his scheme working, he selected a poor, elderly couple – the Richards. Edward and Mary Richards. Ed was a salesman on a pittance of a wage, and poor Mary scrimped and saved, and stretched his meagre salary to make ends meet. One evening the old lady was sitting by the stove, reading *The Lorrain County Herald*, when there was a knock on the door...

(KNOCKING ON WOODEN DOOR)

MARY: *(to herself, moving)* Now who on earth can that be, and at this time of night, too?

(DOOR OPENS)

MARY: Yes?

STRANGER: Mrs Richards?

MARY: Yes.

STRANGER: Pray forgive me for disturbing you, ma'am. May I have a word with your husband?

MARY: I'm afraid my husband's not at home. He has gone to Brixton, and won't be back till tomorrow morning.

STRANGER: Oh. Well, it's of no consequence, Mrs Richards. All I want to do is ask your husband to deliver this great sackful here to its rightful owner. May I please bring it in? I could store it over there, just by your stove.

MARY: Well, I don't really... I'm not at all sure...

STRANGER: I'd leave five dollars to ensure its safe delivery...

MARY: Well, all right. Come in. My goodness, it looks very heavy, that sack.

STRANGER: *(effort)* It is. There!

(HEAVY SACK BANGS ON FLOOR)

Thank you. Let me explain, Mrs Richards. I'm a stranger in these parts. I went out of my way this evening to come to Hadleyburg, so that I can do something that's been on my mind for a long time.

MARY: Oh yes...?

STRANGER: And now my errand is complete. I'll be leaving America in a few days, and I can go with a clear conscience. Now, you see that envelope attached to the red wax seal at the neck of the sack?

MARY: Yes.

STRANGER: Inside that envelope is a paper that explains everything. Please ask your husband to read it. There's no need to break the wax seals. Now, here's the 5 dollar bill, *(moving, retreating)* and I must be on my way. Please don't disturb yourself, ma'am. *(distant)* I'll see myself out.

(DOOR OPENS)

(remote) Goodnight.

(DOOR CLOSES)

HARRIET: I'll guarantee old Mary didn't wait till her husband got back next morning.

MARK TWAIN: Of course not. The stranger hadn't been gone five minutes before curiosity got the better of her, and she opened the envelope.

HARRIET: What did she find?

MARK TWAIN: A document which began: "This sack contains gold coin weighing a hundred and sixty pounds, four ounces."

MARY: Mercy on us! And the door not locked!

MARK TWAIN: Mary Richards flew to it

(HEAVY KEY TURNS TWICE IN LOCK)

and secured it. Then she stood all in a tremble, wondering what else she should do. Thinking of nothing, she finally sat down again, and picked up the paper.

(FADE IN)

STRANGER: I was not born in America, and soon I am returning to my native land. I am grateful to America for all the kindness shown to me during my long stay, but I am especially grateful to one certain person – a citizen of the town of Hadleyburg – who did an act of outstanding personal kindness to me some years ago. I arrived in this town one night, weary and starving hungry. I'd gambled away everything I owned, and didn't have even a single cent in my pocket. Wandering the darkened streets, I chanced to meet this man hurrying home. Thoroughly ashamed of myself, I begged him for help. He did not ignore me. He stood and listened – and then he gave me twenty dollars. Twenty dollars! It was the same as giving me back my life, for that money put me back on my feet. Because of that gift I became a rich man. Even more important than that, a remark that man made has remained with me to this day. Now I have no idea who he was, but I want him found, and I want him to have the money in this sack. This is an honest town, an incorruptible town, and I know I can trust it. This man can be identified by the remark he made to me, full of good advice.

HARRIET: Old Mary Richards must have been in a fine old state reading this.

MARK TWAIN: She certainly was. But that wasn't all. The document went on.

STRANGER: I suggest you publish this document in the local paper, and that a public meeting is called at the town hall under the chairmanship of the Reverend Nicholas Burgess. Let any person claiming to be the man who befriended me provide, in a sealed envelope, the helpful remark he made to me. Mr Burgess may then break the seal at the neck of the sack. Inside he will find an envelope containing the very words. The person who provides the correct remark should be handed all the contents of the sack with my sincere gratitude.

(EDGE OUT)

HARRIET:	I suppose Mary Richards didn't sleep much that night?
MARK TWAIN:	Not a wink. And the moment her husband opened the front door next mmorning, she blurted out the whole story. I don't know what she expected his reaction to be, but it certainly astonished her.
EDWARD:	You say that sack is filled with gold coins and weighs a hundred and sixty pounds? Let me work it out… It's worth forty thousand dollars. Think of it, Mary. A whole fortune. Not one of the six top men in this town is worth more than that. We're rich, Mary, rich. All we have to do is burn that paper. And we never need want for anything for the rest of our lives.
MARY:	What utter nonsense, Edward. That would be thoroughly immoral and dishonest. Anyway, how would we explain a sudden access of wealth to our neighbours – to the rest of the town? Money doesn't grow on trees.
EDWARD:	No, no, you're right, of course, Mary. Please excuse a sudden rush of blood to the head. What I'll do is take this letter to the editor of the Herald. It'll be the biggest story old Harry Cox has had for many a year. It'll set the town ablaze.
MARK TWAIN:	Which is precisely what he did. But when he got back home, he and Mary couldn't help speculating

about who the sackful of gold was really intended for – the man who had once helped a stranger with money and good advice.

MARY: I reckon that stranger got here too late, Ed.

EDWARD: I know what you're thinking. The one man in Hadleyburg who would have handed over twenty dollars to a beggar...

MARY: ...*and* offered a fund of helpful advice, was

EDWARD: }
MARY: } *(together, then they laugh)* Barclay Goodson!

EDWARD: Pity he died six months ago.

MARY: Hadleyburg hasn't really been the same since. He was the living conscience of the town.

EDWARD: And thoroughly disliked because of it.

MARY: Sshhush! Don't say such things, Edward.

EDWARD: Well, it's true. And now Nicholas Burgess and *his* conscience have taken over. Now *he's* setting himself up to be the most hated man in Hadleyburg.

MARY: It's not only his conscience, Ed, as you well know. He's disliked for a very good reason. Isn't it odd that the stranger should have appointed the Reverend Burgess to hand over the money?

EDWARD: Er... Maybe the stranger knows more than the town does.

MARY: What do you mean?

EDWARD: Listen, Mary. Nicholas Burgess isn't a bad man.

MARY: Nonsense!

EDWARD: He's not a bad man, I tell you. All the feeling that was whipped up against him – it was all on account of one thing...

MARY: ...as if that wasn't enough...

EDWARD: ...one thing, Mary, that he wasn't guilty of.

MARY: Excuse me, but everyone in this town knows that he *was* guilty of it.

EDWARD: Mary, I give you my word. He was innocent.

MARY: How do you know?

EDWARD: There's something I've been wanting to tell you for a long time. I was the only person in Hadleyburg who knew he was innocent. I could have saved him. But, you know how wrought up the town was. I didn't have the courage to do it. It would have turned everyone against me. I felt mean – oh, so mean – but I just didn't dare.

MARY: You could have cleared his name? Poor Ed! I don't blame you, not one little bit. Public opinion – one has to be so careful. It would have lost us the good will of so many people. But does he know you could have saved him all that anguish?

EDWARD: He doesn't. He doesn't suspect a thing.

MARY: What a relief! But do you know, I should have guessed. He's always trying to be so friendly. I don't give him any encouragement, but people notice, you know. The Wilsons, the Wilcoxes, even the Harknesses – you'd be surprised how many times they say: "Your friend the Reverend Burgess" in that spiteful way. I wish he wouldn't persist in liking us. I can't think why he keeps it up.

EDWARD: I can tell you. When the affair was hot and everyone was condemning him, a group of fellows planned to grab him and ride him out of town. But I was still feeling so guilty – my conscience hurt so much – that I went to him in secret and warned him. He packed up and left at once, and he stayed away until things had calmed down and tempers had cooled. He's protested his innocence all along, and at last some people are beginning to believe him. So I'm pleased I did it.

MARY: So am I – now. But only think of what the town would have done to you if they'd found out at the time.

EDWARD: I know. It's lucky everyone thought it was Barclay Goodson and his conscience who'd tipped him off. Goodson denied it, of course, and they couldn't prove it was him. Now they'll never know the truth.

MARY: Edward, I'm so pleased you did it. You owed him that much, at least. But of course, Mr Burgess doesn't know anything about this gold business.

EDWARD: No. Not yet.

MARY: Who does know – except for you and me?

EDWARD: Well, only Harry Cox. I gave him that document.

MARY: Only us and the Coxes? Ed, perhaps it's not too late. Us and the Coxes – we could… *(urgent)* Ed, will the Herald be printing by now?

EDWARD: I don't know. I could find out,

MARY: Then go, Edward. Go. Just as fast as you can. Now!

(CROSSFADE TO MUSIC. HOLD A LITTLE. DOWN FOR FOLLOWING, AND CROSSFADE)

COX: I've got it in tomorrow's edition, my dear, and made as much of a mystery about it as I could. But of course there's only one man in this town who could have handed out twenty dollars to a total stranger…

MRS COX:	… and then pontificated about prudence or abstinence or hard work or some such. Barclay Goodson.
COX:	Goes without saying.
MRS COX:	Which means that sackful of gold will go begging. Goodson's got no relatives that I know of.
COX:	What a waste!
MRS COX:	Listen, Harry. At the moment the only people who know about the gold and the secret remark are that Richards couple and us. Harry, can you stop the presses? Is it too late? We don't want the world knowing about this.
COX:	*(beat)* Quick! My hat. *(retreating – calls)* Won't be long. See you soon.

(DOOR OPENS. BANGS SHUT)

MARK TWAIN:	And now Ed Richards and Harry Cox are hurrying through deserted streets from opposite directions. They meet, panting, at the foot of the printing-house stairs.
COX:	*(whispers)* Ed! It's you. Now, listen. Nobody knows about this but us, right?
EDWARD:	*(whispers)* Not a soul. On my honor. *(beat)* Except Mary, of course. But she won't talk.

COX: *(whispers)* Same goes for my Wilhelmina.

EDWARD: *(whispers)* So I was just thinking. If it's not too late…

COX: *(whispers)* My thought precisely.

JOHNNY: *(advancing)* Hi, Mr Cox. What you doin' here?

COX: Come to tell you there's no need to ship the early mail, Johnny. Or any mail, till I tell you. Where have you been?

JOHNNY: Just back from the railroad station, Mr Cox. Sorry, but the mail's already gone.

COX: Gone!

JOHNNY: Yes, siree! Just stabled the horses. They changed the timetable today for Brixton and all towns beyond. Had to get the papers in twenty minutes earlier. Real rush it was. But I did it. All those folks down the line – they'll have their morning Herald tomorrow, just as usual. Yes, siree!

(MUSIC. DOWN FOR FOLLOWING AND OUT)

MARK TWAIN: Hadleyburg's telegraph office was open later than usual that night.

HARRIET: Why was that, Mark?

MARK TWAIN:	Because the printing works foreman at the Herald was the local representative of the Associated Press.
HARRIET:	I don't understand.
MARK TWAIN:	It was a sideline. Three or four times a year the foreman managed to interest AP in a minor story. He'd be asked for 30 words and receive a few dollars for it. Not this time. His despatch got an instant answer: "Send the whole thing, all the details, twelve hundred words." By breakfast time next morning the name Hadleyburg was on every lip in America. Millions of people were discussing the stranger and his money sack – and marvelling at the town's honesty in seeking to find the man it was intended for.

(CROSSFADE)

MRS COX:	I suppose it's just possible that it wasn't Goodson whom the stranger met. It could conceivably be someone else.
COX:	I can't think who, Wilhelmina.
MRS COX:	No. Well, we'll have to go through the charade, I suppose. The only thing I don't like about the whole arrangement is that it's to be in the charge of that Burgess man – Reverend, he calls himself.
COX:	Reverend he is. Now let's forget all that nonsense.

MRS COX: You made enough of it in the paper at the time, Harry.

COX: Yesterday's news. We've got today's and tomorrow's to think about now.

(CROSSFADE TO MUSIC. HOLD A LITTLE. DOWN FOR FOLLOWING AND OUT)

MARK TWAIN: Of course the whole town was agog, speculating about the few words that could unlock a forty thousand dollar fortune.

MAN#1:   What could that remark of old Goodson's have been?

MAN#2:   If we could only guess.

MARK TWAIN: But, of course, they couldn't. Meanwhile the day set aside for the town meeting to be chaired by the Reverend Nicholas Burgess drew closer. With just a week to go, the Richards were sitting at home brooding, when the postman delivered a letter. Mary opened it…

(ENVELOPE TORN OPEN. PAPER)

… but how could she possibly know…

MARY: Oh my goodness me, Ed. Oh my goodness me!

MARK TWAIN: That it came from the stranger who'd left the sack in their house, so many weeks before.

EDWARD: What is it, Mary?

MARY: Read this. Just read this.

(FADE IN)

STRANGER: Dear Mr Richards. I have just learned of the extraordinary events taking place in Hadleyburg, ever since a stranger left a sackful of gold in your house. Well, I happen to know who it was that passing stranger had begged for help. What's more, I know precisely what his generous benefactor said as he handed him the twenty dollars... The worthy citizen was none other than Barclay Goodson, God rest his soul. We were great friends, and on the day in question I happened to be passing through Hadleyburg. We'd spent the evening together, while I awaited the midnight train. We'd eaten and drunk very well, and were both in high spirits as we started back to his house. It was a very dark night, and I'd fallen a little behind him in Hale Alley, when the stranger accosted him. I saw the encounter, and I heard what passed between them. My friend was in an expansive and generous mood. I saw him hand over two ten-dollar bills. Afterwards, as we walked to his house together, he told me how much he disliked most of the eminent men of the town. He made an exception in only one or two cases, and I think you were one of them. He told me that you – I THINK it was you – had once done him a very great service, possibly without realizing just how great it was, and that he wished he could have a fortune to leave when he died, for he would bequeath it to you. Now if it was indeed you, you are his legitimate heir, and you are entitled to the sack of gold. So I'm going to reveal the remark he made to the stranger, well satisfied that if by chance you are not the right man, you will seek and find him, and see that poor Goodson's debt of gratitude is paid. This is the remark. "You are far from being a bad man. Go and reform." – Yours truly. Howard L Stevenson.

(FADE OUT. FULL UP)

HARRIET:	I can imagine Mary's reaction to that.
MARK TWAIN:	She was ecstatic. At one stroke they'd been lifted from abject poverty. They'd be wealthy – as wealthy as the most prosperous family in Hadleyburg. Then a thought struck her.
MARY:	Oh Edward, how lucky that you did poor Godson that great service. And how noble of you never to have mentioned it, but you should have told me. What was it?
EDWARD:	Er... er... er...
MARK TWAIN:	And there, of course, poor Edward Richards was quite stumped. Not for the life of him could he recall any such incident.
EDWARD:	I can't, Mary.

MARY: Why not?

EDWARD: Er … Well, he made me promise. I swore on the
Holy Book never to reveal it.

MARY: Oh well, in that case, Edward, I won't press you.
But it must have been a wonderful service you did
him – and knowing you, I'm sure it was.

HARRIET: How did Edward sleep that night?

MARK TWAIN: To be honest, he didn't. What kept him awake
was his conscience and his memory. The outright
lie he'd told his wife troubled him greatly – but
worse was trying to remember what on earth he
had done for Barclay Goodson. Round and round
in his mind he went, trying to puzzle it out. At
one moment he remembered that Howard L
Stevenson had not been one hundred per cent
sure that Edward Richards was indeed the name
that Goodson had mentioned. A second later he
comforted himself with the thought that Edward
Richards was the only name that Mr Stevenson
had in fact recalled.

HARRIET: So I suppose in the end he convinced himself that
he was indeed entitled to the sack of gold?

MARK TWAIN: Exactly. The only problem was that for the life of
him he couldn't remember what precisely he had
done to earn Goodson's gratitude without, as the
Stevenson letter went,"knowing the full value" of
what he'd done. And then his mind went back

nearly fifty years, and he remembered sweet and pretty Nancy Hewitt, the girl that young Barclay Goodson had fallen in love with, and intended to marry. She'd been a newcomer to Hadleyburg – had arrived in response to an advertisement placed by Bill Benson in the *Lorrain County Times* for an assistant in his drugstore. She'd told Goodson that she was an orphan, brought up in a children's home, without a relative in the world. And then Ed had discovered, purely by chance, that she indeed had a mother, languishing at that very time in the County jail charged with prostitution.

HARRIET: Oh my goodness. Any woman who crossed the boundary of chastity back in the 1840s became known as a "fallen woman" – and a fallen woman bore a stigma that could never be wiped away. Upright citizens like those of Hadleyburg refused to associate with such women – or their offspring. So what did Ed Richards do?

MARK TWAIN: He told Bill Benson, who instantly fired Nancy Hewitt. The story spread like wildfire, and the town made it perfectly clear to Barclay Goodson that any liaison between him and Nancy – who was certainly illegitimate. since her mother wasn't married – was out of the question. This, decided Ed, must be the service he'd rendered Goodson – saving him from marrying a tainted girl. Goodson must have realized what a narrow escape he'd had, and so went to the grave eternally grateful to his benefactor.

(CROSSFADE TO MUSIC. HOLD A LITTLE. DOWN FOR FOLLOWING AND OUT)

MRS COX: Oh my goodness me, Harry. Oh my goodness me.

COX: What is it, Wilhelmina?

MRS COX: Read this. Just read this.

(FADE IN)

STRANGER: Dear Mr Cox. I have just learned of the extraordinary events taking place in Hadleyburg, ever since a stranger left a sackful of gold in your town. Well, I happen to know who it was that passing stranger had begged for help. What's more, I know precisely what his generous benefactor said as he handed him the twenty dollars…

(CROSSFADE TO MARK TWAIN)

MARK TWAIN: Yes, indeed, my dear Harriet. Virtually the selfsame letter that the Richards had received.

HARRIET: You don't mean…?

MARK TWAIN: I do. That identical letter went to each of the six leading citizens of Hadleyburg, and their wives. And all night long, six prominent members of the community tossed and turned, trying desperately to recall what special service they might have done for Barclay Goodson many years before.

HARRIET: And I suppose that while they were engaged in this, their wives were equally busy spending the forty thousand dollars.

MARK TWAIN: Of course. An architect and builder from the next State had recently set up shop in Hadleyburg, but so far he'd had not a single client. All of a sudden his fortunes took a turn for the better. First one lady, then another, then another ventured into his premises to say: "Come round to my house on Monday week, but please not a word to anyone. We're thinking of building." By the end of the day he had six new clients.

HARRIET: Why "Monday week"?

MARK TWAIN: Because the Sunday night had already been chosen for the public meeting at the town hall under the chairmanship of the Reverend Nicholas Burgess. Remember, the original letter had said that any claimant had to provide Burgess, in a sealed envelope, with the helpful remark made to the stranger. Burgess was then to break the seal at the neck of the sack, and inside he'd find an envelope containing the exact words. The person providing the correct remark must be handed all the contents of the sack.

(MIX TO LARGE CROWD CHATTERING. GAVEL BANGS SEVERAL TIMES)
[Note: This scene needs to be punctuated by appropriate crowd reactions]

BURGESS: *(shouts)* Silence! Quiet, everyone!

(CROWD CHATTER FADES)

Do calm down, everybody. Now I know most of Hadleyburg is gathered here in the town hall...

WILSON: *(calls)* Plus half the county, and a crowd of reporters.

BURGESS: Just so, Mr Wilson. But a large crowd shouldn't mean chaos. I think we need to conduct this evening's affair in a spirit of decorum.

WILSON: *(calls)* Just like in church, Reverend Burgess?

(RAUCOUS LAUGHTER FROM CROWD)

BURGESS: Precisely, Mr Wilson. Just like in church. Now, if I can have your attention everybody. You all know something of the reasons I've been asked to chair this extraordinary meeting of the citizens of Hadleyburg. It's all in connection with that sack there – a sack filled to the top, we've been told, with gold coins. By now everyone knows the strange story of how that sack arrived in Hadleyburg, and why we need to assemble this evening. A stranger deposited it one evening in the house of Mr and Mrs Richards here. He said he was acting on behalf of someone who was eternally grateful to one of our fellow-citizens – a generously-spirited man who had taken pity on him many years ago, and handed him no less than twenty dollars to relieve his distress. That sum set him on his feet, and he went on to make his fortune. Now he wished to repay his benefactor. To prove his *bona fides*, any claimant was asked to provide the exact words he uttered as he handed his twenty dollars to the stranger. Those exact words, sealed in an envelope, had to be passed to me in time for this evening's meeting, and I was to check their accuracy by unsealing the neck of this sack, where I understand I will find the exact words used.

WILSON: *(calls)* Well, get on with it.

(CROWD LAUGHTER)

BURGESS: All in good time, Mr Wilson. But I have something more to say. I have to report that I have received not one, but a number of sealed envelopes.

(OOHS AND AAHS FROM THE CROWD)

Yes, ladies and gentlemen. It would seem that quite a few of our upright and honest fellow citizens claim to have handed that twenty dollars to the stranger, to remember what was said to him. and thus to be eligible to receive this sack of gold. *(Calls)* And here are the envelopes. I propose to open the first. Here we go!

(ENVELOPE TEARING)

I will now read out what is here before me: "The remark I made to the stranger in distress was this:

'You are very far from being a bad man. Go and reform.' " This letter is signed. Will the person who sent me this letter please rise.

(CROWD REACTION OF OOH'S AND AAH'S)

This is most puzzling. No less than ... one, two, three...six of our fellow citizens have risen to their feet.

WILSON: *(calls)* Ridiculous. I sent you that letter, Mr Burgess.

BURGESS: It is certainly your signature, Mr Wilson.

MAN#1 }
MAN#2 } But so did I. I signed my letter. So did I.
MAN#3 }

BURGESS: I think I should perhaps open the other letters before breaking the seal on that sack. Now...

(ENVELOPE TEARING)

This is signed by Mr William Pinkerton, our esteemed bank manager. It reads: "The remark I made to the stranger in distress was this: 'You are very far from being a bad man. Go and reform.' "

(CROWD REACTION OF OOOH. ENVELOPE TEARING)

This one is from Mr Harry Cox, the respected manager of our local newspaper. "The remark I made to the stranger in distress was this: 'You are very far from being a bad man. Go and reform.'"

(CROWD LAUGHTER. TEARING ENVELOPES)

This is from Ingoldsby Sargent... this from William Whitworth... and this, John Wharton. Each identical. What are we to deduce from this, ladies and gentlemen?

WILSON:　*(calls)* I'll tell you what I deduce. Someone saw the contents of my letter before it reached you, Mr Burgess. Someone saw it and copied it and sold it to anyone who would buy it. I accuse those five men of corruption. I accuse them of paying some thief for the contents of my letter. Those claims are fraudulent.

MAN#1　　}
MAN#2　　} Monstrous! Disgraceful! Nothing of the sort.
MAN#3　　} Quite untrue. You rogue.

WILSON　*(calls)* Have you read out all the letters. Mr Burgess?

MARY:　*(whispers)* Get ready, Ed. Yours is next.

EDWARD:　*(whispers)* Oh, Mary – the shame, the humiliation. I'll never live it down.

MARY:　*(whispers)* Courage, Ed!

BURGESS: I find I have no more letters, Mr Wilson. Six in all.

MARY: *(whispers)* Oh, bless God. We're saved. He's lost ours.

BURGESS: Of course, none of us yet knows if the comment you all claim to have made as you handed that stranger the twenty dollar bill is the correct one. I think my next move must be to unseal this sack, and see what we learn from what is within. That is what I propose to do right now. Mr Richards – you are nearest that knife there. On the table. Would you be so kind as to pass it to me.

EDWARD: Oh…er…certainly Mr Burgess. Here it is…

(CUT CROWD BACKGROUND)

MARK TWAIN: And this is where a word of explanation is called for.

HARRIET: It most certainly is, Mark. After all, the Richards did get that letter from Howard L Stevenson, with the remark in it. I presume Ed Richards put in his claim?

MARK TWAIN: He certainly did – so why didn't Ed stand up with the other five and challenge Mr Wilson? Is that what puzzles you, Harriet?

HARRIET: Not only that. Why did Mr Burgess say he'd received only six letters? I know there were six leading citizens in Hadleyburg. But if you count in the Richards, he ought to have received seven.

MARK TWAIN: And of course he did. Let me explain. In the first instance, the Richards, although well known in the town, were very poor. They knew their place. Ed Richards certainly wasn't going to stand up in public and challenge the most prominent men in the community. He stayed in his seat and kept his head well down. But in the second, Burgess owned Edward Richards a debt of gratitude – a debt he'd never really repaid. Ed had saved him from being hounded out of town back in the past, and he'd never forgotten it. Once he realized that six leading figures in the town were somehow involved in what looked like a fraud, he decided to say nothing about the letter he'd received from Ed Richards. This was his chance of exchanging one good deed for another.

(UP CROWD BACKGROUND)

BURGESS: I am now about to slice off the seal holding the neck of this sack. There we go.

MAN#1 }
MAN#2 } The document! Read the document! What does
MAN#3 } it say?

BURGESS: Yes, there is a paper here.

WILSON: *(calls)* Well, read it out, then.

(CROWD)

BURGESS: "Citizens of Hadleyburg – I regret to inform you that you have all been the subject of a hoax."

(CROWD)

MAN#1 }
MAN#2 } What? Monstrous! How dare he! What does he
MAN#3 } mean?

BURGESS: Quiet! Let me proceed. "There wasn't any pauper stranger. Nor any twenty dollar handout. Nor any test remark. These are all inventions."

(CROWD)

Quiet please, everybody. Quiet! There's a good deal more. Just look how much there is. It goes on: "These are the facts. Some years ago I passed through your renowned Hadleyburg, and received a deep offence for no reason whatsoever. I was shaken to my core by the insult. And I made up my mind to teach this town of yours, with its reputation for virtue and honesty – a reputation of which you were inordinately proud – a lesson it would never forget. I would teach you that you people of Hadleyburg were far from as pure as you thought you were. You – all of you – were just as corruptible as anyone else. The plan I devised could not work while Barclay Goodson was still alive. Everyone would assume that he was the beneficent citizen who had handed out twenty dollars to an indigent stranger. But as soon as I learned that Barclay Goodson had passed away,

I knew my time had come. So I set my trap and baited it. I may not catch all the men to whom I mailed the pretended test secret, but I shall catch most of them. I hope the result of my little hoax will squelch your vanity and give Hadleyburg a new reputation less to your liking. If I have succeeded, please open the sack and reveal its contents."

(CROWD)

MAN#1	}
MAN#2	} Well open it. Open the sack. What's inside?
MAN#3	} Come on. Get on with it.

BURGESS: Right. Here we go.

(RIPPING FOLLOWED BY TUMBLING COINS)

(calls) But this isn't gold. Friends, these coins are lead – gilded lead. They're nearly worthless.

MAN#1: Mr Chairman, may I suggest you auction off that sack of gilt lead pieces, and donate the proceeds to someone among us who would benefit from them.

MAN#2: I propose the proceeds go to one man not tainted by this shameful episode – Mr Edward Richards.

MAN#3: Yes, Ed Richards. He could certainly do with the money.

(CROWD "RICHARDS! ED RICHARDS!")

EDWARD: *(whispers)* Oh Mary, can we allow this? How can we? Hadn't I better stand up and admit…Oh Mary, what shall I do?

BURGESS: Right, I open the bidding at fifteen dollars. Who will give me fifteen dollars for all the contents of this sack.. Fifteen dollars? You sir? Thank you. Fifteen – twenty? Twenty. Thank you. Twenty-five? Thirty?

MAN#1: *(calls)* Forty!

BURGESS: Forty dollars. Very generous.

MAN#2: *(calls)* Fifty. I bid fifty dollars.

BURGESS: Thank you. Keep it rolling gentlemen. It's a worthy cause. Hadleyburg's reputation is at stake.

MAN#3: *(calls)* One hundred dollars.

BURGESS: A hundred is bid. One twenty? Thank you sir. One fifty?

(VOLUME DOWN ON BIDDING WHICH GOES ON BENEATH FOLLOWING)

MARY: *(whispers)* Edward, I'm all in a tremble. This can't be right.

EDWARD: *(whispers)* It's not right, Mary. I'm just a guilty as the rest of them. I should be in the dock with the other six. I was quite prepared to claim that sack when I thought it contained gold.

MARY: *(whispers)* And I'm guilty along with you, Ed. We're both keeping quiet while Mr Burgess is preparing to hand us a huge sum of money.

EDWARD: Money we've don't deserve and have no right to.

MARY: Oh, but Ed – we're so poor. It'll make such a difference. Oh my goodness, did you hear the last bid?

BURGESS: Eight hundred dollars? Make it nine, someone. Thank you, sir. Very generous. Now who will turn it into a round thousand? One thousand dollars. Thank you.

(CROWD CHEERS)

BURGESS: A thousand dollars. Anyone else? No-one? A thousand dollars it is, then. One thousand dollars for this collection of gilded lead pieces – the proceeds to be handed to Mr and Mrs Richards, who I see sitting right there.

STRANGER: *(calls)* May I have the floor for a moment?

BURGESS: Certainly, sir. I don't think I know your... *[name or who you are...]*

STRANGER: I happen to be passing through Hadleyburg on the way to Cleveland. I was attracted by this gathering of townsfolk, and I've certainly had an entertaining evening. But I think I can bring something really positive to the proceedings.

MARY: *(whispers)* Ed, that's the man. That's the stranger who left the sack in our house. That's him.

EDWARD: *(whispers)* Are you sure?

MARY: *(whispers)* Positive certain. That's him.

BURGESS: Do come forward, sir. That's it. Right here. Now, sir.

STRANGER: Ladies and gentlemen. I am a dealer in rare antiques. In the course of my business I have dealings with people all over the world who specialise in numismatics – that is, in rare coins. I can assure you, ladies and gentlemen, that I have a way to make every one of these lead coins here – coins that we have just valued in total at a thousand dollars – to be worth its weight in gold. In short, given your permission, I can restore the value of this sackful of coins to the forty thousand dollars everyone thought it was worth.

BURGESS: That sounds almost beyond belief. How would you do that – and what would become of the sum you raise?

STRANGER: Let me deal with your second question first. I will give part of the proceeds to your Mr Richards. I would propose handing him ten thousand dollars – and I would do so tomorrow morning.

(CROWD CHEERS)

EDWARD: *(whispers)* Oh, Mary. This gets worse and worse.

BURGESS: And how will you achieve your miracle?

STRANGER: Rarities always depend on some device that arouses comment and curiosity. I was speaking to the manager of my hotel this morning, and I gather that the events that have occurred here in Hadleyburg over the past few weeks have aroused interest all over the United States. Newspapers from New York to Los Angeles have been carrying the story. What I propose, ladies and gentlemen, is to emboss on the head and tail of each of these gilded lead coins the names of the six gentlemen who each claimed to be the generous donor of twenty dollars to a fictitious stranger – the six gentlemen who hoped to acquire forty thousand dollars from a falsehood.

(CROWD CHEERS)

I seem to have general approval for my suggestion. I can assure you that the public would scramble to acquire the coins, and the value of the complete collection would then reach forty thousand dollars, if not more.

(FADE CROWD BENEATH FOLLOWING, THEN OUT)

MARK TWAIN: It was at this point, Harriet, that a certain Theodore Harkness saw a golden opportunity. Harkness was running for the State Legislature. His main opponent happened to be William Pinkerton, Hadleyburg's bank manager – and one of the six claimants to the forty thousand pounds. Now, a new railroad line was being planned, and Harkness had his eye on a parcel of land which he knew would appeal to the developers. Harkness was a speculator at heart. The stakes were high, but the potential rewards were enormous. He made his way to the stranger.

(UP CROWD BACKGROUND)

HARKNESS: *(low)* What's your price for the sack?

STRANGER: *(low)* Forty thousand dollars.

HARKNESS: *(low)* I'll give you twenty.

STRANGER: *(low)* No.

HARKNESS: *(low)* Twenty-five.

STRANGER: *(low)* The price is forty thousand dollars. Not a penny less. Take it or leave it.

HARKNESS: *(low)* All right, all right, you win. I'll come to your hotel tomorrow morning at ten with the cash. Now, I don't want this known. This is a private deal.

STRANGER: *(low)* Agreed. I'll expect you at ten o'clock precisely.

(calls) Mr Chairman, may I ask you to keep the sack for me until tomorrow. Now, which one is Mr Richards? Ah, you sir? I would like to hand you these three 500-dollar notes. Please regard them as a down-payment on the rest of the ten-thousand dollars that I have promised you. I propose to call on you before noon tomorrow with the money.

(FADE CROWD BENEATH FOLLOWING, THEN OUT)

MARK TWAIN: Early next morning the stranger collected the sackful of lead coins, and conveyed them to his hotel. At ten Harkness appeared, and at the stranger's request wrote cheques made out to Bearer totalling forty thousand dollars. At half-past eleven the stranger was knocking on the Richards front door. When Mary opened it, he simply handed her an envelope, raised his hat, turned and walked away.

EDWARD: Oh, Mary, just look at that envelope. That's not cash. It's nowhere near bulky enough. That's a cheque. Two at the most. I feel sick.

MARY: But what's the matter with a cheque, Edward?

EDWARD: Cheques bounce. This'll be a dud. The bank has been defrauded too often by dud cheques. Let me see…

(ENVELOPE TORN OPEN)

Good grief!

MARY: What is it, Edward?

EDWARD: Fan me, Mary. Fan me. These cheques are signed by Theodore Harkness. They're as good as gold.

MARY: But why would Doc Harkness... [*sign cheques for such a large sum?*]

EDWARD: I don't know, Mary. I don't know. There are two checks here made out to Bearer. And they're not just for the remainder of the ten thousand that the stranger promised. These checks add up to forty thousand dollars.

MARY: Dear Lord. It can't be true.

EDWARD: Hold on. There's something else in this envelope. A note.

(FADE IN)

STRANGER: Mr Richards – I'm a disappointed man. Your honesty is beyond the reach of temptation. I thought differently, and I wronged you. I sincerely ask for your forgiveness. I thought that there were seven men in Hadleyburg who would be debauched by the hope of easy money. I was mistaken. You stand head and shoulders above the other six. Take the whole pot. You deserve it.

(FADE OUT)

EDWARD: Oh, if only those beautiful words were deserved, Mary. Once upon a time they would have been. Now I simply can't live with them. Here, take the note, Mary. Put it in the fire.

MARK TWAIN: A few minutes later a messenger arrived at the Richards house with another envelope. It was from Nicholas Burgess.

BURGESS: Ed – You saved me in a difficult time. I saved you last night. It was at the cost of a lie, but I made the sacrifice freely and out of a grateful heart. No one in this town knows better than I how good you are. I was in your debt. I hope I have discharged my obligation. Nicholas Burgess.

(CROSSFADE)

HARRIET: Well, Mark, I suppose you're now going to tell me that the Richards lived happily ever after.

MARK TWAIN: How I'd like to, Harriet. I'm afraid that's not the way things ended up. Firstly Harkness had some of the fake gold coins stamped with a message mocking William Pinkerton, and distributed them all around the town. As a result he won the election with a landslide – and then made his fortune out of a deal with the railroad. But the whole situation was more than poor Mary and Edward Richards could bear. There was no joy for them in their wealth. They grew paranoid. They began to believe that Nicholas Burgess must have told others about their secret. The constant congratulations of their friends and neighbours made them physically ill. The deception at the heart of their situation took its toll on both of them. They fell ill. Doctors could do nothing to relieve their distress. Eventually, lying side by side in bed, they died within minutes of each other – but shortly before he passed away Edward confessed their guilt.

(FADE IN BENEATH FOLLOWING MUSIC PRE-SET TO END AFTER THE CLOSING ANNOUNCEMENT)

HARRIET: Poor people. The temptation was just too great.

MARK TWAIN: You've a soft heart, Harriet.

HARRIET: But what happened when the Richards secret was finally revealed?

MARK TWAIN: Well, Hadleyburg felt that its reputation for honesty and virtue had been irretrievably tarnished – as indeed it had. So they decided to rename their town, and make a new start. And that's precisely what they did.

HARRIET: Well, it's certainly an honest town once more. I can vouch for that.

MARK TWAIN: It's learnt its lesson. You'd have to get up very early in the morning to catch it napping again.

(UP MUSIC. DOWN FOR CLOSING ANNOUNCEMENT. UP MUSIC TO END)

OZMA OF OZ

BY FRANK BAUM
DRAMATISED FOR RADIO
BY NEVILLE TELLER
IN TWO PARTS

Running time: 30' per part (Total: 60')

FIRST BROADCAST ACROSS THE USA
ON 1 NOVEMBER 2017 IN A PRODUCTION BY
SHOESTRING RADIO THEATRE, SAN FRANCISCO

CHARACTERS

APPEARING IN BOTH PARTS 1 AND 2

FEMALE

DOROTHY   *age: 13,14. Kansas accent.*

BILLINA   *A hen. Ability to cluck convincingly*

OZMA   *Mid-20s. The ruler of Oz.*

MALE

TIKTOK   *A mechanical man. Rather jerky speech*

SCARECROW   *Warm, reliable. "If I only had a brain"*

LION   *Cowardly Lion – actually as brave as they come*

TIGER   *Hungry Tiger – ravenous, but with a conscience*

TIN MAN   *"If I only had a heart" – but dependable*

APPEARING ONLY IN PART 1

FEMALE

AUNT EM   *[one speech only]*

MAID

LANGWIDERE   *Princess, absorbed by her personal appearance*

MALE

WHEELER   *Fierce, threatening, but harmless.*

APPEARING ONLY IN PART 2

FEMALE

QUEEN   *Gracious – as a queen should be*

MALE

NOME KING   *Affable on the outside but cunning and devious*

STEWARD   *Big-headed, loud-mouthed*

EVRING   *[two speeches only] Age:12. A prince. A bit formal.*

UNCLE HENRY   *[one line]*

(MUSIC. DOWN FOR OPENING ANNOUNCEMENT. UP MUSIC. MIX TO STORM AT SEA. HOWLING WIND. CRASHING WAVES. DOWN, BUT KEEP BENEATH THE FOLLOWING)

DOROTHY: *(as narrator)* Oh my goodness, what a storm! The sea was like a boiling cauldron. One minute our little ship was being tossed backwards and forwards like a rocking horse; the next we were climbing up the side of a huge wave and then plunging down the other side as if we were on a helter-skelter. The wind howled through the rigging, and the sailors had to hold fast to the ropes and railings to stop being pitched headlong into the sea.

(UP STORM. MIX TO MUSIC. HOLD A LITTLE. DOWN FOR)

The captain had ordered all the passengers into the deckhouse. Keep brave hearts, he told us, don't be scared, and all will be well.

(UP MUSIC. HOLD A LITTLE . DOWN FOR)

Some of the passengers were very frightened. Not me. I'm from Kansas. My name is Dorothy Gale, and I was on board together with my Uncle

Henry. Uncle Henry wasn't very well, because he'd been working so hard on his Kansas farm, and he'd been told to take a sea voyage to get his health back. So he'd left Aunt Em at home to take care of the farm, while he took passage on a ship bound for Australia to have a good rest. And he'd taken me with him, because I was quite an experienced traveller. I'd once been carried by a cyclone as far away as the marvellous Land of Oz, where I'd met with a good many adventures before managing to get back to Kansas. So I wasn't easily frightened, and the storm didn't bother me one little bit.

In fact once we were in the deckhouse and I'd made sure that Uncle Henry was all right, I snuggled down beside him, and actually dozed off.

(UP MUSIC. HOLD A LITTLE. DOWN FOR)

After a while I woke up, but when I reached for Uncle Henry's hand, I found he was no longer by my side. His chair was empty. Now, I had no idea that he'd gone to his sleeping berth to lie down. All I remembered was my Aunt Em's words, before we left Kansas.

AUNT EM: Dorothy, you must look after your Uncle Henry for me. He's not very well, and we both want him to get better, don't we? Now you will watch over him, won't you? I rely on you, Dorothy.

(UP MUSIC. MIX TO STORM. HOLD A LITTLE. DOWN FOR)

DOROTHY: *(as narrator)* I couldn't imagine what had happened to Uncle Henry, so I decided to see if he'd gone on deck. I went over to the door and peered out.

(UP FIERCE STORM)

DOROTHY: *(calling)* Uncle Henry! Uncle Henry! Where are you?

(DOWN STORM, HOLD BENEATH)

DOROTHY: *(as narrator)* I couldn't see very much, so I waited for a lull in the wind, then I dashed forward to where a big square chicken-coop had been lashed to the deck with ropes.

(CHICKENS CLUCKING)

I reached it safely, and found all the chickens very scared by the storm. But I'd no sooner seized hold of the slats, than the wind tore away the ropes that secured the coop to the deck. A second later the coop flew up into the air, with me still clinging on for dear life.

(UP STORM. MIX TO MUSIC. HOLD A LITTLE. DOWN FOR)

Over and over we whirled, this way and that, further and further from the ship. And then, suddenly, the wind dropped – and we dropped with it, like a stone into the churning sea.

(UP MUSIC. MIX TO STORM . DOWN FOR)

When I got the water out of my eyes, I saw that the wind had ripped the cover from the coop, and the poor chickens were fluttering away in all directions. Finally I was left standing on the bottom of the big wooden box, which showed no sign of sinking. As it climbed up to the top of the next big wave, I looked around for the ship, but it was far, far away by now. Down I plunged, and the next time I rose up, the ship had quite disappeared.

(UP STORM. HOLD A LITTLE. DOWN FOR)

DOROTHY: Well, you're in a pretty fix now, Dorothy Gale, I can tell you! And I haven't the least idea how you're going to get out of it.

(UP STORM. MIX TO MUSIC. HOLD A LITTLE. DOWN FOR)

DOROTHY: *(as narrator)* Thank goodness, as night crept on the wind began to drop. Slowly the waves quietened down and began to behave themselves. I was rather wet, but fortunately we'd reached a very warm climate, and I soon began to dry off. Quite exhausted by now, I decided that sleep would be the best thing to pass the time. So I sat down in a corner of the coop, leaned back against the slats, and closed my eyes.

(UP MUSIC. HOLD A LITTLE. DOWN FOR AND OUT UNDER FOLLOWING. SEA LAPPING, OCCASIONAL SEAGULLS)

BILLINA: *(clucking, chicken noises)*

DOROTHY: What's that? What's that noise?

BILLINA: It's me. I've just laid an egg, that's all.

DOROTHY: Goodness me – a yellow hen. Have *you* been here all night, too?

BILLINA: Of course. When the coop was blown away, I clung on to this corner with my claws and my beak. I'm the only chicken left. I nearly drowned, you know. I've never been so wet in all my life.

DOROTHY: Do you feel better now?

BILLINA: Well, since I laid my morning egg, I do. Do you want it for your breakfast? You can have it, you know. I don't care.

DOROTHY: I can't eat a raw egg. Anyway, don't you want to hatch it?

BILLINA: Good heavens, no. I never care to hatch my eggs, even though I lay one every single morning.

DOROTHY: Erm – tell me – how is it you're able to talk? I thought hens could only cackle.

BILLINA: So did I – till this morning. In fact, I can't remember ever having spoken a word, until just now. Strange, isn't it?

DOROTHY: Very. Of course, if we were in the land of Oz, I wouldn't think it odd at all. Many of the animals can talk there. But out here in the ocean, we must be a good long way from the land of Oz.

BILLINA: We may be. But there's land of some sort, isn't there, way over there. On the horizon.

DOROTHY: Good heavens, I do believe you're right. And we're drifting toward it at quite a rate. The tide must be pulling us in. I do hope we'll find something to eat.

BILLINA: Yes, I'm a trifle hungry myself.

DOROTHY: Why don't you eat the egg?

BILLINA: *(affronted)* How dare you! What do you take me for – a cannibal?

DOROTHY: Oh, I do beg your pardon Mrs... Mrs... May I enquire your name, ma'am?

BILLINA: My name is Bill.

DOROTHY: Bill? That's a boy's name.

BILLINA: That's because when I was first hatched they couldn't tell what I was. The little boy on the farm called me Bill, and from then on that's what they all called me.

DOROTHY: But it's not right! If you don't mind, I'll call you Billina. "Eena" makes it a girl's name, you see.

BILLINA: I don't mind at all.

(FADE IN MUSIC BENEATH THE FOLLOWING)

DOROTHY: Then Billina it is. My name is Dorothy Gale. Dorothy to my friends, and Miss Gale to strangers. You may call me Dorothy.

BILLINA: Thank you very much. Look, Dorothy, we're getting very close to the shore. We'll be landing any minute.

(UP MUSIC. HOLD A LITTLE. DOWN FOR FOLLOWING)

DOROTHY: *(as narrator)* The big wooden coop grated gently on the sandy beach. Billina flew out immediately, but I had to climb over the high slats. As soon as I was safely ashore, I took off my wet shoes and stockings and spread them on the sun-warmed beach to dry. Meanwhile the yellow hen was pick-pecking away in the sand.

(CROSSFADE MUSIC TO SEASHORE. WAVES. SEAGULLS. OPEN AIR)

DOROTHY: *(calling)* What are you doing?

BILLINA:	Getting my breakfast, of course.
DOROTHY:	But what can you find?
BILLINA:	Oh, some lovely fat red ants, a few sandbugs, and once in a while a tiny crab. They're very sweet. Shall I find you one?
DOROTHY:	Certainly not. It all sounds disgusting. How can you eat live things, and horrid bugs, and crawly ants. You ought to be 'shamed of yourself.
BILLINA:	What a funny thing to say. Live things are much fresher than dead ones. And you humans eat all sorts of dead creatures.
DOROTHY:	We certainly do not!
BILLINA:	Of course you do. You eat lambs and sheep and cows and pigs and even chickens.
DOROTHY:	But we cook 'em first.
BILLINA:	What difference does that make?
DOROTHY:	A good deal.
BILLINA:	Oh! I almost broke my beak just them. I struck metal.
DOROTHY:	Where? Show me. I'll dig it up.
BILLINA:	Right here. It's not very far down.

DOROTHY: Well, get out of the way then. Now…

(SCRABBLING IN SAND)

Good heavens – a key. A large, golden key. What on earth is that doing here, on the seashore? I wonder what it unlocks, Billlina.

(FADE MUSIC BENEATH FOLLOWING)

I can't see any house nearby.

DOROTHY: *(as narrator)* I put the key into the pocket of my dress. My stockings and shoes were quite dry by now, so I put them on. Then Billina and I set off to explore.

(UP MUSIC. HOLD A LITTLE. DOWN FOR)

DOROTHY: *(as narrator)* As we walked up the beach toward a grove of trees, we came to a flat stretch of white sand. Scrawled in very large letters on its surface were the words: "Beware of the Wheelers". Wondering who the Wheelers might be, we went on, and soon came to the first trees. I was hoping they might be fruit trees, because I was feeling very hungry by now. But imagine my astonishment to find, growing in clusters on all the branches, square paper boxes. On the biggest and ripest of the boxes, the word "Lunch" could be read. Other branches bore tiny little lunch boxes that were quite green, and evidently not yet fit to eat. The leaves of this tree were all paper napkins. I stood on tiptoe and picked the biggest lunch box I could see, together with a few napkins.

(UP MUSIC. HOLD A LITTLE. DOWN FOR)

I sat down and opened it. Inside I found, all nicely wrapped up, a ham sandwich, a piece of sponge cake, a slice of cheese, a pickled cucumber and a big round apple. I ate every little bit of everything.

(UP MUSIC. HOLD A LITTLE. DOWN FOR)

BILLINA: I hope your lunch box was perfectly ripe.

DOROTHY: Oh perfectly. The only green thing was the cucumber, and that just *has* to be green. Now I think we'd better go and explore.

BILLINA: Have you any idea what country this is?

DOROTHY: None at all – but I'm quite sure it's a magic land, or lunch-boxes wouldn't be growing on trees. And if we were in a civilized place like Kansas, a yellow hen like you wouldn't be able to talk.

BILLINA: Perhaps we're in the Land of Oz.

DOROTHY: I'm sure we're not. I've been to the Land of Oz, and it's nowhere near the sea. It's surrounded by desert. So this must be some other magic country. Come on, let's walk up this way.

(UP MUSIC. HOLD A LITTLE. DOWN FOR FOLLOWING AND OUT)

DOROTHY: *(as narrator)* We'd gone only a short distance when, from a path leading from the trees, emerged the most peculiar person I'd ever seen. Dressed in brightly coloured clothes, it seemed like a man, except that it was on all fours, and instead of hands and feet, its arms and legs ended in wheels. Using these wheels, it rolled very swiftly.

(OPEN AIR. SEA. GULLS)

BILLINA: *(squawking in panic)* Run! It's a Wheeler! Run! Come on! Remember that warning in the sand! Run!

DOROTHY: *(as narrator)* So I ran. Looking over my shoulder, I saw a great procession of Wheelers emerging from the trees – dozens and dozens of them, all clad in splendid garments, and all rolling swiftly towards us.

DOROTHY: *(running, panting)* They're sure to catch us. I can't run much farther, Billina.

BILLINA: Climb up this hill. Quick! Up, up! Follow me.

DOROTHY: *(running, panting)* Oh dear! Oh dear!

BILLINA: It's all right. You can slow down. Look, they're all down there, at the bottom. They simply can't roll up this hill, with all these rocks.

DOROTHY: Oh, thank goodness. I must just sit down for a minute and get my breath back.

WHEELER: *(distant, shouting)* We'll get you in the end. You can be sure of that. And when we do, we'll tear you into little bits.

DOROTHY: *(calling)* But why? What harm have I done?

WHEELER: *(distant, shouting)* You stole a lunch box from one of our trees. The punishment is death!

BILLINA: Don't you believe him. I'm sure those trees don't belong to these awful creatures. They're just looking for trouble.

DOROTHY: I think you're right. Let's ignore them. I vote we go on up the hill, right to the very top.

(MUSIC. HOLD A LITTLE. FADE BENEATH FOLLOWING AND OUT)

DOROTHY: Well, there's a lovely view from up here, but not much else.

BILLINA: What about that rock.

DOROTHY: What of it?

BILLINA: The crack there. Doesn't it look like a door, cut into the middle of it? It runs up one side and right down the other.

DOROTHY: Oh, yes. And isn't this a keyhole, Billina? I wonder if that key I picked up on the seashore would fit it?

BILLINA: Why not try?

(KEY TURNS IN LOCK. LOUD CREAK OF DOOR OPENING)

DOROTHY: It's very dim in here. Good gracious! What on earth is that?

BILLINA: Looks like a little man to me.

DOROTHY: So it is. And he's made out of copper. All over. He's all jointed and hinged.

BILLINA: He's just like the old kettle in the barnyard at home.

DOROTHY: I once knew a man made of tin, but he was alive. This one isn't. Oh look, Billina, there's a little notice hanging round his neck.

BILLINA: Well, go on. What does it say? You'll have to tell me. I can't read.

DOROTHY: It says that this is a talking mechanical man operated by clockwork. He thinks, speaks, acts and does everything but live. Manufactured by Smith and Tinker at Evna, Land of Ev.

BILLINA: Well, that's where we must be – the land of Ev.

DOROTHY: Wait a minute. There are some instructions. For thinking, wind keyhole one; for speaking, wind keyhole two; and for walking and action, wind keyhole three. And here's the key.

BILLINA: Well, start with keyhole one.

(WINDING CLOCKWORK)

Nothing's happening.

DOROTHY: Of course it isn't. He's thinking.

BILLINA: I wonder what he's thinking.

DOROTHY: Well, I'll wind up keyhole two, and perhaps he'll tell us.

(WINDING CLOCKWORK)

TIKTOK: Good morning, little girl.. Good morning, Mrs Hen.

DOROTHY: }
BILLINA: } Good morning, sir.

TIKTOK: I thank you for rescuing me.

DOROTHY: Don't mention it. How did you come to be locked up in this place?'

TIKTOK: Well, I was once owned by the cruel King of Ev – his name was Ev-ol-do. He was a most intemperate man. Once, in a fit of rage, he sold his wife and his ten children – five girls and five boys – to the Nome King. After a bit he calmed down and tried to buy them back, but the Nome King refused. Somehow the king blamed me. He locked me up in this rock, threw the key into the ocean, jumped in after it, and was drowned.

DOROTHY: How very dreadful.

TIKTOK: Yes indeed. After a while I just ran down, like a clock that isn't wound up. Until you rescued me, that is.

DOROTHY: I'm very pleased I did. So we're in the Land of Ev, are we?

TIKTOK: We are, indeed.

DOROTHY: Well, I'd better wind up your actions.

TIKTOK: Yes, please.

(WINDING CLOCKWORK)

Thank you so much. From this time forth I am your obedient servant. Whatever you command, that I will do. If you keep me wound up, of course.

DOROTHY: Excuse me, but would you please tell me what you're called?

TIKTOK: My name is Tiktok.

149

DOROTHY: You don't strike, do you?

TIKTOK: Oh, no. And I don't alarm people either. But as I never sleep, I can wake you at any time you like.

(FADE IN CLOCKLIKE TICK-TOCK MUSIC BENEATH THE FOLLOWING)

DOROTHY: That's nice – but I never like being woken up.

BILLINA: You can sleep till I lay my egg. Then, when I cackle, Tiktok will know it's time to wake you.

DOROTHY: Do you lay your egg very early?

BILLINA: Eight o'clock on the dot. And everyone should be up by then, shouldn't they?

(UP MUSIC. HOLD A LITTLE. DOWN FOR FOLLOWING AND OUT)

DOROTHY: Tiktok, can you help us escape from these rocks? The Wheelers are down below, you know, and they threatening to kill us.

TIKTOK: Oh, there's no need to be afraid of the Wheelers.

DOROTHY: Why not?

TIKTOK: Because they are gr...gr...gr *(slows down like a record and stops)*

DOROTHY: Oh dear. What on earth's happened?

BILLINA:	Well, he's run down, of course. You couldn't have wound him up very tight.
DOROTHY:	Oh, well, I'll do better this time.

(WINDING CLOCKWORK)

TIKTOK:	*(suddenly comes to life)* ... great cowards really.
DOROTHY:	Pardon?
TIKTOK:	The Wheelers. They're great cowards. They try to make people believe they're very terrible, but if I had a club in my hands they'd run away as soon as they saw me.
DOROTHY:	Do you have a club?
TIKTOK:	No.
DOROTHY:	Then what shall we do?
TIKTOK:	Wind up my think-works more tightly, and I'll try to devise some other plan.
DOROTHY:	All right.

(WINDING CLOCKWORK)

The best thinker I ever knew was a scarecrow.

BILLINA:	Nonsense!

DOROTHY: It's true! I met him in the land of Oz. He came with me on a journey to the great Wizard of Oz to get some brains, because his head was only stuffed with straw. But his thinking was just as good before he got his brains as afterwards.

BILLINA: I don't believe all that rubbish about the Land of Oz.

DOROTHY: It's all true.

TIKTOK: In the Land of Oz anything is possible because it's a fairy country.

DOROTHY: There, Billina, see? Do you know the land of Oz, Tiktok?

TIKTOK: No, but I've heard about it, because there's only a desert separating it from the Land of Ev.

DOROTHY: How wonderful. So I'm quite close to my old friend the scarecrow. He's the king of Oz now, you know.

TIKTOK: He was. Then he was deposed by a soldier woman called Jin-jur. And then Jin-jur was deposed by a little girl called Ozma. She was the true heir to the throne, and she now rules the kingdom under the title Ozma of Oz.

DOROTHY: What a lot has happened there since I left.

TIKTOK: Now I'll take you to the town of Evna. Follow me down the hill, and I'll deal with the Wheelers. Don't be afraid.

(MUSIC. HOLD A LITTLE. DOWN FOR FOLLOWING, AND OUT)

WHEELER: *(distant, calls)* Halt! Not one step closer. Come any closer, and we'll tear you to pieces.

TIKTOK: Oh, no you won't. Come on, Dorothy.

DOROTHY: Billina, just you stay close.

BILLINA: Oh I will. I will. We chickens can't be too careful.

WHEELER: *(calls)* I said stop.

TIKTOK: But we won't stop. In fact, if you don't get out of the way – you and your friends over there, I'll knock you out.

DOROTHY: He can, you know. He's made of copper. You wouldn't stand a chance.

WHEELER: Oh! Oh, wouldn't we? Well, in that case … *(running away – calling – retreating from mic)* We'll just say goodbye. *(Fading)* Goodbye…

TIKTOK: I told you. They haven't got an ounce of courage between them.

DOROTHY: I once knew a lion who thought he had no courage.

BILLINA: Here she goes again. I suppose that was in the land of Oz.

DOROTHY: It was, as a matter of fact. I wonder what's become of him? He was such a lovely fellow.

BILLINA: I don't believe a word of it.

TIKTOK: This way. This way. We're nearly out of the wood. Come on. There!

DOROTHY: Oh my word. What a pretty scene. Green fields, and fruit trees and…

BILLINA: Just look at those farms. It reminds me of home.

TIKTOK: Never mind the farms. It's the palace over there we need to make for. That's where I used to live.

DOROTHY: It's very beautiful… those fountains – and the spires all sparkling in the sun.

TIKTOK: Come on. Let's get closer.

BILLINA: *(distant, calls)* There's a notice stuck to this door. Come on, Dorothy. I can't read.

DOROTHY: *(approaching)* It says: "Owner absent. Please knock at the third door in the left wing."

TIKTOK: *(moving)* Come on, then. Let's do it.

(MUSIC. DOWN FOR KNOCKING ON DOOR. DOOR OPENS. MUSIC DOWN AND OUT)

MAID: Good day. Do you wish to see the Princess Langwidere?

DOROTHY: Why? Does she live here?

MAID: Of course.

DOROTHY: Then, yes please. We should like to see her.

MAID: I'll tell her you're here, miss. Step in, please, and take a seat in the drawing room. Not you, yellow hen. Shoo!

BILLINA: Shoo yourself! What manners!

MAID: Oh, you can talk, can you?

BILLINA: Well, there's a silly question. Get out of the way.

MAID: Oh, all right. I don't think the princess will like it.

(DOOR CLOSES)

(moving) This way. In there. What names shall I give?

DOROTHY: I am Dorothy Gale, of Kansas, and this gentleman is a machine called Tiktok, and the yellow hen is my friend Billina.

MAID: *(retreating)* I won't be long.

(MUSIC. DOWN FOR FOLLOWING AND OUT)

MAID:	*(approaching)* Excuse me, your Highness.
LANGWIDERE:	What do you think of the head I have on today, Nanda?
MAID:	It's very attractive, your Highness. The hazel eyes go very well with the auburn hair.
LANGWIDERE:	That's what all these mirrors tell me. This head looks very well from every angle. And yet, you know, I've grown rather tired of it. I think I'll choose another head for this afternoon.
MAID:	As you wish, your Highness.
LANGWIDERE:	What is it you want, anyway?
MAID:	You have company, your Highness.
LANGWIDERE:	Really. Who?
MAID:	A Dorothy Gale of Kansas, a Mr Tiktok, and … er … Billina.
LANGWIDERE:	What a strange lot of names. I suppose I'd better see them. But not with this head on. I'll go through to my boudoir, first, and put on Number 17. I think that's the very best of all, don't you?
MAID:	Your number 17 is exceedingly beautiful, your Highness.

DOROTHY: *(as narrator)* Now I must explain to you that the Princess Langwidere had thirty-one heads — one for each day in even the longest month. But, of course, she could only wear one of them at a time, because she had only one neck. Each head was kept in its own little cupboard, and each cupboard had a gold number on the outside.

The heads were all very beautiful, but they were all different — different complexions, different colored hair, different shaped noses, different mouths.

When Nanda and the princess came to cupboard 17, Langwidere took the ruby key which she always carried round her left wrist and unlocked the door.

She handed head number 9 which she'd been wearing to Nanda, then carefully lifted out head 17 and fitted it to her neck. There was only one problem with number 17. The temper that went with it was fiery, harsh and haughty in the extreme, and it often led the princess to do unpleasant things, which she regretted when she came to wear her other heads.

MAID: Very lovely, your Highness.

LANGWIDERE: I am, aren't I? Well, let's go and meet our visitors.

(EDGE OUT. FADE IN)

LANGWIDERE: *(advancing)* Oh! I thought someone of importance had called.

DOROTHY: Then you were quite right. I'm a good deal of 'portance myself, and when Billina lays an egg, she has the proudest cackle you ever heard. As for Tiktok, he's the…*[most amazing machine you ever saw in all…]*

LANGWIDERE: Silence! How dare you annoy me with your senseless chatter. Come here, girl. Closer. Yes… you're quite attractive. Not at all beautiful, you understand. But reasonably pretty, and certainly quite different from my other heads. I believe I'll take your head and give you number 26 for it.

DOROTHY: You certainly won't!

LANGWIDERE: There's no point protesting. I need your head for my collection – and in the land of Ev, my will is law. Head 26 is very lovely.

DOROTHY: I don't care. I'll keep my own head, thank you very much.

LANGWIDERE: You refuse?

DOROTHY: I do.

LANGWIDERE: Then you'll be locked up until you decide to obey me. Nanda, ring for my army.

(HAND BELL RINGS. PAUSE. DOOR OPENS. FEET MARCH IN. ALL HALT TOGETHER)

Captain, carry that girl to the North Tower and lock her up.

(MUSIC. DOWN FOR, HOLD UNDER)

DOROTHY: *(as narrator)* It so happened that at just that moment Tiktok's clockwork ran down. Some of the soldiers led me to a high tower and locked me up. But when the others tried to lift Tiktok, he was so solid and heavy that they couldn't lift him. So they left him standing in the centre of the drawing room.

LANGWIDERE: People will think I have a new statue. Nanda can keep him polished. Oh, and take that hen and put her in the chicken house. Some day I'll have her fried for breakfast.

(UP MUSIC. HOLD A LITTLE. DOWN FOR FOLLOWING. HOLD UNDER)

DOROTHY: *(as narrator)* That night Nanda brought me bread and water for my supper, and I slept on the hard stone floor of my cell. Next morning I leaned out of the window of my prison, high up in the tower. To the east I could see the forest and, beyond it, the ocean. Westward, and just a little way from the palace, the fertile land of Ev suddenly ended, and I could see miles and miles of sandy desert stretching away to the far distance. This, I realized, was the desert that separated the land of Ev from the land of Oz.

Thinking about my old friends in Oz, and wishing I could tell them how much I needed their help, I suddenly saw something on the far distant horizon – something like a cloud – speeding toward me. As it got nearer, I saw that it was a broad green carpet unrolling itself across the desert, while advancing across the carpet was a wondrous procession.

First came a golden chariot drawn by a lion and a tiger, trotting shoulder to shoulder, and I saw at once that the lion was my old friend, the Cowardly Lion. Behind the chariot stretched a great cavalcade, among whom I recognised my old friends the scarecrow and the tin man, along with a parade of soldiers and many others.

Standing inside the chariot was a beautiful girl in flowing robes, a jewelled tiara on her head. In one hand she held reins made of satin; in the other an ivory wand, separated at the top into two prongs. One bore the letter "O" and the other "Z", both formed from glistening diamonds. I guessed at once that she must be the ruler of Oz whom Tiktok had told me about – none other than Ozma of Oz.

(UP MUSIC. DOWN FOR FOLLOWING AND OUT)

DOROTHY: *(as narrator)* As soon as the very last soldier in the procession had reached the land of Ev, the magic carpet rolled itself up and disappeared. I could keep silent no longer.

DOROTHY: *(remote, calling)* I'm here! It's me – Dorothy.

SCARECROW:	*(calling)* Dorothy who?
DOROTHY:	Dorothy Gale, of course. Your friend from Kansas.
SCARECROW:	Good heavens! Hello, Dorothy. What on earth are you doing up there?
DOROTHY:	I'm a prisoner. I'm locked up.
SCARECROW:	Well, just think. You might be much worse off. You can't get drowned, or fall out of an apple tree. Some folks would think they were lucky to be up there.
DOROTHY:	Well I don't, and I want to get down 'mmediately and see you and the Tin Man, and the Cowardly Lion.
OZMA:	Hello, Dorothy. Do you know who I am?
DOROTHY:	Aren't you Ozma of Oz?
OZMA:	Indeed I am. Now tell me, who locked you up?
DOROTHY:	The princess Langwidere. She's horrid.
OZMA:	And why did she lock you up?
DOROTHY:	Because I wouldn't let her have my head for her collection.
OZMA:	I don't blame you. Don't worry, Dorothy. We'll soon have you out of there. I'll go and see the princess myself, this very minute.

(MUSIC. HOLD A LITTLE. THEN DOWN UNDER FOLLOWING, AND OUT)

LANGWIDERE: *(furious)* Ozma of Oz, how dare you enter my palace without an invitation, you and your soldiers. Leave at once.

OZMA: I did not come here to do you harm, Princess Langwidere. I came to free the royal family of Ev from the clutches of the Nome King. As you know, he is keeping the Queen and her ten children prisoners.

LANGWIDERE: *(suddenly sweet)* Oh, I do hope you can free my aunt and my cousins. Then I could hand the kingdom over to them, and be free of all this worry and trouble. Do you know, I have to devote at least ten minutes of each day to affairs of state. Ten minutes! That's ten minutes I could be spending admiring my beautiful heads.

OZMA: I'll certainly discuss how to liberate them shortly, but first you must free another prisoner – the little girl you locked up in your tower,

LANGWIDERE: Oh, of course. I'd forgotten all about her. That all happened yesterday. You can't expect a princess to remember today what she did yesterday. Come with me.

(EDGE OUT. FULL UP)

DOROTHY: *(as narrator)* I was very surprised when the princess and Ozma suddenly appeared at the door of my prison. They took me all the way down the tower and back to the huge drawing room. The first thing I did was to rush into the arms of the Scarecrow, and then the Tin Man hugged me – but not too tight, in case he hurt me. The next thing I did was to wind up Tiktok, so that he could bow properly when introduced to the rest of the company.

DOROTHY: Oh, I've just remembered. Where's Billina?

SCARECROW: Who's Billina?

DOROTHY: She's a yellow hen who's another friend of mine.

LANGWIDERE: She's in the chicken house, in the back yard. My drawing-room is no place for hens.

DOROTHY: Then I must go and rescue her at once. *(retreating)* I won't be long.

DOROTHY: *(as narrator)* Just outside the door I came upon the Cowardly Lion.

(OPEN AIR)

DOROTHY: Oh, Cowardly Lion, I'm *so* glad to see you again.

LION: Ditto, Dorothy. We've had some fine adventures together, haven't we?

DOROTHY: We certainly have. How are you?

LION: As cowardly as ever. Every little thing scares me. But let me introduce you to a new friend of mine, the Hungry Tiger.

DOROTHY: Oh, are you hungry?

TIGER: Dreadfully, dreadfully, hungry.

DOROTHY: Then why don't you eat something?

TIGER: Useless, useless. No matter how much I eat, I stay just as hungry as before. Hungry I was born, and hungry I shall die.

DOROTHY: You poor thing.

TIGER: Yes, I *am* a poor sort of tiger. It's the nature of tigers to be cruel and ferocious, and to pounce on any living thing and devour it. But I have a conscience, and I never eat harmless living creatures. I'm acting as no good tiger has ever acted before. That's why I left the forest and joined my good friend the Cowardly Lion.

DOROTHY: Well, I think that's very wonderful of you. Now, I simply must go and rescue my friend, Billina. *(retreating)* I'll see you both again, very soon.

(CROSSFADE TO MUSIC. HOLD A LITTLE, DOWN FOR FOLLOWING AND OUT)

DOROTHY: May I present my good friend, Billina.

BILLINA: How do you do?

LANGWIDERE: As I have already remarked, I do not usually approve of hens in my drawing room. However, I might make an exception for a *talking* hen.

DOROTHY: Ozma, is the whole of your army composed of officers?

OZMA: All except one. In my Army I have 8 generals, 6 colonels, 7 majors and 5 captains. And then there's one private for them to command. Officers lend dignity to our army.

DOROTHY: I'm sure you're right.

OZMA: And now, we will hold a solemn conference to decide how we are going to liberate the royal family of this fair land of Ev from their long imprisonment. Yes, Tin Man?

TIN MAN: Just to set the background. Word came to our noble ruler, Ozma of Oz, that the widow of the former king of Ev, together with her ten children — five boys and five girls — had been enslaved by the Nome King, and were being held prisoner in his underground palace. Since there was no one in Ev powerful enough to release them, Ozma naturally wanted to help. A friendly sorceress named Glinda presented Ozma with a magic carpet which would continually unfold beneath our feet, making a comfortable path across the desert which divides our two countries. And so here we are.

LANGWIDERE: My uncle Evoldo was a very wicked man. He sold his wife and children to the Nome King. The fact that he regretted what he had done and then drowned himself makes no difference.

OZMA: I quite agree. The Nome king must be made to give up his prisoners. Where are they being held?

LANGWIDERE: No one knows, exactly. What we do know is that the king, whose name is Roquat of the Rocks, is the ruler of the underground world. He has a splendid palace underneath the great mountain to the north of this kingdom. It's rumoured that he has transformed the queen and her children into ornaments, and that he uses them to adorn his magnificent living quarters.

DOROTHY: Goodness gracious me.

LANGWIDERE: That is the rumour. I cannot vouch for it.

OZMA: One thing is quite clear. We must visit King Roquat of the Rocks in his own country. It will be a dangerous undertaking.

DOROTHY: But we must do it, for the sake of the poor prisoners. Mustn't we, Scarecrow?

SCARECROW: We shall do it, although it requires a lot of courage for me to go near the furnaces of the Nome King.

DOROTHY: Furnaces?

SCARECROW: Yes, thousands and thousands of Nomes toil away day and night at their furnaces, making gold and silver and diamonds and rubies. But we'll go, even though I'm only stuffed with straw and a single spark could destroy me.

DOROTHY: How brave you are!

TIN MAN: The furnaces could also melt my tin, but I'm going, too!

DOROTHY: And you're just as brave, Tin Man. Of course you are.

LANGWIDERE: I can't bear heat, so I shall stay at home. But I do wish you all success in your enterprise. I am heartily sick of ruling this stupid kingdom. I need more leisure, so that I can admire my beautiful heads.

OZMA: We don't need you. If I can't succeed with all my brave followers, then for you to undertake the journey would be useless.

LANGWIDERE: How very true. So, if you'll excuse me, *(retreating)* I'll now retire to my boudoir. I've worn this head for quite a while, and I'm tired of it. I want to change it.

(DOOR OPENS AND CLOSES)

OZMA: Will you be coming with us, Dorothy?

DOROTHY: Of course. Me and all my friends. I wouldn't miss this for anything. You'll come, won't you Tiktok?

TIKTOK: I am your slave, Dorothy. Where you go, I go.

DOROTHY: And you, Billina?

BILLINA: To be sure.

(FADE IN MUSIC BENEATH FOLLOWING)

OZMA: Then for the rest of today we will prepare ourselves for the journey. Make sure everyone gets to bed early and has a good rest. For we start for the Kingdom of the Nomes at daybreak tomorrow.

(UP MUSIC. HOLD A LITTLE. DOWN FOR CLOSING ANNOUNCEMENT. UP MUSIC TO END)

END OF PART ONE

(MARCH-LIKE MUSIC. DOWN FOR OPENING ANNOUNCEMENT. UP MUSIC. CROWD CHATTER AS BACKGROUND. DOWN MUSIC, BUT HOLD BENEATH FOLLOWING.)

DOROTHY: *(as narrator)* Everyone was awake before daybreak, and soon we were all eating breakfast in the great dining-room of the royal palace. Ozma of Oz sat at the head of the long table. I sat on one side of her, and the Scarecrow on the other. Lower down were the 27 warriors of Oz, and at the far end sat the Cowardly Lion and the Hungry Tiger, who was eating a great chunk of raw beef as fast as he could. When he'd finished, complaining loudly that he was starving hungry, he and the Lion were harnessed to Ozma's chariot. Then the whole party assembled, ready to start for the Nome king's palace.

(UP MARCH MUSIC. HOLD A LITTLE. DOWN FOR)

First rode Ozma in her golden chariot, with me beside her holding Billina firmly in my arms. Then came the Scarecrow on a sawhorse, with the Tin Man and Tiktok marching side by side just behind him. After these tramped the army, looking brave and handsome in their splendid uniforms. The generals commanded the colonels, and the colonels commanded the majors, and the majors commanded the captains, and the captains commanded the private – and the private marched with an air of proud importance, because it required so many officers to give him orders.

(UP MARCH MUSIC. HOLD A LITTLE. DOWN FOR FOLLOWING AND OUT)

BILLINA:	*(calls)* Stop! Wait!
SCARECROW:	*(calls)* Halt everyone!
TIN MAN:	*(calls)* What's the matter? Why have we stopped?
DOROTHY:	Billina wants to lay her egg, that's all. It won't take a minute.
BILLINA:	*(cackles)*
TIN MAN:	Lay her egg?
DOROTHY:	Yes, Tin Man. She lays one every morning about this time, and it's quite fresh.
BILLINA:	*(cackles, retreating)* If you'll excuse me...
TIN MAN:	And your foolish old hen thinks that this entire calvacade, which is bound on an important mission, should wait while she lays an egg?
DOROTHY:	She won't take long. Honestly!

BILLINA: *(advancing, clucks)* There we are. Job done. Will someone please collect my egg?

SCARECROW: I'll get it. I'll keep it in my pocket. Now *(calls)* Forward March!

(MARCH MUSIC. HOLD A LITTLE. MIX TO REGULAR THUMPING LIKE A PILE DRIVER)

DOROTHY: *(as narrator)* We'd reached a narrow valley lying between two huge mountain peaks. As we marched forward the mountains came closer and closer, until finally there was only a narrow path left, and we were forced to walk in single file.

OZMA: What's that thump-thumping sound?

SCARECROW: I can't imagine, your Highness.

TIKTOK: Perhaps round the next corner…

LION: *(calls)* This is fearful! Fearful!

TIKTOK: What is it, Mr Lion? Let me see! Oh, it's only the giant! He's made out of metal, you know. Just like me.

TIN MAN: Like me, too.

LION: Fearful, fearful. That great big hammer pounding so near my head. One blow would crush me into a doormat.

TIKTOK: I know all about this splendid fellow. He was made for the Nome King by the same firm that made me.

DOROTHY: But Tiktok, why is he banging the roadway with his mallet?

TIKTOK: Well, his duty is to keep people from finding the underground palace.

OZMA: Can he speak and think like you do?

TIKTOK: Oh, no, your Highness. He's made to pound the road, that's all. But he does it very well, don't you think?

SCARECROW: Too well, I'd say. Is there no way to stop his machinery?

TIKTOK: 'Fraid not, Mr Scarecrow. The Nome king has the only key.

SCARECROW: Let me think. Give me a minute. I do have some brains, you know. Ah-ha! I have it. We must run under the hammer, one by one, as it's lifted, and get to the other side before it falls again.

LION: Won't that be terribly dangerous?

TIN MAN: Not if we're quick enough. Just a bit of speed – that's all that's required.

OZMA: We certainly can't get through with this chariot of mine.

SCARECROW: No, we'll have to leave the chariot on this side. Now, who's going first?

LION: Why is everyone looking at me?

SCARECROW: Well, you're leading the procession – you and your friend the hungry Tiger. I know, your Highness, why don't you ride on the Lion's back? He'll get you through. Then Dorothy can ride through on the Tiger.

DOROTHY: What a good idea. You first, Ozma. Cling fast to his mane. I've ridden the Lion myself, and that's the way I held on.

DOROTHY: *(as narrator)* So Ozma clung onto the Lion's mane. The Lion crouched in the path and eyed the swinging mallet carefully, until he knew just the instant it began to rise. Then he made a sudden leap straight between the giant's legs, and before the mallet struck the ground again, the Lion and Ozma were safe on the other side.

(FADE IN MUSIC BENEATH FOLLOWING. LOSE THUMPING)

I was next, on the Hungry Tiger. We got through just as easily. When everyone saw that it could be done they lined up and, one by one, braved the giant mallet. Soon the whole party was on the other side, and we proceeded on our way, leaving the giant to pound the path behind us.

(UP MUSIC. HOLD A LITTLE. DOWN FOR)

After a while we approached the furthermost edge of the Kingdom of Ev. We were now close to the Nome king's dominions, and his splendid underground palace could not be far away.

(SHORT BURSTS OF MOCKING LAUGHTER. LOSE MUSIC)

DOROTHY: Who's that? Who's laughing at us?

LION: This is scary. Oh dear, oh dear.

OZMA: There are all sorts of creatures flitting about.

TIKTOK: Don't mind them, your Highness. They're only the Nomes.

DOROTHY: Who are the Nomes?

TIKTOK: Rock fairies. They serve the Nome king. They won't harm us – but someone will have to call for the king. We'll never find the entrance to the palace unless he lets us in.

DOROTHY: I think it had better be you, Ozma. He won't take notice of any of us.

OZMA: I suppose you're right. Are you ready? *(calls imperiously)* I demand that the Nome king appear to us.

(BURSTS OF MOCKING LAUGHTER)

TIKTOK: Excuse me, your Highness, but you mustn't command the Nome king. After all, you don't rule him as you do your own people in the Land of Oz.

OZMA: Quite right, Mr Tiktok. I'll try again. *(calls)* I request the Nome king to appear to us.

(BURSTS OF MOCKING LAUGHTER)

TIKTOK: Try begging him.

OZMA: Begging? Shall Ozma of Oz humble herself? I put it to everyone here – do you want your ruler to plead with the wicked Nome king?

(ALL SHOUT: "NO")

DOROTHY: *I'm* not afraid to plead with him. Let me call the Nome king.

TIGER: Do – and if he makes hash of you, I'll willingly eat you for breakfast tomorrow morning.

DOROTHY: Oh, Hungry Tiger, you wouldn't. Your conscience wouldn't let you. Now just stand to one side, will you? *(calls)* Please, Mr Nome king, come here and see us.

(LOUD PROLONGED CREAKING SOUND)

SCARECROW: The rock face! It's opening.

TIN MAN: You've done it, Dorothy.

NOME KING: *(remote, on echo)* Enter!

LION: This is fearful. It could be a trick. Oh dearie, dearie me.

OZMA: Never mind. We came here to rescue the poor queen of Ev and her ten children. We must run some risks if we're to succeed. Follow me!

            (MUSIC. HOLD A LITTLE. DOWN FOR FOLLOWING AND OUT. FADE IN)

            (hushed) This must be the throne room. It's very dim.

DOROTHY: *(hushed)* There. At the far end. Is that the Nome king?

TIN MAN: *(hushed)* He's exactly the same colour as the rock he's sitting on.

TIKTOK: *(hushed)* That's not a rock. That's his throne. Can't you see it's studded with diamonds and emeralds and rubies.

DOROTHY: *(hushed)* He looks just like Santa Claus – only he's not the same colour.

NOME KING: *(remote, laughing)* I heard that! And you may be right. Come along, seat yourselves over here, by me. You, my dear, on the other side. That's right.

OZMA: Thank you. Now, your majesty, I am the ruler of the Land of Oz, and I've come here to ask you to release the good queen of Ev and her ten children. I understand you have enchanted them and are holding them here as your prisoners.

NOME KING: Oh, no, no, my dear. You're quite mistaken. They aren't my prisoners – they're my slaves, bought fair and square from the king of Ev. The purchase was entirely above board.

OZMA: But for him to do that was quite wrong.

NOME KING: According to the laws of Ev, the king can do no wrong. He was perfectly within his rights to sell his family to me, if he wanted to. He did it in exchange for a long life.

DOROTHY: Then you cheated him. He didn't have a long life. He jumped into the sea and was drowned.

NOME KING: That's scarcely my fault. I did give him a long life, but he destroyed it. I have no intention of giving up the queen and her children on that account. They belong to me, and I shall keep them.

OZMA: If you've made them your slaves, you're treating them very cruelly.

NOME KING: Once again, you are very much mistaken. I cannot abide cruelty of any kind. Since the queen and her children were very delicate, I transformed them into ornaments and bric-a-brac of various sorts, and I dispersed them around the palace. They do no work of any nature. They merely stand around and look decorative. I really think I've treated them with the utmost kindness.

OZMA: But what a fate you've subjected them to. And meanwhile the kingdom of Ev is in urgent need of a royal family to govern it. Free them, and I will give you eleven ornaments to replace each one you lose.

NOME KING: And if I refuse?

OZMA: Then with my army and my friends here I will conquer your kingdom and force you to obey.

NOME KING: *(laughing)* You? And your army? And your friends? *(calls)* Come with me. All of you. Come…

(CREEP MUSIC BENEATH FOLLOWING)

DOROTHY: *(as narrator)* He led us to a little door at one side of his throne room. This he opened, and we stepped out onto a balcony which commanded a wonderful view of his underground world. A vast cave extended for miles under the mountain, and in every direction furnaces and forges were glowing brightly, with Nomes at each of them hammering on precious metals or polishing gleaming jewels. All around the walls, built into the solid rock, were thousands of doors of silver and gold extending in rows far into the distance.

Suddenly the Nome king reached for his belt, from which dangled a golden whistle…

(SHRILL WHISTLE)

… At once all the silver and gold doors flew open, and from every one marched solid ranks of Nome soldiers. There were so many that they quickly filled the immense underground cavern, and forced the busy workmen to abandon their labours.

(UP MUSIC. CROSSFADE TO NOME KING)

NOME KING: This is but a small part of my army. Let me disperse them, and we will return to the throne room.

(SHRILL WHISTLE. FADE IN)

NOME KING: Well, Ozma of Oz. What have you to say now?

OZMA: I don't know what to say. It would be foolish to fight, for our brave army of 27 would soon be wiped out.

TIGER: One thing you could do is to ask where the kitchen is. I'm starving.

SCARECROW: It seems to me that our best plan is to wheedle his majesty into giving up his slaves.

NOME KING: That's the most sensible thing I've heard today. It's folly to threaten me, but I'm so kind-hearted that

I invariably yield to coaxing and wheedling. Why doesn't someone try it?

OZMA: Oh, all right. Now, your majesty, I am very keen to liberate the queen of Ev and her children, who are at present ornaments and bric-a-brac in your palace. Tell me how I might do this?

NOME KING: Well, are you willing to take a few risks yourself?

OZMA: Oh, yes. Yes indeed.

NOME KING: Then I'll make you an offer. You'll have free access to all the rooms in my palace. You may examine everything they contain. Then you may touch eleven different objects, saying the word "Ev". If any of those objects happens to be the queen or one of her children, they'll instantly be changed back, and I'll let you leave my kingdom with them.

OZMA: What happens if I don't succeed in freeing them all?

NOME KING: Then each of your friends and followers may have the same chance.

OZMA: Oh, thank you. Thank you for your kind offer.

DOROTHY: I don't think the king has finished, Ozma.

NOME KING: Not quite. For I have one condition to make.

OZMA: What is that?

NOME KING: If none of the eleven objects you touch proves to be any of the royal family, then you yourself will be instantly transformed into an ornament. The same will apply to any of your friends who may follow you. This is the risk you said you were willing to take.

(BURST OF MUSIC. HOLD A LITTLE. DOWN FOR FOLLOWING AND LOSE)

DOROTHY: Ozma, don't you do it. If you guess wrong, you'll be enslaved yourself.

OZMA: But I'll have eleven guesses. Surely I'll be able to guess one object in eleven. If I do, I'll have rescued one member of the royal family and be safe myself. Then the rest of you can try, and we'll soon free all the king's slaves.

SCARECROW: But what if we fail?

LION: Yes, think of that. It's a fearful prospect. I'd look nice as a piece of bric-a-brac for the rest of my life!

OZMA: So we mustn't fail. Having come all this way to free these poor unfortunate people, it would be weak and cowardly of us to give up. Your majesty, I accept your offer.

NOME KING: Then come with me, my dear. You may start your search at once.

(MUSIC. DOWN FOR FOLLOWING. HOLD BENEATH)

DOROTHY: *(as narrator)* It was only much later that Ozma told me what happened next. The Nome king led her into his vast underground palace, and there he left her. It was magnificent. The walls and floors were all made of marble, while the ceilings were great stone arches that rose far above her head. She wandered from room to room, each one adorned with exquisite draperies and beautiful furniture – sofas and polished tables and easy chairs upholstered in silk and velvet. And everywhere – on mantels and shelves and brackets and side-tables – were clustered scores of ornaments of every description. There were vases and human figures and animals and bowls and vases and paperweights – shapes too numerous to mention. Hundreds and hundreds – no, thousands – of them, made of every sort of material you could think of: iron and steel and pewter and metal and glass and china and ivory and precious stones. It was only then that Ozma began to realize how much the odds were stacked against her actually finding even one of the eleven objects she was seeking. She had nothing at all to guide her. A silver candelabra with ten branches caught her eye

OZMA: This may be the Queen of Ev and her ten children. I'll touch it. "Ev".

DOROTHY: *(as narrator)* But nothing happened. So she wandered into another room. There she saw a china lamb.

OZMA: This may be one of the children. "Ev"

DOROTHY: *(as narrator)* Again, nothing. On she went. Three guesses. Four. Five. All wrong.

OZMA: Oh dear. This is getting serious. Ah, a little porcelain shepherd all in blue. This *must* be one of the boys. I'll touch it. "Ev". Nothing. That's six guesses, all wrong.

DOROTHY: *(as narrator)* Six turned into seven, seven into eight, eight into nine and nine into ten.

OZMA: One guess left – and my own fate depends on the result. I must take my time. Let me see – let me see. I know. I'll leave it to chance. I'll close my eyes ... like this ... and I'll creep forwards ... like this ... and I'll stretch out my hand ... like this ... and the very first thing my fingers touch... Ah! "Ev"!

(CLASH OF CYMBALS)

DOROTHY: *(as narrator)* Disaster! Ozma had vanished – and the Nome king had gained a new ornament, a pretty grasshopper, formed from a single emerald.

NOME KING: *(bursts out laughing)*

TIKTOK: What's happened? Has she failed?

NOME KING: She has. But that's no reason why one of you shouldn't succeed. The next one to try can have twelve guesses instead of eleven, since there are now twelve people transformed into ornaments. Now, who is it to be?

DOROTHY: *(as narrator)* I'm not going to dwell on the next few hours – they're too painful to describe in detail as, one by one, each of our party left to try their luck. Not one of them found any of the trapped prisoners, and one by one were themselves transformed into ornaments. Billina had crept into a hollow underneath the Nome king's rocky throne, but the rest of us sat in the throne room. Every time I offered to go next, but every time one of the others insisted on going first. So finally, sitting facing the king, were Lion, Tiger, Scarecrow, Tiktok – and me.

NOME KING: This has gone on long enough. It's after midnight. Tomorrow is another day – we can conclude our business then. *(calls)* Chief Steward!

STEWARD: *(approaching)* Your majesty?

NOME KING: Show these guests to the sleeping apartments. Then come back here, and you can escort me to my own bedroom.

(MUSIC. DOWN THEN FADE BENEATH FOLLOWING)

DOROTHY: *(as narrator)* Now, everyone had forgotten about Billina, including me. As I told you, she'd tucked herself into a little nook beneath the Nome king's throne, and had gone to sleep. Suddenly the sound of the king calling for his steward woke her up, but scared of being discovered, she kept very quiet. And this is what she heard.

STEWARD: *(approaching)* They're all safely locked into their sleeping quarters, your majesty.

NOME KING: Good.

STEWARD: But I don't know why you waste so much time on them. Why didn't you just turn them all into ornaments at once, instead of playing this game with them, one by one?

NOME KING: Because it amuses me, that's why. I'm getting an enormous amount of pleasure in seeing them fail, one by one.

STEWARD: But suppose some of them happen to guess right?

NOME KING: There's not much chance of that. Do you know how many ornaments I have, scattered through the rooms of this palace?

STEWARD: I do not, your majesty.

NOME KING: Well, taking into account the newest additions to my collection, three thousand, five hundred and eighty seven. Three thousand, five hundred and eighty seven! How is anyone to pick out the few correct ones from that lot? The odds are astronomic. In any case, how could they guess that my prisoners are the only ornaments with a touch of royal purple in their decoration? Those few are scattered amongst thousands of ornaments decorated with every color of the rainbow. Take my word for it, Steward, they wouldn't settle on the purple ones in a month of Sundays.

STEWARD: Well, your majesty, if I may say so, I think you're acting very foolishly even to run the risk of losing.

NOME KING: You may not say so, Steward. You are going too far.

STEWARD: All the same, if you come to grief, remember that I told you so. I'd never take the chances you're taking. If I wore the magic belt that gives you so much power, I'm sure I'd make a much wiser king than you are.

NOME KING: *(angry)* Now you *have* overstepped the mark. Get out of my sight. One more piece of impudence like that and I'll send you to work in the furnaces. Out! Out!

DOROTHY: *(as narrator)* Tucked beneath the Nome king's throne, Billina heard every word of this conversation. As the king left to go to bed, Billina tucked her head under her wing and went to sleep. She woke up next morning to find me and my few remaining friends back in the throne room, facing the Nome king.

TIGER: I'm starving hungry.

NOME KING: I ordered breakfast for you all. Didn't you have any?

TIGER: It was only a bite, your majesty. But what good is a bite to a hungry tiger?

STEWARD: He ate 17 bowls of porridge, a platter full of fried sausages, 11 loaves of bread, and 21 mince pies.

NOME KING: Goodness gracious. What more could you possibly want?

TIGER: Something alive, that I can chase and kill. But of course my conscience wouldn't allow me to do that, so I'll have to be an ornament and forget my hunger. I volunteer to go next.

NOME KING: Absolutely impossible. I most certainly will not allow any clumsy beasts to roam through my palace, breaking all my pretty ornaments. Once your other friends have tried and failed to find my prisoners, you may return to the upper world and go about your business.

LION: Does that apply to me too?

NOME KING: It certainly does. Lions are just as clumsy as tigers.

DOROTHY: In that case, it really is my turn to find your prisoners.

TIKTOK: No, no, Dorothy. I am your servant. It is up to me to go first.

SCARECROW: Tiktok's quite right, Dorothy. He has to go before you do.

DOROTHY: Oh, all right. Scarecrow. If you say so.

TIKTOK: *(retreating)* Wish me luck, Dorothy!

DOROTHY: *(calling)* Oh, I do. We all do.

LION: }
TIGER: } *(calling)* Good luck, Tiktok. Do your best.
SCARECROW: } You show them, Tiktok.

(MUSIC. HOLD A LITTLE, THEN DOWN FOR FOLLOWING, AND HOLD UNDER)

DOROTHY: What is Tiktok doing now, your majesty?

NOME KING: Let me use my magic powers. Ah, he's doing nothing. He's standing perfectly still in the middle of a room.

DOROTHY: Oh, I expect he's run down. I forgot to wind him up this morning. How many guesses has he made?

NOME KING: All that he's allowed, except one. Suppose you go in and wind him up, and then you can stay there and try to find my prisoners yourself.

DOROTHY: All right.

SCARECROW: It's my turn next.

DOROTHY: Oh, Scarecrow, you haven't the strength to wind Tiktok up. Your hands are only gloves stuffed with straw. No, it has to be me.

SCARECROW: I suppose so. Run along, little Dorothy, and may good luck go with you.

(UP MUSIC. HOLD A LITTLE. DOWN FOR FOLLOWING AND OUT)

DOROTHY: *(as narrator)* I wandered through the palace until I came upon Tiktok standing motionless in the middle of a huge, beautifully furnished room, filled with dozens and dozens of wonderful ornaments. I quickly wound up the machine man's action, speech and thoughts.

TIKTOK: Thank you, Dorothy. I now have only one guess to make.

DOROTHY: Oh, be very careful, Tiktok, won't you?

TIKTOK: I'll do my best, but I'm afraid the Nome king has beaten us. He must have known that there was very little chance of anyone finding his prisoners. He took a gamble, but it has paid off.

DOROTHY: I fear you're quite right, Tiktok. Well, make your guess, and if you fail, I'll watch to see what shape you're changed into.

TIKTOK: All right. Now, let's see… Ah, how about this ivory figurine? This looks very special. Now…"Ev"

(CLASH OF CYMBALS)

DOROTHY: *(as narrator)* In a flash Tiktok had vanished. I

looked in every direction, but it was impossible to find one new ornament among so many. So in the end I thought I'd better get on with making my own guesses. I walked through the rooms, examining all the knick-knacks very carefully, but there was nothing to show which ones might be the Nome king's prisoners. Like Ozma, I decided that it must simply be a matter of guessing right. So I touched two or three, calling out "Ev", but none of my guesses proved correct. And then I came upon a pretty little purple kitten fashioned out of porcelain.

DOROTHY: Oh, how sweet. I'll choose you. "Ev".

(CLASH OF CYMBALS, FOLLOWED BY RINGING OF HANDBELL. FADE BELL)

EVRING: Where am I? What's happened to me?

DOROTHY: Well, I do declare! I've really done it.

EVRING: Done what?

DOROTHY: Saved myself from being an ornament. And saved you from being a purple kitten for ever.

EVRING: A purple kitten?

DOROTHY: That's what you were, a moment ago. Don't you remember standing up there on the mantel?

EVRING: I most certainly do not. I am a prince of Ev, and my name is Evring. I remember my father, the king, selling my mother and all his children to the cruel Nome king. I can't remember much else.

DOROTHY: Well, now that you're yourself again, I'm going to try to save some of your brothers and sisters, and perhaps also your mother. So come with me.

DOROTHY: *(as narrator)* I seized the boy's hand and hurried here and there, trying to decide which object to choose. My next guess was a failure, so was the next and the next. Finally, when I'd used up all my guesses, I decided to return to the Nome king with my one success. But while all this was going on, certain events had been taking place in the throne room.

(CROSSFADE TO BRIEF BURST OF MUSIC. QUICKLY DOWN AND OUT)

BILLINA: *(loud prolonged cluck-clucking)*

NOME KING: Good gracious! What's that?

SCARECROW: Why, it's Billina. I wondered what had happened to her.

NOME KING: What do you mean by making a noise like that?

BILLINA: I've got a right to cackle, I guess. Especially since I've just laid my egg.

NOME KING: Laid an egg? In my throne room? How dare you do such a thing?

BILLINA: I lay eggs wherever I happen to be.

NOME KING: *Thunder-ation!* In my kingdom, eggs are poison.

BILLINA: Poison? I'll have you know that all my eggs are warranted strictly fresh and up to date. Poison, indeed!

NOME KING: Listen to me. Eggs belong only to the outside world – the world you come from. Here, in my underground kingdom, they are rank poison. We nomes can't bear them around.

BVILLINA: Well, you'll have to bear this one around. I've just laid it.

NOME KING: Where? Where did you lay it?

BILLINA: Under your throne.

NOME KING: *(scream)* Take it away, take it away. I can't sit up here with an egg underneath me. Get rid of it. This very instant.

BILLINA: I can't. I haven't any hands.

SCARECROW: I'll take the egg. I'm making a collection of Billina's eggs. There's one in my pocket now that she laid yesterday. I'll put this one in my other pocket, so that they don't break each other.

NOME KING: Get away from me, you... you scarecrow, you.

BILLINA: Stop!

SCARECROW: Why, what's wrong?

BILLINA: Don't remove that egg unless the king allows me to enter the palace and guess, just like the others have done.

NOME KING: You? You're only a hen. How could you be more successful than the others?

BILLINA: I can try. And if I fail, you'd have another ornament.

NOME KING: That's true. I can never resist the chance of adding to my collection. Very well, you shall have your way. It'll be a good punishment for daring to lay an egg in the royal presence. Now, Scarecrow, get rid of that egg.

SCARECROW: Right away.

(HANDBELL RINGS)

NOME KING: Well, well, well. The girl has actually done it.

SCARECROW: Done what?

NOME KING: She's made one correct guess. Just one. It's too bad. I never thought she'd do it. Ah, here she is.

DOROTHY: *(remote, approaching)* I trust you'll keep your word, your majesty. I've found one of your prisoners and released him. This is Prince Evring.

NOME KING: I always keep my promises, no matter how foolish they are. But I'll make an ornament of that yellow hen, to replace him.

DOROTHY: Billina! Where on earth have you been?

BILLINA: Good morning, Dorothy. I've laid my egg for today – and now I'm going to try my luck at freeing the prisoners.

DOROTHY: Oh, no, Billina. You'll never succeed. You'll just be turned into one of those ornaments.

BILLINA: You never know. I may surprise you all by guessing right.

NOME KING: Guessing right? You stupid hen. How can you guess right when all your betters have failed?

BILLINA: I shall not dignify that with a response. Let me pass, please.

NOME KING: Absurd feathered fool!

BILLINA: *(retreating)* Feathered I may be, but I'm no fool even if I *am* a chicken. *(cluck-cluck)*

NOME KING: I hope I've seen the last of that bird. Hens are bothersome enough at the best of times, but when they can talk they're simply dreadful.

DOROTHY: *(as narrator)* Billina, of course, knew the Nome king's secret, and it didn't take her long to identify all the ornaments which had a touch of royal purple in their colouring. Finally, the yellow hen noticed a large purple footstool. "Ah ha" she thought. She placed a claw upon it and said "Ev". At once the footstool vanished, and a lovely lady, tall and slender and most beautifully robed, stood before her.

BILLINA: Good morning, ma'am. Welcome back to the land of the living.

QUEEN: Who is addressing the Queen of Ev?

BILLINA: My name, your majesty, is Billina. Down here, ma'am. The yellow hen at your feet.

QUEEN: Ah, indeed. The yellow hen. I've never encountered a hen that speaks before.

BILLINA: Nor have I, ma'am, if truth be told. Not even myself, before I found myself in the sea, floating off the land of Ev. Then it all seemed to come quite naturally. The important thing is that I have saved you from the Nome king, and you are a slave no longer.

QUEEN: Then I thank you most gratefully. But, my children... Tell me, I beg of you... Where are my children?

BILLINA: Fear not. They are all safe, every one of them, even though they have been enchanted – all, that is, except young prince Evring who is with my friend

Dorothy. Come with me, ma'am, and watch me disenchant the whole lot of them – your family, and Ozma the ruler of Oz who came all the way here to help you, and all her friends and helpers.

DOROTHY: *(as narrator)* Soon the whole of Ozma's company, together with the Queen of Ev and nine of her ten children were gathered together in one of the great rooms of the palace.

OZMA: Now let us all go back to the Nome king, and see what he has to say for himself.

(MARCH MUSIC. DOWN FOR)

DOROTHY: *(as narrator)* So off they started. Ozma went first, with the queen and her train of little princes and princesses following. Then came Tiktok and the Scarecrow, with Billina perched upon his straw-stuffed shoulder. After them marched the Tin Man, while the 27 officers and the private brought up the rear.

As they reached the hall, the doors flew open before them…

(FADE MUSIC BENEATH FOLLOWING)

and they all stopped and stared into the huge cavern. For the room was filled with the mail-clad warriors of the Nome king, rank after rank, standing in orderly array, their battle-axes poised as if to strike down their foes. And in the center of this terrible army sat the Nome king on his throne of rock, his face distorted with rage and most dreadful to behold.

NOME KING: I have been betrayed. Someone has tricked me — and I know who it is. It's that girl Dorothy. Seize her!

LION: *(roar)* Anyone who comes anywhere near Dorothy will have me to deal with. Anyone want to fight a lion?

TIGER: *(growl)* And me as well. Who wants to take on a particularly hungry tiger?

NOME KING: Well, get on with it. Seize her.

STEWARD: Would you mind enchanting those wild beasts first, your majesty?

NOME KING: You lily-livered crew. Oh well, let the girl alone. She can't escape us, anyway. As for the rest of you, starting with Ozma, surrender all of you. You're my prisoners.

BILLINA: But you promised that if I guessed correctly, my friends and I could depart in safety. And you always keep your promises.

NOME KING: Ah, but did you guess correctly? Or did someone betray my secret? Who is the traitor? Come on. Tell me his name.

(CREEP MUSIC BENEATH FOLLOWING)

DOROTHY: *(as narrator)* But Billina said not a word. Ozma, however, had no intention of surrendering. She rallied her troops and ordered them to rush forward. The captain of the Nomes was so surprised by this sudden onslaught that he forgot to command his warriors to fight, and the first rank went down like ninepins. The others were pressed so closely behind that they fell backwards like a set of dominoes. One by one the ranks of the Nome soldiers fell back until they were all lying on the ground, kicking their legs in the air.

The Nome king, furious, marched over the top of them until he was facing Ozma and her friends. But before he could take any action, the Scarecrow drew one of Billina's eggs from his pocket and hurled it straight at the little monarch's head. It hit him squarely in the left eye, where the egg smashed and covered his face and hair and beard with its sticky contents.

NOME KING: *(roar of rage)* Ow! Help! Help!

STEWARD: It's an egg! An egg! Run for your lives!

DOROTHY: *(as narrator)* And how they did run. The warriors fairly tumbled over each another in their efforts to escape the fatal poison of that awful egg. While all this was going on, Billina flew over to Dorothy.

BILLINA: *(urgent whisper)* Get his belt! Get the Nome king's belt! It's the source of all his magic. Go on – it unbuckles at the back. Quick, Dorothy, quick.

(UP MUSIC. HOLD A LITTLE. DOWN FOR
FOLLOWING. HOLD MUSIC UNDERNEATH)

DOROTHY: *(calls)* Your majesty, we shall now leave your kingdom – all of us. And you will allow us all to go.

NOME KING: *(furious)* I will do nothing of the kind. You will all be instantly transformed into scorpions. All of you. Every one. NOW! *(puzzled, anxious)* What's wrong? Why is my magic not working?

STEWARD: You're not wearing your magic belt, your majesty. Where is it? What have you done with it?

NOME KING: It's gone! It's gone – and I'm ruined.

DOROTHY: It's not gone. *I* am wearing it.

NOME KING: You... You...

DOROTHY: Be careful. You don't know what I may do with my magical powers.

NOME KING: *(splutters in frustration)* You ... you don't know how to use my belt. It's no use to you. Give it back, and I'll let you go free.

DOROTHY: I'm keeping the belt. And now we're leaving.

NOME KING: Oh, yes? Well tell me how you propose to do that? Where's the entrance? It's all solid rock, isn't it? You're trapped.

DOROTHY: Of course we're not. *(calls)* Belt, open the passage.

(CLASH OF CYMBALS)

Come along, everybody. Goodbye your majesty!

(UP MUSIC)

CAST: Goodbye, farewell, let's go, come along, come on, good riddance, get moving, bye-bye, cheerio… etc., etc.

(HOLD MUSIC. FADE IN THUMP-THUMP OF GIANT'S HAMMER. MUSIC DOWN FOR FOLLOWING)

OZMA: Getting past the giant, Dorothy – it's going to be much more difficult than before. We have all these royal children now.

DOROTHY: Don't worry Ozma. Remember – I have the magic belt. *(calls)* Belt, stop the giant thumping!

(THUMPING STOPS)

Right everyone, through the giant's legs. Quickly. Let's get as far away from the Nome king as possible.

(UP MUSIC. DOWN FOR FOLLOWING, THEN OUT)

DOROTHY: *(as narrator)* We found Ozma's golden chariot, harnessed up the Lion and the Tiger, and set off.

When our cavalcade arrived at the royal palace of Ev, a great crowd of people had gathered to welcome the queen and her ten children. There was much shouting and cheering, and people threw flowers in our path. We found the princess Langwidere in her boudoir, admiring one of her heads, and I can't tell you how glad she was to be rid of her royal duties.

(FADE IN CROWDS BENEATH FOLLOWING. FADE OUT AS QUEEN STARTS TO SPEAK)

Then the queen led her eldest son, Prince Evado, to the great French doors that opened onto a balcony. Facing the huge crowds that had gathered outside the palace, she spoke into the microphone.

(EXTERIOR. QUEEN'S SPEECH ON ECHO, AS IF FROM LOUDSPEAKERS)

QUEEN: People of Ev. I present to you your future ruler, King Evardo. He is 15 years of age, has 15 silver buckles on his jacket, and is the 15th Evardo to rule the land of Ev.

(GREAT CROWD ROAR, AS AT FOOTBALL MATCH. CROSSFADE TO MUSIC. DOWN FOR)

DOROTHY: *(as narrator)* The royal reception that followed wasn't the only one I attended. For Ozma invited me to return with her to the land of Oz for a visit. We crossed the desert using Ozma's magic carpet, and entered Oz by way of the Munchkin territory.

The king of the Munchkins met us at the border, and that evening he entertained us right royally at his palace. Next morning we set out for the Emerald City, Ozma and I in her golden chariot, drawn by the Cowardly Lion and the Hungry Tiger. Everywhere the people turned out to greet their beloved Ozma, and all of us.

That evening we all sat down to a splendid feast in the royal palace. Ozma sat at the head of the table, with me on her right and Billina on her left. Then came the Scarecrow, the Tin Man and Tiktok with baskets of flowers in front of them, because they didn't need food. The Lion and the Hungry Tiger sat together, because they certainly did. Then came the 26 army officers with the private standing behind them. After a while the Scarecrow rose to speak. He congratulated Ozma on the success of her mission, and proposed her health.

Ozma stood up. She presented gold medals to each of the 26 officers, and promoted the private on the spot to be commander of her bodyguard. The Tin Man was given a new axe studded with diamonds, the Scarecrow a jar of complexion powder, and Tiktok two bracelets set with sparkling emeralds. Then she turned to me.

OZMA: Dorothy Gale of Kansas, I present you with this golden coronet, and hereby create you a princess of Oz.

(UP MUSIC. HOLD A LITTLE. DOWN FOR FOLLOWING AND LOSE)

DOROTHY: *(as narrator)* I passed several very happy weeks in the land of Oz. One day, sitting in Ozma's private room, I noticed a very odd picture hanging on the wall – it kept changing. First it was a meadow, then a lake, sometimes a village. I asked Ozma about it.

OZMA: Yes, it's a wonderful invention. Whatever place or person I want to see, I need only say so, and there it is in front of me.

DOROTHY: May I try it?

OZMA: Of course, Dorothy.

DOROTHY: Show me my aunt Em. How is she? What is she doing?

(MAGIC SOUND – PERHAPS TINKLE)

Oh there she is. Dear aunt Em, washing dishes by the kitchen window. And there's the farm. And Toto…

OZMA: Who's Toto?

DOROTHY: My dog. Just look at him snoozing in the sun. How marvellous. Everything's all right, back in Kansas. Oh – Uncle Henry! I wonder what he's doing? Show me Uncle Henry.

(MAGIC SOUND – PERHAPS TINKLE)

And there he is, in Australia I suppose, sitting in an easy chair, smoking his pipe. But he looks ill and very sad, doesn't he? He doesn't seem to be getting better. He must be worried about me. Ozma, dear, I simply have to go to him at once.

OZMA: Well, there's your magic belt. I have it here. Why not buckle it round you, and order it to take you to your uncle?

DOROTHY: What a wonderful idea. Wait a minute, though. Once I was away from Oz, wouldn't it lose its magic, just like my silver shoes did last time? Wouldn't it be better for you to keep the belt, and use it to wish me to join my uncle Henry?

OZMA: You're right, Dorothy. Here, I'll wrap it round me. Now Dorothy, every Saturday morning, at exactly eight o'clock, I'm going to ask my magic picture to show me what you are doing. If you wave your right hand as the clock strikes eight. I'll know you want to come back to Oz, and I'll tell the magic belt to bring you here.

DOROTHY: Oh thank you, Ozma. So it isn't goodbye. It's only *au revoir*.

OZMA: *Au revoir*, dear Dorothy. Belt, transport Dorothy to her uncle Henry.

(CLASH OF CYMBALS. FADE IN)

DOROTHY: ... no, I wasn't drowned at all. And I've come to nurse you and get you well again. And Uncle Henry you must promise to get well as soon as possible

UNCLE HENRY: I'm better already, my darling.

(MUSIC. DOWN FOR CLOSING ANNOUNCEMENT. UP MUSIC TO END)

END OF PART 2

THE THINKING MACHINE:

THE PROBLEM OF CELL 13

BY JACQUES FUTRELLE
DRAMATIZED FOR RADIO
BY NEVILLE TELLER

Running time: 30'

FIRST BROADCAST ACROSS THE USA
ON 18 APRIL 2018 IN A PRODUCTION BY
SHOESTRING RADIO THEATRE, SAN FRANCISCO

CHARACTERS IN
ORDER OF APPEARANCE

RANSOME   *Mid-40s A doctor. Professional friendly manner.*

VAN DUSEN   *Mid-50s, A super intelligence. Described as "wizened" but with "an enormous head". Impatient and rather dismissive of people who can't keep up with him. You can almost hear that brain working.*

FIELDING   *Mid-40s. Professional man.*

MARTHA   *Early 60s. Typical African-American servant of the 1900s. Feisty. She's probably the only one who can manage Van Dusen – or dares to.*

WARDEN   *Late-40s. Prison governor. Pretty much a disciplinarian, but a reasonable man. A friend of Ransome, so he deals more gently with him.*

SCOTT   *50s. A jailor with years of experience, who's seen it all. Born and bred in New England.*

ELEANOR HATCH   *Mid-30s. A hard-boiled woman journalist who's fought her way up in a man's world. There weren't all that number around in 1900, but those who'd made it were good! Resourceful, in control of the situation – and always out for a story.*

(MUSIC. DOWN FOR OPENING ANNOUNCEMENT. UP MUSIC. FADE SLOWLY)

RANSOME: Such a thing is impossible.

VAN DUSEN: Nothing is impossible.

FIELDING: My dear Van Dusen, what an extraordinary thing to say.

VAN DUSEN: I mean it.

RANSOME: You may have more letters after your name than before it, Van Dusen, but I challenge you all the same.

FIELDING: What about airships? You're not saying that one day we'll be able to fly?

VAN DUSEN: Not impossible at all, Fielding. They'll be invented some time – sooner rather than later, I'd say. I'd do it myself, but I'm busy.

RANSOME: *(laughs)* No wonder the newspapers call you the Thinking Machine.

FIELDING: *(laughs)* Augustus S. F. X. Van Dusen, to whom nothing is impossible.

VAN DUSEN: Nor is it.

RANSOME: Admit it, Van Dusen – there are some things that can't just be *thought* out of existence.

VAN DUSEN: Like what, Ransome?

RANSOME: Erm... Well, take prison. No man can *think* himself out of a cell. If he could, there'd be no prisoners.

VAN DUSEN: What a man could do is apply his brain and ingenuity so that he could *leave* a prison cell, which amounts to the same thing.

FIELDING: Van Dusen! You can't mean what you're saying.

VAN DUSEN: Indeed I can – and do.

RANSOME: Suppose you were locked in a cell in death row, unable to communicate with other prisoners. Are you saying you could escape?

VAN DUSEN: Most certainly.

FIELDING: Only if you entered the cell with tools that could enable you to get out.

VAN DUSEN: Not at all, Fielding. Lock me in any prison, anywhere, wearing only what is necessary. Treat me precisely as any prisoner under sentence of death. I guarantee to escape within a week. One week.

RANSOME: This time, Van Dusen, you've gone too far. At last the Thinking Machine has outsmarted himself.

VAN DUSEN: I would get out.

RANSOME: Are you serious, Van Dusen?

VAN DUSEN: Deadly.

FIELDING: Would you be willing to try it?

VAN DUSEN: Of course. May I ring for my housekeeper?

FIELDING: Please do. Now let's get this clear. You're arrested without warning and locked in a death cell with no chance to communicate with friends.

VAN DUSEN: Exactly.

(KNOCK ON DOOR. DOOR OPENS)

MARTHA: *(remote throughout scene)* Here I is, professor. All the way from the kitchen. I guess you want something.

VAN DUSEN: I certainly do, Martha. I'm going away. Tonight.

MARTHA: Tonight? Ain't that a bit sudden? You want me to pack?

VAN DUSEN: That won't be necessary.

MARTHA: How long you planning ... *[to be gone, professor...]?*

VAN DUSEN:	I shall be back exactly one week from tonight.
MARTHA:	A week? With no clean underwear? What you thinkin' of, professor?
VAN DUSEN:	Never you mind about that, Martha. Next Thursday, at half-past nine, these gentlemen and one or two others will take supper with me, here.
MARTHA:	Got it. Supper for five next Thursday at half past nine.
VAN DUSEN:	Oh, and please remember. Dr Ransome is very fond of artichokes.
MARTHA:	Oh, I knows that already. Yes sir. Is that everything?
VAN DUSEN:	Thank you, Martha.

(DOOR CLOSES)

RANSOME:	I'll take my artichokes with a pinch of salt. Now, how about the death cell in Auburn Prison? The warden's a great friend of mine.
VAN DUSEN:	Auburn Prison is quite acceptable.
FIELDING:	And what will you wear?
VAN DUSEN:	As little as possible. Underwear, a shirt, trousers, socks, shoes.

FIELDING:	You'll allow yourself to be searched, of course.
VAN DUSEN:	Of course.
RANSOME:	Then kindly allow me to use your telephone.
VAN DUSEN:	You're welcome.

(RECEIVER LIFTED. HANDLE OF 1900 TELEPHONE TURNED)

RANSOME: Hullo. Hullo, operator? Please connect me to Auburn Prison. *(pause)* Oh, hullo. May I speak with the Warden, please. *(pause)* My name is Dr Charles Ransome. Mr Mead is a friend of mine. *(pause)* Hullo. Hullo, Warren. Oh, very well, thank you.

(SLOW FADE OUT OF THE FOLLOWING)

Now this may come as something of a surprise, but I have a rather unusual request to make of you, and I do hope you'll be willing to go along...

(MUSIC. DOWN FOR FOLLOWING AND FADE BENEATH)

WARDEN: Well, my officers have searched you thoroughly, Professor Van Dusen, just as we would a convicted felon.

VAN DUSEN: And you've found nothing except the clothes on my back.

WARDEN: That is so.

RANSOME: Warren, I must ask you this. Would it be at all possible for him to communicate with someone outside the prison?

WARDEN: That, Charles, I can assure you, will be totally impossible. He will not be supplied with writing materials of any sort. I've been warden here for 13 years. In all that time not one prisoner in the condemned cell has ever succeeded in making contact with anyone outside.

FIELDING: How about your jailers, Mr Mead? After all Professor Van Dusen is a wealthy man, unlike most of your prisoners, I imagine. Could they be tempted? Would they deliver a message for him?

WARDEN: They would not, Mr Fielding. I've hand selected the officers who'll be guarding him – men of the utmost probity. Every word he utters will be reported to me, and they'll hand over anything he may give them.

VAN DUSEN: Which is exactly as I would wish it to be.

RANSOME: Just one thing, Warren. If things get too much for him during the coming week, and he asks for his liberty, you will of course free him.

WARDEN: That goes without saying. Rest assured, Professor Van Dusen, you have only to say the word. You aren't a convicted felon. You're being incarcerated only for the purpose of proving – or rather disproving – your claim. Though I must admit a certain personal interest in the experiment. I am convinced that this institution is escape proof. It would cause me no little concern to be proved wrong.

VAN DUSEN: Then, Mr Mead, I apologize in advance for the worry I'll be causing you. Gentlemen, before you leave I should like to make three small requests. You may grant them or not, just as you please.

FIELDING: No special favours, now.

VAN DUSEN: I'm not asking for any. All I'd like is some tooth powder, and one 5-dollar and two 10-dollar bills.

RANSOME: Warren, is there anyone that our friend will be in contact with who could be bribed with 25 dollars?

WARDEN: Twenty-five hundred wouldn't do the job.

FIELDING: Well, let him have them, then. They won't get him out.

RANSOME: You said three requests.

VAN DUSEN: It's just that I'd like my shoes polished, if you don't mind.

WARDEN: That's not a problem. Ordinary prisoners are required to polish their own boots; those on death row have it done for them. Just hand them over to my officer when you get to your cell. Come along, gentlemen. This way.

(EDGE OUT. EDGE IN – HALF ECHO)

WARDEN: And here we are. Mr Flanagan, if you please.

(KEY ON METAL. KEY TURNS IN LOCK. DOOR CREAKS OPEN. SQUEAKING OF RATS)

This where we keep condemned murderers. No one in it can possibly communicate with the outside. You'd stake your reputation on that, eh Mr Flanagan? His office is just over there; he can hear everything.

RANSOME: What's that terrible squeaking?

VAN DUSEN: Rats. Dozens of them. Am I right, Warden?

WARDEN: I'm afraid we are somewhat plagued by them – especially in this block.

VAN DUSEN: Never mind. They can keep me company. Now, Warden, could you tell me what the time is, exactly?

WARDEN: Let's see. It's just on eleven-seventeen.

VAN DUSEN: Thank you. Well one week from tonight, at half-past eight, I'll be joining you three gentlemen, as free as a bird.

RANSOME: Will you indeed?

VAN DUSEN: Indeed I will.

WARDEN: And where do you intend this meeting to take place?

VAN DUSEN: Why in your office, of course, Warden. Where else?

WARDEN: Your self-confidence, Professor, is entirely misplaced. Nobody has ever escaped from Auburn prison. Here you are, and I guarantee that here you will stay – unless you yourself ask to be released. I wish you good night. If you please, Mr Flanagan.

(HEAVY CLANG OF METAL CELL DOOR BEING SHUT, AND KEY TURNING IN LOCK. MUSIC. HOLD A LITTLE. DOWN FOR FOLLOWING AND OUT UNDERNEATH)

VAN DUSEN: *(as narrator)* As soon as I heard their footsteps retreating down the corridor, I started taking very careful stock of my situation. By standing on the bed and peering through the closely barred window, I could see that Auburn prison was a huge structure set in the middle of a great open yard which was surrounded by a wall of solid masonry eighteen feet high. On top of this was a five-foot fence of steel rods, each ending in a sharp point.

The prison yard was twenty-five feet wide in all directions and was brilliantly lit by great arc lamps set on all four walls of the prison. The feed wire to the lamp fixed high above my cell ran within a few feet of my window. The yard was patrolled by armed guards. When I had satisfied myself on all those matters, I lay down on my bed and had a sound night's sleep.

Next morning, after ablutions and a modest breakfast, I was left to my own devices. Again I stood on the bed and peered through the window. I soon deduced that the river lay not too far beyond the prison walls, because I could hear the faint pulsing of motor boats. Then came the distant sound of boys at play and the sound of a ball hitting a bat, and I gathered that a playground lay between the prison walls and the river.

I looked at the window bars, and could see that there wasn't a trace of rust on them. Peering down I couldn't see the ground, but it was clearly only three or four feet below the cell window – an easy drop, if the window were big enough and the iron bars could be removed.

There was nothing in the cell except the iron bed, so firmly put together that it was impossible to dismantle, and a chamber pot of heavy porcelain. There wasn't even a table, a chair, or a bit of crockery. The jailer stood by while I ate, and then took away the wooden spoon and bowl that I'd used.

VAN DUSEN: Before you go, jailer. I get very thirsty. Do you think I could have a little water in the cell with me?

SCOTT: I'll ask the warden.

VAN DUSEN:	When do I see you next?
SCOTT:	I bring you food at 6 a.m., at noon and at 6 in the evening. At 9 p.m. there's a tour of inspection.
VAN DUSEN:	*(as narrator)* And that was to be the sum total of my human contact. When I had completed a thorough examination of my cell, I sat down on the bed to think. I was disturbed by a rat, which ran across my foot and then scampered away to a dark corner, frightened at its own daring. I squinted into the darkness, and thought I could see more than one pair of beady eyes staring at me. I got to my feet and took a step towards them. There was a great squeaking and scampering of feet, and then silence.
	I got down on my hands and knees and felt around in the darkness. After a moment I came upon a small round opening in the floor. When I felt inside the opening it seemed to be a disused drainage pipe.

(KEY TURNS IN METAL LOCK. METAL DOOR HANDLE)

SCOTT:	*(remote, advancing)* Midday. Here's your lunch. Sit on the bed. I'll put the tray on your lap. Oh, and here's the water you asked for. The warden says you may keep this bowl, but you must show it to me when I ask. If you break it, you won't get another.
VAN DUSEN:	I'll guard it with my life, jailor. No, I can't go on calling you jailor. What's your name?

SCOTT: Zack Scott.

VAN DUSEN: *(eating)* Well, Mr Scott. Things must stay pretty much the same in prison. Any improvements here in the past few years?

SCOTT: Nothing in particular. We had new plumbing about seven years ago.

VAN DUSEN: Really? I can tell there's a river over there. How far away is it?

SCOTT: Only about a hundred yards.

VAN DUSEN: Really?

SCOTT: There's a baseball ground before you get there.

VAN DUSEN: Yes, I can hear the boys playing. OK, Mr Scott. I guess that will keep body and soul together till this evening.

SCOTT: Right. I'll take your tray.

VAN DUSEN: Thank you, Mr Scott. I look forward to your next visit.

(EDGE OUT. FADE IN)

SCOTT: *(remote, advancing)* What on earth are you doing down there?

VAN DUSEN: Got you!

SCOTT: What have you got?

VAN DUSEN: Just look at this? Stop wriggling!

SCOTT: My God – a rat! Ain't you got anything better to
                do than catch rats?

VAN DUSEN: I shouldn't have to. It's disgraceful they're here at all.
                Take this one away and dispose of it. It's a water rat.
                If you release it outside, it'll make its way to the river.

SCOTT: Give it here. But I warn you – this is the first and
                last time I do this. *(retreating)* You can stop
                catching them as from now. And I'll be telling the
                warden all about it.

VAN DUSEN: *(calling)* Then perhaps he'll do something about
                his prison being infested by vermin.

                **(HEAVY CLANG OF METAL CELL DOOR BEING
                SHUT, AND KEY TURNING IN LOCK. MUSIC.
                HOLD A LITTLE. DOWN FOR FOLLOWING AND
                OUT UNDERNEATH)**

SCOTT: Have a look at this, Warden.

WARDEN: What is it?

SCOTT: This was thrown out of the window of Cell 13
                half an hour ago.

WARDEN: Show me. A 5-dollar bill wrapped around a piece
                of torn shirting. Who's on guard duty?

SCOTT: Flanagan. Of course he brought it straight to me.

WARDEN: Good heavens. There's something written on the linen. *(deciphering)* "Finder please deliver to Dr Charles Ransome". Ah-ha – plan of escape number one has gone wrong. But why did he want to contact Dr Ransome?

SCOTT: More to the point, sir, where did he get the pen and ink to write with?

WARDEN: Oh, my goodness. You're right. Let's see what he was going to say to Dr Ransome. It's wound up pretty tight. Now what's this? Some sort of code. Can't make head or tail of it. I think I'll have a word with the professor. Come with me, Scott.

(EDGE OUT. EDGE IN)

WARDEN: Still catching rats? It seems to be your favourite occupation.

VAN DUSEN: It's disgraceful. These rats – there are scores of them.

SCOTT: Other occupants of this cell have been able to stand them.

WARDEN: Professor, I'm afraid I'll have to take your shirt from you. I've brought you a standard prison garment. The stripes are quite decorative. Please change.

VAN DUSEN:	If you insist.

WARDEN:	I'll take that one, if you please. Now let me see. As I thought. This note of yours was torn from your shirt. Now, what did you write this with?

VAN DUSEN:	That, Warden, is surely for you to find out.

WARDEN:	Scott, search the cell.

(MUSIC. DOWN FOR FOLLOWING AND OUT)

SCOTT:	Day three, professor, and you're no nearer escaping.

VAN DUSEN:	The prison's drainage pipes, Mr Scott – they lead to the river, don't they?

SCOTT:	They do, but they're much too small for you to crawl through, if that's what you're thinking.

VAN DUSEN:	How true. Those arc lights out there. They keep me awake.

SCOTT:	Turn your face to the wall.

VAN DUSEN:	Who looks after them?

SCOTT:	Man from the company.

VAN DUSEN:	You have no electricians in the building?

SCOTT:	No.

VAN DUSEN: I should think you could save money if you had your own man.

SCOTT: None of my business, professor.

VAN DUSEN: Mr Scott, I came into this prison thinking I could make my escape. I wonder, would you consider a financial reward for helping me get out?

SCOTT: No.

VAN DUSEN: Fine hundred dollars. Remember, I'm not a criminal. There's nothing illegal in what I'm suggesting.

SCOTT: No.

VAN DUSEN: A thousand?

SCOTT: No. I'll have your tray. Thanks. You can offer me what you like, but I couldn't get you out. You'd have to go through seven locked doors, and I only have the keys to two of them. Just admit it, Professor. You've set yourself a hopeless task. There's no escaping from Cell 13.

(MUSIC. DOWN FOR FOLLOWING AND OUT)

WARDEN: Another note?

SCOTT: Yes, Warden. He threw this down about half an hour ago. Bartelli was on duty. He brought it straight to me.

WARDEN: Well it's Monday. He's been with us for four days. He must be getting desperate. He's tried sending a coded message and he tried bribery. What's he up to this time? Let's see. "Only three days more."

SCOTT: What does he mean?

WARDEN: Well, it's either a cry of despair, or it's a boastful warning to us. I wonder which?

SCOTT: But, Warden, where did he get the white linen shirting to write on?

WARDEN: Indeed. And we still haven't discovered either a writing implement or any ink. How does the fellow manage it?

(FADE OUT. FADE IN)

SCOTT: It's happened again, Warden.

WARDEN: What's happened again?

SCOTT: He's dropped something out of his cell window. The guard immediately brought it to me.

WARDEN: Who was on duty?

SCOTT: Flanagan again, sir. He's a good man. One hundred percent reliable.

WARDEN: I'll note this on his record. See if I can manage a bonus at Christmas. Show me.

SCOTT: It's only a five dollar bill, Warden. He called out to Flanagan: "That's for you."

WARDEN: A five dollar bill? What do you mean a five dollar bill?

SCOTT: What's the matter, sir?

WARDEN: The matter, Scott, is that he went into that cell with one five dollar and two ten dollar bills. He threw one five dollar bill out into the yard with a message two days ago. Where did he get another five dollar bill? Where?

SCOTT: I couldn't say, Warden.

WARDEN: Take three of your best men, Scott, and search that cell again with a fine-tooth comb. Search it as it's never been searched before. I want you to test each and every bar on that cell window. Examine the walls, the floor, the ceiling. Dismantle the bed. That man is making a fool of us.

(EDGE OUT. FULL UP)

SCOTT: I'm sorry, sir. Nothing. Nothing at all.

WARDEN: All right, men. You may go.

(FEET ON CONCRETE)

Now, Professor van Dusen. Turn out your pockets, if you will.

VAN DUSEN: By all means. I imagine these will be of interest to you.

WARDEN: Good God, man. How on earth did you get hold of five one-dollar bills?

VAN DUSEN: That, I'm afraid Warden, is my business.

WARDEN: Did any of my men change this money for you? On your word of honour, Professor.

VAN DUSEN: I'm not obliged to answer that, Warden. But I will tell you that no, none of your men are responsible.

WARDEN: Then how, in the name of all that's holy…?

VAN DUSEN: I'll tell you all about it on Thursday night. In your office.

WARDEN: Such impudence! Remember, Van Dusen, pride comes before a fall.

(MUSIC. DOWN FOR FOLLOWING. HOLD UNDER THROUGHOUT)

WARDEN: Oh no, Scott. Don't tell me there's something else.

SCOTT: I'm afraid so, sir. It's getting worse. He threw another note out of his cell window – but this time he followed it with a 50-cent piece.

WARDEN: I don't believe it.

SCOTT: Here it is, Warden. A half-dollar coin.

WARDEN: And the note?

SCOTT: It read: "Day 5. Only two days more."

WARDEN: Where is he getting the linen, the pen, the ink? To
                   say nothing of the money. How is he doing it?

                   (UP MUSIC. DOWN FOR FOLLOWING. HOLD
                   UNDERNEATH THROUGHOUT)

RANSOME: My dear Charles. This is just to confirm that Mr
                   Alfred Fielding and I will be presenting ourselves
                   at the prison gates tomorrow evening at half-
                   past seven. We gather that our friend, Professor
                   Van Dusen, has not yet escaped, for we have
                   heard nothing from him, and so we presume you
                   will be releasing him at around half-past eight.
                   We expect to meet him in your office shortly
                   afterward.

                   (UP MUSIC. DOWN FOR FOLLOWING. HOLD
                   UNDERNEATH THROUGHOUT)

SCOTT: Another note, sir. He writes: "Looking forward to
                   our meeting, tomorrow evening at 8.30."

WARDEN: The impudence of the man!

                   (UP MUSIC. DOWN FOR FOLLOWING. HOLD
                   UNDERNEATH THROUGHOUT)

WARDEN: Come in, Scott. Six-thirty. Just two hours to go. Everything all right in cell 13?

SCOTT: Yes, sir. He didn't eat much, though. I left him lying on his bed. He complained about the arc lights. Said they kept him awake.

WARDEN: Well, he won't be spending another night in the cell. We'll wait till eight-thirty, just to disprove his claim, then we'll bring him here. He and his friends can all go home together. And so much for his much-vaunted escape.

            (UP MUSIC. DOWN FOR FOLLOWING. LOSE UNDER)

WARDEN: Yes, Scott?

SCOTT: Dr Ransome and his colleague have arrived, sir, but the guard on the river side reports that his arc light has failed. It's pretty dark on that corner.

WARDEN: Phone the electric company, and get some men down here as quickly as possible. This is a prison. That light needs fixing urgently.

SCOTT: Yes, sir.

WARDEN: Meanwhile, get someone to escort Dr Ransome and his friend up here to my office.

SCOTT: *(retreating)* Right away, Warden.

(MUSIC. DOWN AND OUT QUICKLY UNDER FOLLOWING. FADE IN)

WARDEN: Well, welcome once again to Auburn, gentlemen.

RANSOME: We've heard nothing from Van Dusen all week, Warren. Has he been all right?

WARDEN: He's in the pink of condition. He's made one or two feeble attempts to bribe his way out. But he was safe and sound and locked in Cell 13 only a quarter of an hour ago.

FIELDING: It looks as though his claim to escape is about to be proved wrong.

WARDEN: Resoundingly wrong – together with his assertion of meeting us all here in my office in... let me see... just over half an hour's time.

FIELDING: Yes, that was his boast. Can the Thinking Machine have got it all so wrong?

RANSOME: No one is perfect, Fielding. Not even the Professor.

(KNOCK ON DOOR)

WARDEN: *(calls)* Yes? Who is it? Come in.

(DOOR OPENS)

SCOTT: *(remote, advancing)* Sorry to disturb you, Warden, but this letter has just been brought over by the guard. He says it was delivered to the gate by hand. It has "Urgent" on the envelope.

WARDEN: Thanks, Scott. Let me see...

(ENVELOPE RIPPED OPEN)

Incidentally, have the electricians arrived?

SCOTT: Yes, sir. They're hard at work right now.

WARDEN: Ye gods and little fishes!

RANSOME: What is it?

WARDEN: This letter. It's a special delivery.

FIELDING: Yes. What of it?

WARDEN: Look where it's from.

FIELDING: Cell 13?

RANSOME: But... but what is it?

WARDEN: An invitation to supper. This evening at 9.30. At Van Dusen's residence! The cheek of the man. How was this letter delivered to our gatehouse? Scott, get over to Cell 13 this instant and see that he's still in there.

SCOTT: *(retreating)* Yes, sir. I'll be back in just a few minutes.

RANSOME:	It looks as though we've been under-estimating our friend.
WARDEN:	Nothing of the sort. This is all some sort of trick that he's managed to pull. But he's inside that cell. That I'd wager.
FIELDING:	I'm tempted to ask how much you'd wager, Warden – but I won't. We'll all know soon enough.
RANSOME:	Let me have a look at that letter, Warren, would you? Thanks. Yes... it's Van Dusen's handwriting, there's no question of that.

(TELEPHONE BELL SINGLE RING. RECEIVER LIFTED)

WARDEN:	Hullo. Yes, guard, what's up? Reporters? How many? Oh well, I can manage two. Get someone to escort them up here.

(RECEIVER REPLACED)

Word of Van Dusen's claims must have got out. Two reporters have arrived. If they're hoping for some dramatic turn of events, they'll be disappointed. And I don't mind the world knowing how secure Auburn Prison is. Yes, Scott?

SCOTT:	*(remote, advancing)* He's in his cell, all right, sir. He's not catching rats for once. He's in bed fast asleep.

(DOOR CLOSES)

WARDEN: There, I told you. Despite all his games and tricks, he's certainly not escaped from his cell.

RANSOME: What games and tricks?

WARDEN: Well, somehow – heaven knows how – he managed to get hold of a pen of some sort and an endless supply of white linen on which to write, and he's been dropping notes out of his cell window. And then – again, I can't imagine how – he acquired a whole lot of dollar bills from somewhere. To say nothing of a half-dollar coin. We've searched him and his cell time and again, but there's no explanation that I can see. And then, how did he mail this letter from his cell? Perhaps he'll enlighten us on all this, once we release him.

(KNOCK ON DOOR. DOOR OPENS)

SCOTT: *(remote)* The two reporters, sir.

WARDEN: *(half-whisper)* Not a word about all this before them, gentlemen. I'd never hear the last of it. *(aloud)* Ah, good evening. I know you, Miss Hatch. We've met before.

ELEANOR: Indeed we have, Warden. May I introduce my colleague?

VAN DUSEN: Good evening, Warden. Gentlemen. Please excuse me, I may be a trifle early. I believe it's not quite eight-thirty.

WARDEN: What on…? Where on…? How on…?

VAN DUSEN: You seem lost for words, Warden. As for me, I'm a man of mine. I said I'd escape from your condemned cell, and I did so. I said I'd meet you here this evening at 8.30, and here I am. If I'd wagered a thousand dollars on doing what I said I'd do, I'd be a wealthy man.

RANSOME: My dear Van Dusen, you've put us all to shame.

FIELDING: You must tell us how you did it.

VAN DUSEN: All in good time. Miss Hatch, gentlemen, would you care to accompany me back to my cell.

ELEANOR: I'd certainly love to see it. I have a camera with me. I'll take a few pictures, if I may.

SCOTT: But I saw you lying in bed not ten minutes ago.

VAN DUSEN: Then perhaps you'd come with us as well, Mr Scott. Follow me.

(MUSIC. DOWN AND OUT. FADE IN)

VAN DUSEN: Your men tested the bars on this window of mine only two days ago. Isn't that right, Mr Scott?

SCOTT: It certainly is. And as I reported back to the Warden, they're as firm as the day they were fixed.

VAN DUSEN: Really? Then how do you explain this, Mr Scott?

(CLATTER OF METAL RODS HITTING EACH OTHER AND THE FLOOR)

ELEANOR: I must get a shot of that. Hold it one second.

WARDEN: Miss Hatch – please! You'll make a mockery of Auburn prison, and bring ridicule on my officers. I'll have to ask you to leave.

ELEANOR: No, Warden. I do assure you that the only effect of my story will be to enhance the reputation of the Thinking Machine, Professor Van Dusen. The high security achieved at Auburn Prison has never been in doubt, and I will do nothing to damage your record.

WARDEN: Oh, very well. What's this in the bed?

VAN DUSEN: A wig. Let me turn down the covers.

FIELDING: Good grief, what have you got in there? A hardware store?

VAN DUSEN: Merely thirty feet of strong rope, a dagger, ten feet of electric wire, a powerful pair of pliers – see this? – a small hammer, and...

WARDEN: A pistol? This is too much.

VAN DUSEN: I disagree, Warden. It was an essential part of the bare necessities I required to effect my escape.

WARDEN: I dare say you'll enlighten us shortly on how you acquired them and achieved your miracle?

VAN DUSEN: Over supper at my house – a supper I'm certain my housekeeper will have arranged precisely according to my instructions, right down to your artichokes, Ransome. Shall we make our way?

(CROSSFADE TO MUSIC. FADE MUSIC BENEATH FOLLOWING. FULL UP. CROCKERY, CUTLERY)

VAN DUSEN: But do you both admit that it was a fair test?

RANSOME: Most certainly. And you proved your point, van Dusen. Mind you, I'd say that you are the only person in the United States of America who could have done what you did.

WARDEN: Yes, how did you do it?

ELEANOR: That's certainly something my readers will want to know – from the horse's mouth, as it were. I'll take down the Thinking Machine's own words. Mind you, I must admit to having had a hand in it all.

WARDEN: What's that, Miss Hatch? What sort of hand?

ELEANOR: I think it would be best if the professor gives his own account.

VAN DUSEN: Yes, well… Let me start at the beginning. My agreement was to go into a prison cell, carrying nothing and wearing only a few basic clothes, and to leave that cell within a week. I had never seen Auburn prison. When I went in I asked for some tooth powder, two ten and one five-dollar bills and to have my shoes blacked. It wouldn't have mattered seriously if my requests had been refused. But you agreed to them.

WARDEN: Well, except for the money, any condemned prisoner would have been allowed those things.

VAN DUSEN: Exactly. What you didn't take into account is that anything is dangerous in the hands of someone who knows how to use them. Anyway, next morning I learned from Mr Scott that except for my three mealtimes, I would be left alone in my cell, so straight after breakfast I undertook a detailed examination of my surroundings.

WARDEN: What was there to learn?

VAN DUSEN: A great deal. First that the river lay not far away from the perimeter wall. And second that there was a boys' playground between the wall and the river. Both these facts were later confirmed by Mr Scott.

WARDEN: Anything else?

VAN DUSEN: Indeed yes. That the feed wire to the arc light above my cell ran within a few feet of my window. It was while I was sitting pondering the various possibilities that a rat ran over my feet.

WARDEN: Those rats. You did keep on about them.

VAN DUSEN: With good reason. For they suggested an interesting line of thought. I stood up suddenly and clapped my hands – and hey, presto! They vanished. I watched to see where they disappeared to. It was in one corner of the cell. I went down on my hands and knees and searched around.

ELEANOR: And what did you find, professor?

VAN DUSEN: An old drain pipe – long unused and half-choked with dirt. But this was where the rats had disappeared, and obviously the way they came in. But where did they come from? A drain pipe would probably lead to the river, or near it. That first day, when Mr Scott brought me my meal, he told me two important things, though he probably didn't realize it. One was that a new system of plumbing had been put into the prison about seven years ago, and the second was that the river was only three hundred yards away. That told me that the drainage pipe was part of the old system, and that it led down toward the river.

ELEANOR: But you couldn't know whether it ended in water or on dry land.

VAN DUSEN: You're ahead of me, Miss Hatch. But you are quite right. That was one thing I had to find out.

WARDEN: And how did you manage that?

VAN DUSEN: By catching several of them. Mr Scott was surprised to see me at this, but all I did was examine them, one by one, Each was completely dry – but more than that, I discovered that they weren't the usual type found in houses. They were field rats. So then I knew that the drainage pipe ended on dry land, outside the prison walls. From that moment, Warden, I devoted no little effort to leading you astray.

WARDEN: You certainly led me and my men a merry dance, professor. But you have a great deal more explaining to do.

VAN DUSEN: All in good time. The first thing was to try to make you believe I was trying to communicate with you, Ransome. So I wrote a note on a piece of linen that I tore from my shirt, addressed it to Dr Ransome, tied a five-dollar bill to it, and threw it out of the window. I knew the guard would take it to you,

WARDEN: Hold on, professor. You say "I wrote a note" as if you had pen and ink in front of you. You had neither. How did you write a note?

VAN DUSEN: May I direct your attention to these boots of mine, Warden – the boots you so obligingly blacked for me just a week ago.

ELEANOR: Why, they're scraped clean, right down to the leather.

VAN DUSEN: Precisely, Miss Hatch. That was my ink. As for my pen, the metal tips of my shoe laces served perfectly.

FIELDING: Van Dusen, you're a perfect wonder!

VAN DUSEN: It's simply a matter of using one's brain, as I told you originally.

WARDEN: But then I took your white shirt away and gave you a striped prison shirt instead. Yet you went on writing your notes.

VAN DUSEN: I had already removed nine inches of linen. I had it rolled up in a ball and in my mouth when you next searched the cell.

WARDEN: Nine inches of linen? Where did you get that from?

VAN DUSEN: The fronts of all white evening shirts are of triple thickness. I simply pulled away the third layer. I knew you wouldn't notice. Nor did you,

RANSOME: You have a great deal more explaining to do, Van Dusen. You obviously got in touch with someone outside the prison.

ELEANOR: Guilty, Dr Ransome.

RANSOME: You, Miss Hatch?

ELEANOR: I'm afraid so.

VAN DUSEN:	I knew that drainpipe led to somewhere outside the prison. I knew that rats came into my cell and went back there. I knew that there was a boys' playground close by. So the first thjing I needed was a long and reliable thread. I hope I don't embarrass you, Miss Hatch, if I pull up my trouser legs. Here… And here.
ELEANOR:	I've seen much worse than your legs, Professor, in my journalistic career.
VAN DUSEN:	It's not my legs I'd draw to your attention, but my socks. As you see, there's very little left of them. I unravelled them, and had easily a quarter of a mile of thread. On my remaining linen I wrote a note to my dear friend, Miss Eleanor Hatch – I knew she'd help me, if only for the newspaper story she'd get from it.
ELEANOR:	I'd have helped in any event.
VAN DUSEN:	Thank you. I tied my ten-dollar bill to the letter, and wrote "Finder please deliver to Miss Eleanor Hatch of *The Daily American* who will give you another ten dollars." I took one of the rats, tied the note to one leg, fastened my thread to another, and turned him loose in the drain pipe. He scuttled away as if his life depended on it. I reckoned that once he was outside he'd probably gnaw off the linen.
FIELDING:	Wasn't that a very risky thing to do, professor? You had no idea of what might happen. I mean

the thread may have got broken before the rat reached the outside?

VAN DUSEN: Yes, Fielding, a thousand things may have gone wrong. I was on tenterhooks for hours. But one thing gave me some confidence.

RANSOME: And that was…?

VAN DUSEN: The thread in my hand almost ran out. That suggested that my letter had indeed reached the outside.

ELEANOR: I was in my office at around five that afternoon when I was told a young lad wanted to see me. He'd been playing baseball, and had spotted the note. Of course I gave him his ten dollars. Then I carefully followed the instructions in the note. Before I got the boy to show me where he'd found it, I arranged for some spools of silk, some twine and a roll of light wire to be delivered. I waited till two in the morning, and then began the search. The note said that when I found the end of the thread, I was to follow it back to the drainpipe, and give it a twitch. Once the professor had answered, I was to attach the silk to the end of the thread, and to the end of the silk I was to attach the wire.

VAN DUSEN: I lay awake that night with my end of the thread wrapped round my finger. It was nearly half-past three when I felt the thread twitch. Then I began to pull it in. There was always the possibility that it might snag somewhere and break. Fortunately, nothing if the sort occurred, and so I acquired some of the things I needed to effect my escape.

ELEANOR: And then we tested the pipe to see if it could act as a speaking tube.

VAN DUSEN: We found it did. Though I had to speak softly, I was able to make Miss Hatch understand that I needed some nitric acid.

WARDEN: But we searched the cell repeatedly. We never found these items.

VAN DUSEN: Of course not. I simply slipped them back into the drain pipe and guarded the top with a dead rat.

WARDEN: Yes, I remember.

VAN DUSEN: Before leaving, Miss Hatch passed change for ten dollars up the pipe. Now I needed the guard to get used to seeing me at my cell window. As I stood there, I took to dropping notes and money down to him. I'd already learned from Mr Scott that the prison was dependent on an outside electrical company if anything went wrong with the arc lamps.

WARDEN: So it was you...?

VAN DUSEN: I'm afraid so, Warden – once Miss Hatch had supplied me with the nitric acid I'd asked for. I severed the feed wire, which was quite close to my cell window, and…

WARDEN: Hold your horses, professor. There were bars on your window. Your cell was inspected several times on your last day.

VAN DUSEN: Cutting the steel bars was not difficult, using the nitric acid. But it did take time. Hour after hour. There I stood looking down at the guard, and occasionally he looked up at me, especially when I dropped money. But all the time I was working on those bars with wire dipped in acid. What else? Miss Hatch supplied the wig that was necessary to my plan. The special delivery letter I wrote with a fountain pen kindly supplied by Miss Hatch, and sent it down the drain pipe to her.

WARDEN: But you left the prison grounds, and came back in. How on earth…?

VAN DUSEN: Perfectly simple. I'd already cut the electric wire. When they switched them on, and the one above my cell didn't light, I knew the guard would go to report to you. The yard was dark. I removed the bars, crept out of the window – it's only a few feet above the ground – replaced the bars, and stayed in the shadows until the group of electricians arrived. Miss Hatch, dressed in uniforms and with a forage cap on, was one of them.

ELEANOR: I'd come carrying overalls and a cap. I handed them to the professor. As soon as he was dressed, we made our way out of the gatehouse.

VAN DUSEN: As we left I told the guard we needed something from the van. Out of his sight, we quickly discarded the overalls, and reappeared as two reporters asking to see you. We saw you. That's all.

RANSOME: Wonderful! Perfectly amazing.

WARDEN: Too many coincidences. You'd never have got out without them.

VAN DUSEN: I assure you, Warden, that there were at least two other ways I could have escaped from that cell.

WARDEN: How did Miss Hatch manage to come in with the electricians?

ELEANOR: You'd be surprised what the Press can achieve, Warden. But in this instance, there was no difficulty at all. My father happens to own the electricity company.

WARDEN: }
RANSOME: } *(laughter – hold till lost by music)*
FIELDING: }
VAN DUSEN: }

(MUSIC. HOLD FOR A LITTLE. DOWN FOR CLOSING ANNOUNCEMENT)

BOX AND COX

BY J M MORTON
ADAPTED FOR RADIO
BY NEVILLE TELLER

Running time: 30'

FIRST BROADCAST ACROSS THE USA
ON 21 OCTOBER 2015 IN A PRODUCTION BY
SHOESTRING RADIO THEATRE, SAN FRANCISCO

CHARACTERS IN
ORDER OF APPEARANCE

NARRATOR

MRS BOUNCER *Mid-50s – their landlady*

JAMES COX *Early 20s*

JOHN BOX *Early 20s*

"COX AND BOX" OVERTURE BY SIR ARTHUR SULLIVAN:
HTTPS://WWW.YOUTUBE.COM/WATCH?V=HZZ-NJFZ7FC

(BOUNCY MELODY FROM "COX AND BOX"
OVERTURE BY SIR ARTHUR SULLIVAN (1
MIN 12 SECS AFTER START). DOWN FOR
OPENING ANNOUNCEMENT. UP MUSIC. FADE
BENEATH NARRATOR)

NARRATOR: Well, here we are in London, England, about a hundred years ago. And this is what they call a "bed-sitter". The bed we can't actually see, since it stands in a recess, shielded by a drawn curtain. The sitter part is the rest of the room which contains a plain wooden table a couple of wooden chairs, and a worn-out couch. As for the rest of the furnishings, there's a basin and a cold water tap in one corner. The cooking arrangements consist of a single gas ring perched rather precariously on a washstand. The one bit of comfort is an old-fashioned open coal fire, before which young Mr James Cox is currently warming himself as he combs his hair with one hand, while holding a small looking-glass in the other.

(KNOCK ON DOOR)

MRS BOUNCER: *(remote, calls)* Mr Cox! It's me, Mr Cox!

COX: *(calls)* Come in, Mrs Bouncer.

(DOOR OPENS)

MRS BOUNCER: *(remote, advancing)* Good morning, Mr Cox. I hope you slept well?

COX: I can't say I did, Mrs B. I'd be much obliged if you could provide me with a plumper pillow. The one I have seems to have about a handful and a half of feathers at each end, and nothing whatever in the middle.

(DOOR CLOSES)

MRS B.: Anything to accommodate you, Mr Cox.

COX: Thank you. Then, perhaps, you'll be good enough to hold this mirror while I do up my tie.

MRS B.: Certainly. Like this? Why Mr Cox, I do declare you've had your hair cut.

COX: Cut? I've had it mowed! It's very kind of you to mention it, but I don't need reminding of how absurd I look. Now where's that hat? Whoops!

MRS B.: Oh my goodness, Mr Cox. You can't wear that.

COX: I certainly can't. My head's shrunk by at least a size-and-a-half. That's the result of having your hair cut. This hat fitted me quite tight before. Luckily I've got two or three more. Here you are – what about this? Oh, no, it's worse than the other one. Hold on, this one seems to wobble about rather less than the others.

MRS B.: Very nice, Mr Cox. Very stylish.

COX: And now I'm off! By the way, Mrs Bouncer, I wish to draw your attention to something that's been bothering me for some time. I've noticed that my supply of coal gets used up remarkably fast.

MRS B.: Mr Cox!

COX: And not only the coal, Mrs Bouncer. I've recently observed a steady reduction in my supplies of wood, tea, sugar and matches.

MRS B.: Lor, Mr Cox! You surely don't suspect me!

COX: I don't say I do, Mrs B. On the other hand, I don't believe it's the cat.

MRS B.: Is there anything else you've got to grumble about, sir?

COX: Grumble! Mrs Bouncer, do you possess such a thing as a dictionary?

MRS B.: Now what would I be doing with a dictionary?

COX: Let me lend you mine. Here. Now if you turn to the letter G…

(RUSTLE OF PAGES)

yes, here we are..."Grumble" – to complain without a cause." Without a cause, Mrs B. Now that's not my case. And now that we're on the subject, I'd like to know why I frequently find my room full of smoke.

MRS B.: Why – I suppose the chimney …

COX: The chimney doesn't smoke tobacco, Mrs B. I'm speaking of tobacco smoke. I hope, Mrs Bouncer, *you're* not guilty of cheroots or Cuban cigars?

MRS B.: Mr Cox! As if I would.

COX: You're not partial to a pipe?

MRS B.: I am not, sir. As you very well know.

COX: Then, how is that…

MRS B.: Why – I suppose… Yes – that must be it…

COX: At the moment I entirely agree with you, Mrs B – because I haven't the remotest idea what you mean.

MRS B.: Why the gentleman who's got the attic is hardly ever without a pipe in his mouth – and there he sits for hours, and puffs away into the fire-place.

COX: Ah, then you mean that this gentleman's smoke, instead of emulating all other sorts of smoke and going *up* the chimney, thinks it proper to take the contrary direction?

MRS B.: Why...

COX: Then, I suppose the gentleman you're speaking of is the same individual that I invariably meet coming up the stairs when I am going down, and going down the stairs when I am coming up!

MRS B.: Why – yes – I...

COX: From his appearance, I should unhesitatingly put him down as someone connected with the printing trade. His hands are invariably covered with printers' ink.

MRS B.: You are quite correct, sir – and a very respectable young gentleman he is.

COX: Except that he smokes. Well, I must be off. *(retreating)* Good morning to you, Mrs Bouncer.

(DOOR OPENS)

MRS B.: You'll be back at your usual time, I suppose, sir?

COX: *(remote)* Yes – nine o'clock. You needn't light my fire in future, Mrs B – I'll do it myself. Don't forget the pillow!

(DOOR CLOSES)

MRS B.: *(close)* Thank goodness he's gone! I declare I was all in a tremble for fear Mr Box would come in before Mr Cox went out. Luckily, they've never met yet – and what's more, they're not likely to. For Mr Box is hard at work at a newspaper office all night, and doesn't come home till the morning, and Mr Cox is busy making hats all day long, and doesn't come home till night. So I'm getting double rent for my room, and neither of my lodgers is any the wiser. What a capital idea of mine that was! But I haven't an instant to lose. First of all, let me put Mr Cox's things out of Mr Box's way.

(OBJECTS MOVED QUICKLY, CLOSET DOOR OPENS AND SHUTS)

I really must beg Mr Box not to smoke so much. I was so dreadfully puzzled to know what to say when Mr Cox spoke about it. Now, then, to make the bed – and don't let me forget that what's the head of the bed for Mr Cox becomes the foot of the bed for Mr Box – people's tastes do differ so.

(CURTAIN DRAWN BACK HASTILY, BEDCLOTHES)

And what's the matter with this pillow may I ask? The idea of Mr Cox presuming to complain!

(CURTAIN DRAWN)

BOX: *(remote, shouts)* Keep your own side of the staircase, sir?

(DOOR OPENS)

(approaching, shouts) It was as much your fault as mine.

MRS B.: Lor, Mr Box! what *is* the matter?

BOX: Mind your own business, Bouncer!

MRS B.: Dear, dear, Mr Box! What a temper you're in, to be sure! You're quite pale!

BOX: What colour would you have a man be, when he's been setting up long leaders for a paper all night?

MRS B.: Oh, but then you've all the day to yourself.

BOX: So I hope! Far be it from me to hurry you, Bouncer, but I intend getting undressed, and going to bed.

MRS B.: Oh, of course, Mr Box. *(retreating)* I'm on my way.

BOX: Stop! Can you inform me who the individual is that I invariably encounter going down stairs when I'm coming up, and coming up stairs when I'm going down?

MRS B.: Oh... yes... That must be the gentleman in the attic, sir.

BOX: Really. Well, there's nothing particularly remarkable about him, except his hats. I meet him in all sorts of hats – white hats and black hats, hats with broad brims, and hats with narrow brims, Stetsons, Fedoras, golfing caps – in short, I have come to the conclusion that he must be professionally associated with the hatting trade.

MRS B.: He is indeed, sir. And by the way, Mr Box, he begged me to ask you, as a particular favour, not to smoke quite so much.

BOX: Did he, just? Then you may tell my lord hatter, with my compliments, that if he objects to the smell of tobacco, he'd better remove himself to some adjoining parish.

MRS B.: Oh, Mr Box! You surely wouldn't deprive me of a lodger?

BOX: It would come to precisely the same thing, Bouncer, because at the slightest attempt to put my pipe out, I give you warning that I shall give you warning.

MRS B.: Fair warning, Mr Box. Now, do you want anything more of me?

BOX: On the contrary – I've had quite enough of you!

MRS B.: Well I never! *(retreating)* Goodbye, Mr Box.

(DOOR SLAMS SHUT)

BOX: Quite extraordinary, the trouble I always have to get rid of that woman! She knows I'm up all night, yet she seems determined to stop me sleeping by day. Now, let me see – shall I take my nap before I swallow my breakfast, or shall I take my breakfast before I swallow my nap? I mean... No – never mind! I've got a rasher of bacon in one of my pockets... somewhere ... Oh, here it is – and a bread roll. The next thing is to light the gas-ring. Where are my matches?

(MATCHES)

Now, this is too bad of Bouncer! I had a whole box full, three days ago, and now there's only one match left! I'm perfectly aware that she makes free with my coal and my sugar and my tea – but I did think my matches would be sacred! I'd better use this last one to light the gas ring.

(HISS OF GAS. MATCH STRUCK, GAS IGNITES)

And blow me down if she hasn't been using my frying pan as well! The last thing I cooked on it was a pork chop, and now it smells strongly of herring! Well, the bacon will soon overcome that.

(SIZZLE OF BACON ON PAN)

(yawns) I can scarcely keep my eyes open. Tell you what, I'll just lie down for a bit while the bacon fries itself.

(CURTAINS DRAWN APART. BED CREAKS)

Aahh! *(yawns)*

(CURTAINS DRAWN SHUT. SHORT BURST OF
MUSIC. DOOR OPENS. DOWN MUSIC FAST)

COX: *(close)* Wonders will never cease! I was eleven minutes late this morning, and I was sneaking into the shop when my venerable employer, with a benevolent smile on his aged face, says: "Cox, I shan't want you today – you can have the day off." Heaven knows what I'll do – but I must have my breakfast first. That'll give me time to reflect. I've bought a mutton chop, so I shan't want any dinner. Good gracious! I forgot the bread. Hullo, what's this? A roll, I do declare! That's lucky! Now, then, to light the gas ring. That's my box of matches. Who's dared to touch them.

(MATCH BOX)

Why, it's empty! I left one in it – I'd swear to it. Goodness gracious, the gas ring is alight – and the frying pan is on it. And what's that on the frying pan? Bacon? Bacon it is! Well upon my life, Mrs Bouncer has a nerve. She takes my last match and my frying pan to cook her breakfast! No, no – I won't put up with.

(PAN RATTLES AGAINST METAL)

Out of that pan with you! In you go, mutton chop. Now, then, to tackle Mrs Bouncer. *(retreating)* I won't have it. I really won't!

(DOOR OPENS AND SHUTS WITH A BANG)

BOX: *(remote calling)* Come in, if it's you Mrs Bouncer.

(BED CURTAINS DRAWN BACK)

I wonder how long I've been asleep? Goodness gracious – my bacon! Hullo! what's this? A chop! Whose chop? Mrs Bouncer's I'll be bound – she thought she'd cook her breakfast while I was asleep with *my* frying pan, too. But where's my bacon? Ah, here it is. Well, this time Bouncer's gone too far! You'll never see this chop again.

(SASH WINDOW PULLED UP AND THEN DOWN)

Out of the window with it. Let's give the cats of the neighbourhood a treat. So much for Bouncer's breakfast, and now for my own! *(retreating)* And now to tackle the Bouncer.

(DOOR OPENS)

COX: *(remote, advancing)* Who are you, sir?

BOX: Come to that – who are *you*?

COX: What are you doing here?

BOX: Come to that what are *you* doing here?

COX: Go to your attic, sir.

BOX: *My* attic, sir? *Your* attic, sir!

COX: Printer, I shall do you a frightful injury, if you don't instantly leave my apartment.

BOX: *Your* apartment? You mean *my* apartment, you contemptible hatter, you.

COX: *Your* apartment? I like that! Look here, sir

                (PAPER)

        Mrs Bouncer's receipt for the last week's rent, sir...

                (PAPER)

BOX: Ditto, sir!

COX: }
BOX: } Mrs Bouncer! *(both call)* Mrs Bouncer!

MRS B: *(remote approaching)* What's the matter? Oh my goodness! Mr Cox. And Mr Box. May I introduce you?

BOX: Certainly not. Remove that hatter! Instantly!

COX: I have no wish to be acquainted with that printer! Turn him out. Immediately!

MRS B: Well, gentlemen, I would, but it's not as simple as it may appear…

COX: Madam, explain yourself!

BOX: Yes, I demand an explanation! Whose room is this?

COX: Come on, Bouncer. Speak up. You let this apartment to me, didn't you?

BOX: Nonsense. I'm your tenant, aren't I?

MRS B.: No!

COX: There! You heard that, sir. This room belongs to me!

MRS B.: Not exactly.

COX: Not exactly? What do you mean, woman?

MRS B.: Well… It sort of…belongs to both of you! *(sobs)*

COX: }
BOX: } Both of us!

MRS B.: *(sobbing)* Oh, dear gentlemen, don't be angry – but you see, Mr Box only being at home in the day time, and Mr Cox at night, I thought I might venture, until my little back second floor room was ready…

COX:	}
BOX:	} And when will it be ready?

MRS B.: Tomorrow…

COX: I'll take it!

BOX: So will I!

MRS B.: Excuse me – but if you both take it, you may just as well stop where you are.

COX:	}
BOX:	} True.

COX: I spoke first, sir…

BOX: Then you may have it, Mr Cox. The little back second floor room is yours. Now, sir, please go away.

COX: Go away? I shall do no such thing.

MRS B.: Don't quarrel, gentlemen, please. I'll get the other room ready at once. *(retreating)* Now *do* keep your tempers.

(DOOR CLOSES)

BOX: I'm quite worn out. I need my sleep. I think I'll go to bed.

COX: I beg your pardon! I cannot allow anyone to rumple my bed.

BOX: *Your* bed? It's my bed, and I've been working all night. You may retire to your bed in the little back second floor as soon as it's ready.

COX: Look, we may be doomed to share the same room for a few hours longer, but I don't see any need to lose our tempers. After all, I've no violent animosity to you, sir.

BOX: Nor have I any rooted antipathy to you. Besides, it was all Mrs Bouncer's fault.

COX: Entirely. Why don't we sit down, Mr Box?

BOX: Very well, Mr Cox! After you.

COX: Can this couch bear the weight of us both?

BOX: Let's test it!

(CREAK AS BOTH SIT ON COUCH)

(cough. Pause) Er…have you visited the music hall recently, Mr Cox?

COX: No, sir – my …er … intended, that is, my future wife, doesn't approve.

BOX: So you're to be married? I congratulate you. My hand, sir

COX: *(sighs)* Thank you. And there's no need to get up, sir. She won't be coming here.

BOX: Oh, I understand. You've got a snug little establishment somewhere else on the sly. Cunning dog…

COX: No such thing, sir. But my intended wife happens to own a small hotel at the seaside…

BOX: Really? Where?

COX: …and during the holiday season – which fortunately is rather long – we see little of each other. But as the season is nearly over, I fully expect to be blessed with the sight of my beloved before too long. Are *you* married, Mr Box?

BOX: Me? Er – not exactly!

COX: Ah – a happy bachelor!

BOX: Not precisely!

COX: Oh! a widower? My condolences, sir.

BOX: Er – not exactly a widower either. Not absolutely!

COX: You are not by any sad chance divorced?

BOX: Divorced! Certainly not, sir.

COX: You'll excuse me, Mr Box, but I don't exactly understand how you can help being one of them. Every man alive must be either married or unmarried, or if not, the surviving partner of a previous marriage.

BOX: That may well be the case. But, you see, I'm not alive!

COX: Sir, you are talking in riddles. You're as alive as I am.

BOX: No, I'm perfectly serious. I've been dead for the last three years!

COX: What utter poppycock!

BOX: If you won't believe me, I'll refer you to a very large and respectable circle of disconsolate friends.

COX: My dear Mr Box, if a man on the eve of committing matrimony could indeed leave this world, and yet stop in it, I should be very pleased to know how. Very pleased.

BOX: Oh, then I gather you're not frantically attached to your intended?

COX: Not exactly. And yet, at present, I'm aware of only one obstacle to doting on her.

BOX: And what is that?

COX: The fact that I can't abide her!

BOX: Then there's nothing easier. Do as I did.

COX: I will! What was it?

BOX: Drown yourself!

COX: I don't quite…

BOX: Listen to me. Three years ago it was my misfortune to engage the affections of a blooming, though somewhat middle-aged, widow at a certain seaside resort.

COX: *(close)* How strange! Just my case, three months ago.

BOX: Well, her attentions became so embarrassing that I seriously considered enlisting in the Guards.

COX: *(close)* So did I. How very odd!

BOX: But they wouldn't have me. They actually had the effrontery to say that I was too short.

COX: *(close)* I wasn't tall enough either!

BOX: So I had to content myself with a marching regiment – I signed up!

COX: *(close)* So did I. What a coincidence!

BOX: I'd no sooner done so, than I was sorry for it.

COX: *(close)* So was I.

BOX: My infatuated widow offered to buy my discharge, on condition that I'd lead her to the altar.

COX: *(close)* My case exactly!

BOX: I hesitated – but at last I agreed.

COX: *(close)* I consented at once!

BOX: Well, Mr Cox, the day fixed for the happy ceremony at length drew near – in fact, too near to be pleasant. So I suddenly discovered that I wasn't worthy to possess her. When I told her so, instead of being flattered by the compliment, she flew on me like a tiger. I fought back. Suddenly something whizzed past me, within an inch of my ear, and smashed into pieces against the mantelpiece. It was the slop-basin. I retaliated with a tea cup. We parted, and the next morning I was served with a notice for breach of promise.

COX: What happened?

BOX: I faced ruin. So I left my home early one morning, with one suit of clothes on my back, and another tied up in a bundle, under my arm. I arrived on the cliffs, opened my bundle, deposited the suit of clothes on the very edge of the precipice, took one look into the yawning gulf beneath me, and walked off in the opposite direction.

COX: So you disappeared – the suit of clothes was found…

BOX: Exactly. And in a jacket pocket was found a piece of paper, with these affecting farewell words: "This is your work, Penelope Ann!"

COX: Penelope Ann! Did you say Penelope Ann?

BOX: Penelope Ann!

COX: Originally widow of William Wiggins?

BOX: Indeed. How did you…?

COX: Then you must be the lamented, long lost Box!

BOX: I am!

COX: What a coincidence. And I was about to marry the interesting creature you so cruelly deceived.

BOX: Congratulations. I give you joy! And now, I think I'll go and take a stroll.

COX: No, you don't! I'll not lose sight of you till I've restored you to the arms of your intended.

BOX: *My* intended? You mean *your* intended.

COX: No, sir – yours!

BOX: How can she be *my* intended, now that I'm drowned?

COX: You're no such thing! And you proposed to her first!

BOX: What of that? I came to an untimely end, and you popped the question afterwards.

COX: You are much more worthy of her than I am. I give her up to you. My generosity knows no bounds.

BOX: I wouldn't rob you for the world! *(retreating)* Good morning, sir!

COX: Stop!

BOX: Let go of me, hatter, or you'll regret it.

COX: Pooh to that!

BOX: An insult – under my very nose! I demand satisfaction sir.

COX: }
BOX: } *(calling)* Mrs Bouncer! Mrs Bouncer!

               (DOOR OPENS)

MRS B.:   Goodness gracious me. What a to-do. What is it, gentlemen?

BOX: Pistols for two!

MRS B.: Yes, sir. *(retreating)* At once, sir.

COX: Stop! You don't mean to say that you keep loaded firearms in the house?

MRS B.: Oh, no, Mr Cox – they're not loaded.

COX: Then produce the murderous weapons instantly!

MRS B.: *(retreating)* I won't be a minute.

(DOOR CLOSES)

BOX: What's your opinion of duelling, Mr Cox?

COX: I think it's a barbarous practice.

BOX: So do I, sir. To be sure, I don't so much object to it when the pistols are not loaded.

COX: No – I dare say that *does* make a difference.

BOX: And yet, on the other hand, doesn't it strike you as rather a waste of time, for two people to fire pistols at another, with nothing in 'em?

COX: No, sir – no more than any other harmless recreation.

BOX: Tell me – why do you object to marrying Penelope Ann?

COX: Because, as I've observed already, I can't abide her. You'll be happy with her.

BOX: Happy? Me! Knowing that I've deprived *you* of such a treasure? No, no, Cox! I won't have her!

COX: Nor will I.

BOX: Here's an idea. Suppose we draw lots for the lady.

COX: Fair enough, Mr Box.

BOX: Or, what do you say to dice?

COX: Dice, by all means.

BOX: *(close)* That's lucky! Mrs Bouncer's nephew left his pair here yesterday. We sometimes throw for a trifle – and he always throws sixes. I know those dice are loaded. *(loud)* They're over here. Here we are.

COX: *(close)* I've no objection at all to dice. I lost one pound, seventeen shillings and sixpence, at last Barnet Races, to a very gentlemanly looking man, who had a most peculiar knack of throwing sixes. I suspected they were loaded, so I gave him another half-crown, and he gave me the dice.

BOX: Now then, sir! Here are my dice. Where are yours?

COX: I have them here. Let's sit at the table.

                    (CHAIRS LEGS SCRAPE ON WOODEN FLOOR)

                    Will you lead off?

BOX: As you please. The lowest throw, of course, wins Penelope Ann?

COX: Of course.

                    (DICE RATTLE AND THROWN ON TABLE)

BOX: Sixes!

COX: Well thrown, sir. Let's see what I can do

                    (DICE RATTLE AND THROWN ON TABLE)

                    Sixes!

BOX: That's a pretty good throw of yours.

                    (DICE RATTLE AND THROWN ON TABLE)

                    Sixes!

                    (DICE RATTLE AND THROWN ON TABLE)

COX: Sixes!

BOX: Those aren't bad dice of yours, Mr Cox

COX: Yours seem pretty good ones, Mr Box.

BOX: Suppose we change?

COX: Very well. Here you are. Many thanks. You make a start.

(DICE RATTLE AND THROWN ON TABLE)

BOX: Sixes!

(DICE RATTLE AND THROWN ON TABLE)

COX: Sixes!

BOX: This is perfectly absurd. Let's try something else. I have it! Suppose we toss for Penelope Ann?

COX: The very thing I was going to suggest!

(COINS)

BOX: *(Close)* Now where's on earth's my tossing shilling? Ah, here it is!

COX: *(Close)* Where's that lucky sixpence of mine? I've got it!

BOX: Now then, sir – heads win?

COX: Or tails lose – whichever you prefer.

BOX: It's the same to me, sir. Then, heads I win. Here goes!

(SLAP OF PALM ON BACK OF HAND)

Heads!

COX: I'll toss now, if you don't mind. Heads I win.

(SLAP OF PALM ON BACK OF HAND)

Heads!

BOX: My turn.

(SLAP OF PALM ON BACK OF HAND)

Heads!

COX: Now me.

(SLAP OF PALM ON BACK OF HAND)

Heads!

BOX: Stop! Allow me to examine that coin of yours. As
                I suspected – your sixpence has got no tail, sir!

COX: Just a moment – let me see your coin. Your
                shilling, sir, has got two heads.

BOX: Cheat!

COX: Swindler!

(DOOR OPENS)

MRS B.: *(remote, advancing)* Gentlemen, gentlemen. I'm afraid I can't find the pistols, but I've bought you a letter. It came by the last post, yesterday. I'm sure I don't know how I forgot it, for I put it carefully in my pocket. Here it is, Mr Cox. *(retreating)* Now I simply must go and finish that room in the attic.

(DOOR CLOSES)

COX: The post-mark decidedly says "Southend-on-Sea."

BOX: Oh – a tender epistle from Penelope Ann, no doubt.

COX: Then you'd best read it, sir. Here.

BOX: Me, sir?

COX: Of course. You don't suppose I'm going to read a letter from your intended?

BOX: *My* intended! Look, it's addressed to you – C.O.X.

COX: You call that a C.? I'd say it was most definitely a B.!

BOX: Utter nonsense! Open it!

(TEARING ENVELOPE, PAPER)

COX: Goodness gracious!

BOX: Here, let me see.

(PAPER)

Gracious, goodness!

COX: Give it here.

(PAPER)

"Southend-on-Sea – May the 4th. Sir, – I am sorry to have to inform you that yesterday, May the 3rd, your intended wife suffered a fatal accident..."
He means *your* intended!

BOX: No, *yours*! However, it's of no consequence now, but she unquestionably was yours. Go on.

COX: "Poor Mrs Wiggins went out for a short excursion in a sailing boat – a sudden and violent squall soon after took place, which it is supposed, upset her, as she was found, two days afterwards, keel upwards."

BOX: Poor woman!

COX: The boat, sir! Not Mrs Wiggins. "As her business agent, I proceeded to examine her papers, amongst which I soon discovered her will; the following extract from which will, I have no doubt, be satisfactory to you. 'I hereby bequeath my entire property to my intended husband.'"

And to think that I tossed for such a woman!

BOX: Or that I staked such a treasure on the hazard of dice!

COX: Mr Box, I can't sufficiently thank you for your sympathy.

BOX: I'm sure, Mr Cox, you couldn't feel her loss more, if she'd been your own intended!

COX: *If* she'd been *my own* intended? She *was* my own intended!

BOX: *Your* intended? I like that! Haven't you just been insisting that this letter was addressed to me? And did you not remark, quite correctly, that I proposed to her first?

COX: To which you very sensibly replied that you'd come to an untimely end.

BOX: I deny it! The fortune's mine!

COX: Mine!

BOX: I'll go to law!

COX: So will I!

BOX:	Stop – a thought strikes me. Instead of going to law about the property, suppose we divide it?
COX:	Equally?
BOX:	Equally. I'll take two-thirds.
COX:	That's fair enough – and I'll take three-quarters.
BOX:	That won't do. Half and half!
COX:	Agreed! There's my hand on it…
BOX:	And mine.
	(REMOTE BUT VERY CLEAR, RAT-TAT-TAT ON FRONT DOOR)
COX:	Hullo! Did you hear that? It's the postman again!
BOX:	Postman yesterday – postman today.
	(DOOR OPENS)
MRS B.:	*(remote, advancing)* Another letter, Mr Cox!
COX:	Another trifle from Southend-on-Sea..
	(TEARING ENVELOPE, PAPER)
	Goodness gracious!
BOX:	Let me see that.

(PAPER)

Gracious goodness!

(PAPER)

COX: Give that back! "Happy to inform you – false alarm…"

BOX: "Sudden squall – boat upset – Mrs Wiggins your intended…"

COX: "Picked up by a steamboat…"

BOX: "Carried into Boulogne…"

COX: "Returned here this morning…"

BOX: "Will start by early train, to-morrow…"

COX: "And be with you at ten o'clock, exact."

BOX: Cox, I congratulate you.

COX: Box, I give you joy!

BOX: I'm sorry that most important business of the Colonial Office will prevent my witnessing the truly happy meeting between you and your intended. *(retreating)* Good morning to you, sir!

COX: Oh, no, Box. You're not the one to leave. It's obviously up to me to do so. Not for worlds would I disturb the rapturous meeting between you and your intended. *(retreating)* Good morning to you, sir!

BOX: You'll excuse me, but our last arrangement was, that she was *your* intended.

COX: No, yours!

BOX: Yours!

(CLOCK STARTS TO CHIME TEN)

COX: Oh, my goodness. Ten o'clock.

(REMOTE EARLY 20TH CENTURY MOTOR VEHICLE APPROACHES AND COMES TO HALT OUTSIDE WINDOW)

BOX: Do you hear that? A cab's stopping at the door! *(Moving)* No – it's an omnibus!

COX: *(Moving)* Let me see. A lady's getting out.

BOX: There's no mistaking that majestic person – it's Penelope Ann!

COX: Your intended!

BOX: Yours!

COX: Yours!

BOX: Listen. She's coming up the stairs!

COX: Shut the door!

(DOOR SLAMS. KNOCKING ON DOOR)

MRS B.:   *(remote)* Mr Cox! Mr Cox!

COX: *(calls)* I've just stepped out!

BOX: *(calls)* So have I!

MRS B.:   *(remote)* Mr Cox. Open the door. It's only me –
                    Mrs Bouncer!

COX: Only you? Then where's the lady?

MRS B.:   *(remote)* Gone!

COX: Upon your honour?

BOX: As a gentleman?

MRS B.:   *(remote)* Yes, and she's left a note for Mr Cox.

COX: Give it to me!

MRS B.:   *(remote)* Then open the door!

COX: Slide it under!

(ENVELOPE TORN OPEN. PAPER)

Goodness gracious!

BOX: Let me see that.

(PAPER)

Gracious goodness!

(CREEP IN MELODY FROM "COX AND BOX" AS IN OPENING UNDER THE FOLLOWING)

COX: "Dear Mr Cox, pardon my candour…"

BOX: "But being convinced that our feelings, like our ages, are not in tune…"

COX: "I hasten to inform you that I am about to be married…"

BOX: "To Mr Knox."

COX: Hooray!

BOX: Three cheers for Mr Knox! Hooray, hooray, hooray!

(UP MUSIC. THEY DANCE. DOOR OPENS)

MRS B.: *(calls. approaching)* The little second floor back room is ready!

COX: I don't want it!

BOX: No more do I!

(MUSIC DOWN AND OUT UNDER FOLLOWING)

After all, why should we be parted?

COX: Why should we be torn asunder?

BOX: Cox, you'll excuse the apparent insanity of the remark, but the more I look at you, the more certain I am that you're my long lost brother.

COX: That's exactly what I was about to say to you.

BOX: Tell me – for heaven's sake tell me – do you have such a thing as a strawberry mark on your left arm?

COX: No!

BOX: Then you are! You are indeed my long lost brother.

COX: And you are mine! And of course we stop where we are!

BOX: Of course!

(CREEP IN MUSIC UNDER FOLLOWING – PRE-SET TO ENABLE PIECE TO END STRAIGHT AFTER CLOSING ANNOUNCEMENT)

MRS B.:   Oh, gentlemen, what wonderful news.. Then I shall let my little second floor back room to someone else.

COX: You do that, Mrs Bouncer. And make your fortune. Between you and me, I'm rather partial to this apartment.

BOX: So am I. I feel quite at home here.

COX: Everything so clean and comfortable...

BOX: And I'm sure the mistress of the house, from what I have seen of her, is very anxious to please.

MRS B.: Indeed I am.

COX: I knew it. I vote, Box, that we stick by her, and continue to share this excellent room.

BOX: Agreed! There's my hand upon it. Then Box...

COX: And Cox...

BOX: }
COX: } Are both highly satisfied!

(UP MUSIC. DOWN FOR CLOSING ANNOUNCEMENT. UP MUSIC TO TRIUMPHAL END)

THE TURN OF
THE SCREW

BY HENRY JAMES
DRAMATIZED FOR RADIO
BY NEVILLE TELLER

Running time: 60'

FIRST BROADCAST ON
BBC RADIO 4 ON 25 JULY 2008

CHARACTERS IN
ORDER OF APPEARANCE

ARABELLA   *30s. Educated mid-Victorian accent. Society wife*

GRIFFIN   *40s. Educated mid-Victorian accent. Professional man.*

CHARLOTTE   *30s. Educated mid-Victorian accent. Society wife*

DOUGLAS   *60s. Educated mid-Victorian accent. Gentleman of means.*

SIR GEORGE   *Mid-30s. Educated mid-Victorian accent. Charming man-about-town used to getting his own way with women. Perfectly able to dazzle and bemuse an impressionable, out-of-town young lady by a combination of apparent sincerity and an appeal to her better nature. No doubt good-natured at base, he's nevertheless thoroughly selfish and intent pretty exclusively on his own pleasures. Thoroughly self-satisfied when, finally, he gets his own way.*

GOVERNESS   *Aged 20. Educated mid-Victorian accent. Unworldly, impressionable and highly strung. It's* unclear whether she actually sees the ghosts, or whether they're the outcome of her own fevered imagination – but they're certainly real to her. Because of her upbringing (a vicar's daughter) and her strong sense of right and wrong, she conceives it her duty to protect her young charges from the evil influences of Quint and Miss Jessel – a duty that turns into an obsession. She comes to see it as a battle between good and evil, a battle finally for the very soul of Miles. The question has been asked whether, by the end of the piece, she has actually tipped over into madness. She is sexually highly charged – though in typical Victorian fashion the sexual impulses are hidden. She certainly falls for the children's uncle – she's even dreaming of meeting him at the moment she first sees Quint. The unspoken debaucheries of Quint and Miss Jessel – separately and together – underlie the vehemence of her hatred for them. She is more than half in love with Miles – just look at the language she uses in talking of him (in the final scene, she even compares him to a bridegroom on his wedding journey). When Miss Jessel appears before Flora, the little girl is described as pushing a stick into the hole in a piece of wood. Rampant sex hovers beneath the surface of what the governess says and feels.

MRS GROSE   50s. Uneducated but astute countrywoman who has become a valued family retainer. Warm-hearted and trusting, she's swept along by the governess's obsessive urge to snatch the children from the clutches of Quint and Miss Jessel, even though she herself never sees either apparition. Bewildered, perplexed by what the governess tells her, she is protective of the two children to the last.

FLORA
8 years old. Educated mid-Victorian accent. A sweet, innocent child – but, on occasion, so very sweet as to arouse suspicion of whether there isn't a rather cunning little person underneath. In her big scene with the governess, she is either genuinely frightened to death by her, or she's putting on a very good act indeed. We mustn't know which.

MILES
10 years old. Educated mid-Victorian accent. Soft-spoken but very self-assured – a perfect little gentleman. The crime for which he was expelled from school was probably no more than repeating a selection of four-letter words and expounding the functions and activities they represent. Like Englishmen of his time, he's inhibited – especially in front of women – and he finds it difficult, if not impossible, to say clearly what he has done. Has he been corrupted by Peter Quint and is in league with him – or is all that part of the governess's fevered imagination? Well, in the final scene, when she sees Quint, he fails to. Perhaps he's being hounded to his death by devils actually created by the governess. In short, perhaps (except for his misdemeanour at school) he really is the innocent little boy she first thinks him. It's all a mystery! Keep 'em guessing!

(MUSIC. DOWN FOR OPENING ANNOUNCEMENT. UP MUSIC. FADE BENEATH VICTORIAN DRAWING ROOM. SIX CHARACTERS WELL SPACED. LOG FIRE. FADE IN CLAPPING AND EXPRESSIONS OF APPRECIATION, ESPECIALLY FROM WOMEN)

ARABELLA: How deliciously gruesome!

GRIFFIN: And every word the gospel truth.

CHARLOTTE: You can't expect us to believe that, Mr Griffin. But it's an ideal ghost story for a Christmas Eve.

ARABELLA: Yes, isn't it nice being chilled to the marrow in front of a roaring fire?

DOUGLAS: Of course, what made your tale peculiarly horrible was the involvement of the little boy. But if the presence of one child gives an extra turn of the screw, so to speak, what would you say to *two children?*

ARABELLA: Why, that it would give two turns, of course, Mr Douglas...

CHARLOTTE: ...and that we'd want to hear all about it.

DOUGLAS: Well, as your host I suppose I'm under an obligation to keep my house-guests entertained... though I must admit the events I have in mind are far from entertaining. Quite the reverse. It was all ... too horrible. Beyond everything. It outdoes your tale, Griffin, ten-fold. Nothing I know even touches it...

GRIFFIN: For sheer terror?

DOUGLAS: For sheer ... dreadfulness.

ARABELLA: How delicious!

CHARLOTTE: *(pause)* Well, Mr Douglas...?

DOUGLAS: *(moving)* I have ... in my desk here ... excuse me ...

(BENEATH FOLLOWING ROLLTOP OPENS. KEY UNLOCKS – SMALL DRAWER OPENS. PAPERS)

locked in a drawer ... *(searches)* a manuscript ... ah! A most beautiful hand – see! A woman's. She's been dead these twenty years. I first met her here, in this house. *(moves and sits)* I was in my second year at Oxford. When I came down in the long vac, I found that she'd been engaged as a governess for my sister. Oh, but she was such a charming person. I was ten years younger than she was, but she seemed to find it easy to talk to me. Don't grin like that, Griffin – yes, I liked her very much indeed. If I hadn't, I doubt if she'd ever have told me about those dreadful … those terrible events. She'd told nobody else.

GRIFFIN: And the manuscript? How did you come by that?

DOUGLAS: Oh, I asked her to write it later – some years later – and she agreed. I thought the facts ought to be set down.

ARABELLA: Well, let's hear them.

DOUGLAS: All in good time. First I must sketch in the background, or nothing will make any sense. We must go back more than fifty years. My friend was then just twenty, the youngest daughter of a country parson. Under the necessity of earning a living,

(UNDER FOLLOWING FADE IN LONDON STREET 1850. HORSE-DRAWN CARRIAGE STOPS. FRONT DOOR BELLS RINGS FROM INTERIOR. FRONT DOOR OPENS. MURMUR FROM BUTLER OF "THIS WAY, IF YOU PLEASE". FOOTSTEPS ON MARBLE)

she'd responded to an advertisement for a governess, and had been required to attend for interview in London. She'd never been in London before, and she found herself outside a house in Harley Street that impressed her as vast and imposing. Soon she was seated before a gentleman – a bachelor in the prime of life – a figure such as she'd only ever experienced in dreams, or in the pages of novels: handsome, bold, rich, pleasant, kind...

(EDGE OUT. QUICK FADE IN. LONDON DRAWING ROOM. 1850)

SIR GEORGE: I should be so very much in your debt. I've done all I can for those two poor little souls – I assure you I do take my responsibilities as their guardian most seriously – but they require the sort of care and attention that I personally could never provide.

GOVERNESS: Have they recovered from the shock of their parents' death?

SIR GEORGE: Oh, I think so. Children are so resilient, aren't they? But to be perfectly frank with you, I'm not sure that I have – quite. I was very close to my brother – and he and his wife died in India in most tragic circumstances. I won't burden you with the details.

GOVERNESS: And ... where are the children? Above – in the nursery?

SIR GEORGE: Oh, they're not here. The family seat is in Essex, and it seemed much more suitable for the children to live there than in town. Don't you agree?

GOVERNESS: Oh, I do.

SIR GEORGE: That's where I trust you'll take charge of them for me.

GOVERNESS: But who's looking after them at present?

SIR GEORGE: Well, at the moment the little boy – Miles – is away at school. He's only just ten, and I wouldn't have chosen to send him away, but unfortunately the young lady whom I'd engaged to care for the children's education died quite suddenly, and I had no alternative. Flora, his little sister, is being cared for by the housekeeper, Mrs Grose. An excellent woman, been with the family for years – at one time she was my mother's personal maid. Of course Bly also has the usual staff – cook, housemaid, dairywoman, gardener and so forth. But as governess, you would be in supreme authority – you'd be *in loco parentis*.

GOVERNESS: That's rather a … daunting prospect.

SIR GEORGE: Oh, please don't be daunted, I beg you. The children are both delightful – they won't be a bother to you. You'll adore Flora on sight – and Miles is a pleasure to be with. He'll be back at Bly shortly for the school holidays. You'll find the house very comfortable, and the grounds are extensive. I'm sure you'll be very satisfied with life at Bly – and you'd be doing me such a personal favour.

GOVERNESS: In that case, I can scarcely refuse.

SIR GEORGE: You'll not regret your decision, I'm sure. But there is just one thing that I must ask of you. I do hope you'll be able to grant it.

GOVERNESS: I'll do my best. What is it you want?

SIR GEORGE: For you to take over at Bly completely and to consult me about nothing. Nothing at all. You see, my own affairs occupy all my time and attention. Often they require me to leave the country at short notice. I'd like you to deal with everything yourself. Money will be sent to you regularly by my solicitors. Use it as you see fit, but – please – do not communicate with me. In short, I want you to take complete charge and to give me peace of mind about the children. I know I'm asking a great deal of you – but will you do this for me?

GOVERNESS: I will.

(EDGE OUT. FULL UP. AS FIRST SCENE)

DOUGLAS: She told me that when, for a moment, disburdened, delighted, he held her hand to thank her, she already felt rewarded.

ARABELLA: But was that all her reward?

DOUGLAS: She never saw him again.

CHARLOTTE: Good gracious! That, in itself, is … odd.

DOUGLAS: You'll learn why. Shall I start reading the manuscript?

GRIFFIN: Yes, get on with it, Douglas.

(PAPER)

DOUGLAS: Very well. *(clears throat)* She starts: "I remember the whole beginning as a succession of flights and drops. The mood of optimism – indeed near-exaltation…

(CROSSFADE TO GOVERNESS AS NARRATOR)

GOVERNESS: *(as narrator)* …of optimism – indeed near-exaltation – in which I'd agreed to take on the position soon faded, and on the journey to Bly I spent the long hours of bumping, swinging coach full of doubts. At the stopping place I was met by a vehicle from the house, and it was late in the afternoon of a glorious June day that we turned into the drive at Bly… And there stood the house – a magnificent edifice flanked by two crenellated towers.

(BENEATH FOLLOWING HORSE-DRAWN FLY STOPS ON GRAVEL; GOVERNESS DESCENDS AND WALKS)

GOVERNESS: *(as narrator)* … There immediately appeared at the door a civil person, holding a little girl by the hand, and she dropped me as decent a curtsey as if I'd been mistress of the place.

(COUNTRY. OPEN AIR. JUNE AFTERNOON)

MRS GROSE: Welcome to Bly, Miss. Welcome indeed. We've been looking out for you all afternoon.

GOVERNESS: Good afternoon. You must be Mrs Grose. And you – you're Flora?

FLORA: How do you do? I hope you had a pleasant journey.

GOVERNESS: Well, Flora, it was very long and tiring, and I'm certainly pleased to be here at last.

MRS GROSE: Oh, Miss, you must be yearning for a cup of tea. Do please follow me. *(moving)* I alerted cook as soon as we spied your carriage. Then I'll show you to your room and you'll be able to rest and freshen yourself before dinner...

(FADE OUT. FADE IN - HOUSEKEEPER'S ROOM)

GOVERNESS: *(distant – hesitant)* Mrs Grose? May I...?

MRS GROSE: Oh, come in, Miss, do. Miss Flora all tucked up for the night?

GOVERNESS: And asleep already. What an adorable child she is – and so lovely. I don't think I've ever seen a more beautiful little girl.

MRS GROSE: She's certainly that, Miss.

GOVERNESS: And the little boy – Miles – does he look like her?

Is he too so very remarkable?

MRS GROSE: *Most* remarkable, Miss. If you think well of her, you'll be quite carried away by the little gentleman.

GOVERNESS: I'm afraid I'm rather easily carried away. I was carried away in London.

MRS GROSE: In Harley Street?

GOVERNESS: Indeed.

MRS GROSE: Well, Miss, you're not the first – and you won't be the last.

GOVERNESS: *(laughs)* Oh, I've no pretensions to being the only one!

(EDGE OUT. FADE IN DRAWING ROOM AT BLY)

MRS GROSE: *(approaching)* A packet has just arrived in the postbag for you, Miss. It's from the master.

(PACKET IS OPENED BENEATH FOLLOWING)

GOVERNESS: Thank you, Mrs Grose. Please wait a moment. This may contain instructions that concern us both.

(SIR GEORGE ON DISTORT)

SIR GEORGE: I enclose an unopened letter, which I recognise is from the headmaster – and the headmaster's an

	awful bore. Read him, please. Deal with him. But tell me nothing of the matter. Not a word! I'm off!
GOVERNESS:	*(reading)* Good gracious! What does it mean? The child's been dismissed from his school.
MRS GROSE:	Master Miles? But aren't they all…?
GOVERNESS:	Sent home? Yes, for the holidays. Miles is not to return. The headmaster won't allow him back.
MRS GROSE:	But – what has he done?
GOVERNESS:	It doesn't actually say. "I regret that it will be impossible to keep him." It can only mean that Miles is an injury to the others.
MRS GROSE:	Master Miles! An injury! He's scarcely ten years old.
GOVERNESS:	So *you've* never known him bad?
MRS GROSE:	Oh, I don't pretend that, Miss – thank God.
GOVERNESS:	You mean that a boy without spirit…
MRS GROSE:	… is no boy for *me!*
GOVERNESS:	Nor me. But not to the degree to contaminate… to corrupt…

(FADE OUT. FADE IN HOUSEKEEPER'S ROOM. CROCKERY. THEY'RE DRINKING TEA)

GOVERNESS: Tell me, Mrs Grose. The lady who was here before – what was she like?

MRS GROSE: The last governess? She was also young and pretty – almost as young and pretty as you, Miss.

GOVERNESS: Indeed? He seems to like us young and pretty.

MRS GROSE: *(sharp)* Oh he did! *(attempt to recover herself)* I mean, that's his way – the master's.

GOVERNESS: But who were you speaking of at first?

MRS GROSE: Why the master, of course. Who else?

GOVERNESS: And what happened to her? Did she die here?

MRS GROSE: No. She went off.

GOVERNESS: She was taken ill, you mean, and went home?

MRS GROSE: No, she left at the end of the year for a short holiday, and never returned. I was expecting her back when I heard from the master that she was dead.

GOVERNESS: But of what?

MRS GROSE: He never told me.

(FADE OUT. FULL UP)

GOVERNESS: *(as narrator)* The next day I went with the carriage to collect Miles from the inn at which the coach had put him down. The moment I set eyes on him I felt – exactly as with his little sister – that I was seeing him in a great glow of freshness and purity, outside and in. He was incredibly beautiful, but what I took him to my heart for, there and then, was an indescribable divine air of knowing nothing in the world but love. It would have been impossible to carry a bad name with a greater sweetness of innocence.

(EDGE IN. HOUSEKEEPER'S ROOM)

GOVERNESS: It's grotesque, Mrs Grose. Grotesque. You have only to look at the boy. He's innocence itself – too good, I dare say, for the horrid, unclean world of the boarding school.

MRS GROSE: So what will you do about the letter?

GOVERNESS: Nothing! I shall do nothing at all!

(EDGE OUT. FULL UP)

GOVERNESS: *(as narrator)* And so we settled into an agreeable way of life. The attraction of my small charges was a constant joy. Both of them had a gentleness that was quite unpunishable. In Miles especially there was something extraordinarily sensitive, yet extraordinarily happy, that struck me anew each day. He had never for a second suffered. I took this as a direct disproof of his having really been chastised at school. To me, therefore, he was an angel. The best way to picture it all is to say that

I was dazzled by the purity and innocence of the children – and that I was off my guard.

The best of those long summer days was what I used to call my own hour – the period after teatime and bedtime had come and gone for my pupils, and the daylight slowly dwindled.

(CREEP MUSIC BENEATH FOLLOWING)

One evening, at the end of a long June day, with the children tucked up in bed, I'd come out – as so often – for a stroll. On these evening walks of mine I'd often played with the idea, as in a story, of unexpectedly encountering a handsome and charming stranger. That evening, coming suddenly into view of the house, it seemed as if my imagination had, in a flash, turned real. He did stand there! – but high up, at the very top of one of the two crenellated towers that flanked the house.

But this figure, in the clear twilight, wasn't the person I'd initially supposed – it was a man I'd never seen before, in Harley Street or anywhere else. While I took it in, the sounds of evening fell into an intense hush. The man who looked at me over the battlements was as definite as a picture in a frame. I thought with extraordinary quickness of each person he might have been – and wasn't. We were too far apart to call to each other but, after a moment, never taking his eyes from me, he slowly walked to the opposite corner of the platform. Here he stopped and, still fixing me with his gaze, turned away. That was all I knew.

(FULL UP VICTORIAN DRAWING ROOM AS IN
OPENING SCENE. CROSSFADE)

DOUGLAS: *(reading)*… with his gaze, turned away. That was all I knew.

CHARLOTTE: A mysterious figure on top of a tower. How deliciously gothic!

DOUGLAS: Exactly – and she was wracked by curiosity and dread. Was there a 'secret' at Bly – a mystery of Udolpho, an insane, an unmentionable relative kept in unsuspected confinement?

ARABELLA: And was there?

DOUGLAS: Be patient. Meanwhile – perhaps to spare Mrs Grose – the governess said nothing of her encounter, but day after day tried to puzzle out the truth. She could arrive at no satisfactory explanation. She was quickly convinced that she'd not been the object of a trick played on her by the servants. Finally, there was only one sane inference: someone had taken a monstrous liberty and wandered into Bly to enjoy the view, then stolen out.

CHARLOTTE: But that wasn't the case?

DOUGLAS: No, indeed. The horrific truth was revealed one Sunday evening, a few weeks later. It had rained so persistently that day that there was no question of going to church in the morning. But during the afternoon the rain eased…

(CROSSFADE TO CHURCH BELLS FROM A DISTANCE. ENTRANCE HALL AT BLY)

GOVERNESS: *(calling)* I'll be with you in a moment, Mrs Grose.

MRS GROSE: *(distant - calling)* Don't hurry yourself, Miss. We've plenty of time before evensong.

GOVERNESS: *(calling)* It's my gloves. I left them in the dining-room.

(HEAVY DOOR OPENS. SHE WALKS FORWARD)

(Gasp of horror)

GOVERNESS: *(as narrator)* The day had been grey and wet, but there was sufficient light, as I crossed the threshold, for me to see the articles I wanted on a chair by the tall windows. At the same instant...

(CREEP MUSIC BENEATH. KILL MUSIC ON START OF FOLLOWING SPEECH)

...I became aware of a person on the other side of the window looking straight in. One step into the room sufficed. This was the person who'd already appeared to me – but this time with a nearness that made me catch my breath. And this time something happened that hadn't happened before. His deep hard stare quitted my face for a moment, and he looked round the room. On the spot there came to me the shock of knowing, without a doubt, that it wasn't for me he had come. He'd come for someone else.

GOVERNESS: *(terror – shouts)* Mrs Grose! Mrs Grose! Quickly!

MRS GROSE: *(distant, approaching, calling)* Coming, I'm coming. Why whatever's the matter, Miss? You're as white as a sheet.

GOVERNESS: Oh, Mrs Grose. Just now... Through that window...

MRS GROSE: What was it?

GOVERNESS: An extraordinary man. Looking in. He's gone...

MRS GROSE: Have you seen him before?

GOVERNESS: Once. On the old tower.

MRS GROSE: You didn't tell me.

GOVERNESS: No, I wasn't... I wanted... I should have. I've been dying to tell you.

MRS GROSE: What's he like?

GOVERNESS: He has no hat. Red hair, close-curling, a long pale face – and arched eyebrows. Certainly not a gentleman.

MRS GROSE: A gentleman? Never.

GOVERNESS: You know him then?

MRS GROSE: How is he dressed?

GOVERNESS: In somebody's clothes. They're smart, but they're not his own.

MRS GROSE: *(distressed)* They're the master's!

GOVERNESS: You *do* know him!

MRS GROSE: Quint! Peter Quint! The master's valet, when he was here!

GOVERNESS: When the master was?

MRS GROSE: He never wore a hat, but he did wear ... well, there were waistcoats missing. They were both here, last year. Then the master went, and Quint was alone with us. In charge.

GOVERNESS: And what became of him?

MRS GROSE: *(pause)* He died!

GOVERNESS: *(appalled)* Died!

MRS GROSE: Yes. Mr Quint's dead.

(MUSIC. DOWN AND FADE UNDER. HOUSEKEEPER'S ROOM)

MRS GROSE: You say he was looking for someone else?

GOVERNESS: He was looking for little Miles. *That's* who he was looking for.

MRS GROSE: But how do you know?

GOVERNESS: I know! I know! And *you* know, my dear! He wants to appear to the children.

MRS GROSE: But why?

GOVERNESS: I wonder… You know, it's odd, but my pupils have never mentioned the time they were with him – never even mentioned his name.

MRS GROSE: Oh, the little lady doesn't remember…

GOVERNESS: But Miles? Miles would remember. He'd know about his death…

MRS GROSE: Don't try him! Please!

GOVERNESS: Never by the least reference. And you tell me they were great friends.

MRS GROSE: Oh, it wasn't Miles. It was Quint's own fancy. Quint was much too free.

GOVERNESS: Too free? With *my* boy!

MRS GROSE: For several months they were inseparable. They spent hours together. I didn't like it.

(EDGE OUT. FULL UP)

GOVERNESS: *(as narrator)* We talked late into that Sunday night, and I learned a good deal about the months Peter Quint had passed at Bly – an evil time that ended one winter's morning when he was found dead on the road from the village. A fatal wound to his head was later determined to have been produced by a slip in the dark on a steep icy slope. And yet, free with information though Mrs Grose had been, I remained haunted by the shadow of something she hadn't told me, something she'd kept back. That something was about to be revealed to me in all its horror.

On Tuesday afternoon I took Flora for a walk in the grounds. Miles wished to finish a book he was reading, and we left him indoors. The day was exceptionally warm, and we made our way to the edge of the lake where I took out my stitching. I'd become fully engaged in my work when I suddenly became aware that on the other side of the lake there was ... an alien object, a spectator. I can feel once more the spasm of my effort not to look over. What I did was to transfer my gaze to little Flora. In that very instant she turned her back to the water, picked up a flat piece of wood that happened to have a hole in it and, with the idea perhaps of producing a mast, was intently tightening a twig into the hole.

I waited some seconds, and then I felt ready to face what I had to face...

(HOUSEKEEPER'S ROOM)

GOVERNESS: They *know!* Oh, Mrs Grose, it's too monstrous. They know!

MRS GROSE: And what on earth... *[do they know?]*

GOVERNESS: Why all that *we* know – and heaven knows what more besides! Two hours ago, in the grounds ... Flora *saw!*

MRS GROSE: She's told you?

GOVERNESS: Not a word. That's the horror! She kept it to herself! A child of eight!

MRS GROSE: Then how do you know?

GOVERNESS: I was there. I saw with my own eyes. She was perfectly aware.

MRS GROSE: Of *him?*

GOVERNESS: Of *her!*

MRS GROSE: Her?

GOVERNESS: Another person – but of quite as unmistakable horror and evil. A woman in black, pale, dreadful, on the other side of the lake. I was there with the child.

MRS GROSE: Have you seen her before?

GOVERNESS: Never. But the child has. You have! My predecessor

– the one who died.

MRS GROSE: Miss Jessel? But how can you be sure?

GOVERNESS: Ask Flora. She's sure. No, for God's sake *don't!* She'll lie.

MRS GROSE: How *can* you?

GOVERNESS: Because I'm quite clear – Flora doesn't want me to know. But the child must be protected from that woman – from what she wants.

MRS GROSE: What does she want?

GOVERNESS: To get hold of her.

MRS GROSE: Dear Lord! This person – she was in black, you say?

GOVERNESS: In mourning. Extraordinarily beautiful – but infamous.

MRS GROSE: Miss Jessel *was* infamous – they both were. But she was a lady, and he… he came from the gutter. He did whatever he wished.

GOVERNESS: With her?

MRS GROSE: With them all.

GOVERNESS: And what did she die of?

MRS GROSE: I never knew. I didn't want to know. I imagined – and I still imagine. And what I imagine is dreadful…

(MUSIC. FADE AND HOLD UNDER)

GOVERNESS: *(as narrator)* Over and over in the small hours I could repeat to Mrs Grose that with the children's voices in one's ears, their fragrant faces against one's cheek, nothing mattered but their vulnerability and their beauty. To gaze into their eyes and pronounce their loveliness a trick of premature cunning was to be guilty of a terrible cynicism. And yet, as we spoke, hints of something less than total innocence forced themselves on me…

(FADE MUSIC BENEATH FOLLOWING)

MRS GROSE: I didn't like Miles spending so much time with Peter Quint. I spoke to Miss Jessel about it. She told me to mind my own business.

GOVERNESS: Did you speak to Miles?

MRS GROSE: He wouldn't speak of it. He never mentioned anything that passed between him and Quint.

GOVERNESS: And Miss Jessel? Did he speak of her?

MRS GROSE: Never! Never!

GOVERNESS: But you could see that he knew what was between the two wretches? That he was covering and concealing it?

MRS GROSE: Oh, he couldn't prevent…

GOVERNESS: Your learning the truth? I dare say! But, heavens, see what they succeeded in making of him! Now that letter from his school seems less … incomprehensible.

MRS GROSE: Well, if he was such a fiend at school, how is he such an angel now?

GOVERNESS: Yes, indeed. Ask me that again one day.

(EDGE OUT. FULL UP)

GOVERNESS: *(as narrator)* I waited and waited. Stranger than I can express was the effort to struggle against my new insights. I used to wonder how my little charges could help guessing that I thought strange things about them. There were moments when I caught them up by an irresistible impulse and pressed them to my heart. As soon as I'd done so, I used to wonder: 'What will they think of that? Doesn't it betray too much?' But both children were at this period extravagantly fond of me. They'd never wanted to do so many things for their poor protectress…

(FULL UP VICTORIAN DRAWING ROOM AS IN OPENING SCENE. CROSSFADE)

DOUGLAS: *(reading)* …extravagantly fond of me. They'd never wanted to do so many things for their poor protectress.

ARABELLA: Yes, well clearly Miles wasn't the little innocent she imagined him to be.

CHARLOTTE: "Imagined" – exactly. That woman's imagination ran riot.

DOUGLAS: Why – do you believe she didn't see Quint and Miss Jessel?

CHARLOTTE: Well, we have only her own word for both encounters. She was alone when she saw Peter Quint. And when she claimed to see Miss Jessel, Flora denied seeing anything.

DOUGLAS: Flora *said* she didn't. Now I never met Flora, but I did get to know the woman who wrote this account – and I assure you she was incapable of telling a falsehood. What she claimed to have seen, she saw.

GRIFFIN: Ah, but was it all self-delusion? She was a most impressionable young woman, wasn't she? It's clear she was quite bowled over by the children's uncle.

DOUGLAS: Perhaps, Griffin, perhaps. Oh, would you help me fill up our guests' glasses?

(MOVEMENT. GLASSES, POURING)

ARABELLA: So there's more to come?

DOUGLAS: Oh, a great deal more.

CHARLOTTE: I'm interested in these apparitions. Did the governess see them again?

DOUGLAS: Several times. You know she shared a room with Flora. Well, one evening she hadn't gone to bed but sat reading by the light of a candle. Suddenly she had the feeling of something ... astir in the house. She took her candle, went out and locked the door, and walked down the passage till she came in sight of the tall window at the turn of the staircase. At that instant, unaccountably, her candle went out, and in the moonlight she saw a figure walking up the stairs. It had reached the landing halfway up. The light from the window was quite sufficient for her to recognise Quint. When it saw her, it stopped and stared long and hard at her. She felt he knew her as well as she knew him. After a long intense moment, she saw the figure turn and pass straight down the staircase into the darkness.

ARABELLA: Inside the house! The figure had come indoors!

CHARLOTTE: The horror's getting closer!

DOUGLAS: But there was an even greater shock awaiting her when she got back to the room. She found Flora's bed empty, and the child up and gazing through the window. She questioned the child closely but the little girl maintained she'd awoken, found the governess not in the room, and had looked out to see if she had gone for a walk.

(FULL UP BEDROOM)

GOVERNESS: You were looking for me out of the window? You thought I might be walking in the grounds?

FLORA: Well, you know, I thought someone was.

GOVERNESS: And did you see anyone?

FLORA: Oh *no!* Of course not. If *you* weren't out there, who could be?

(EDGE OUT. FULL UP)

GOVERNESS: *(as narrator)* But I must move on with the record of what was hideous at Bly. Days, weeks passed without another encounter. I recognised the signs, the portents, the *feeling* of that June evening when I had my first sight of Peter Quint – but I continued unmolested. The summer turned, and autumn dropped upon Bly with its grey skies and scattered dead leaves. Then, suddenly, there came an incident after which the business seems to have been pure suffering.

One evening I went to bed in the room I shared with little Flora, and slept till about one o'clock. When I woke it was to sit straight up, as completely roused as if a hand had shaken me. I'd left a light burning, but it was now out, and I felt an instant certainty that Flora had extinguished it. I climbed out and went straight, in the darkness, to her bed. She wasn't in it. A glance at the window enlightened me. The child had squeezed in behind the blind and was again peering out into the night. She was, I was certain, face to face with the apparition we had met at the lake. Her concentration was so intense that nothing I did disturbed her. I slipped into a wrap and slippers, and quickly made my way out into the corridor and down one flight of stairs to a room on the flank of the house, beneath the tower. I went over to the window and looked out. On the lawn stood a person, motionless and, as if fascinated, looking up at something above me. There was clearly another person above me – on the tower. But the presence on the lawn wasn't in the least what I had conceived. It was poor little Miles.

(FADE IN. HOUSEKEEPER'S ROOM)

GOVERNESS: ... of course I rushed down to bring him in.

MRS GROSE: What did he do?

GOVERNESS: As soon as I appeared on the terrace, he came across to me. I took his hand without a word and led him back to his room.

(EDGE IN. BEDROOM)

GOVERNESS: Miles, you must tell me now – and all the truth. What did you go out for? What were you doing there?

MILES: Oh, it's so simple! Just so that you should do this.

GOVERNESS: Do what?

MILES: Think me – for a change – *bad!* **(hugs her)** 'Mmmm… **(kiss).**

GOVERNESS: I see you didn't undress at all?

MILES: No, I sat up in bed and read. At midnight, I went out. When I'm bad, I'm *bad!*

GOVERNESS: I see. But how could you be sure that I'd know?

MILES: Oh, I arranged that with Flora. She was to get up and look out. That would disturb you. To see what she was looking at, you'd also look out – and see! Which you did!

(FADE IN HOUSEKEEPER'S ROOM)

GOVERNESS: But it doesn't add up, Mrs Grose, does it? I awoke by chance, not by Flora's design. No, no, the four – Quint, Miss Jessel, Miles and little Flora – perpetually meet. Depend upon it. If there were nothing else, the systematic silence of the children would be proof enough. Never, by a slip of the tongue, have they so much as alluded to either of their old friends – any more than Miles has alluded to his expulsion. Oh yes, we may sit here and look at them – but even while they pretend to be lost in their fairy-tale, they're steeped in their vision of the dead restored to them!

MRS GROSE: Heaven help us.

GOVERNESS: They're not mine – they're not ours. They're his and they're hers. Quint and that woman want to get to them.

MRS GROSE: But for what?

GOVERNESS: For the love of all the evil the pair put into them. To destroy them, of course.

(FADE IN OPEN AIR, COUNTRY, LATE SUMMER. CHURCH BELLS. DOWN FOR)

GOVERNESS: *(as narrator)* And so the curtain rose on the last act of my dreadful drama. The night had brought a touch of frost, and the autumn air that Sunday morning was bright and sharp. Walking to church, I had little Miles at my side, while in advance of us were his sister and Mrs Grose…

(UP BACKGROUND. FADE UP GOVERNESS, MRS GROSE, MILES AND FLORA WALKING ON ROAD. AFTER FIRST SPEECH, GOVERNESS AND MILES STOP – THE OTHERS MOVE AWAY)

MILES: Look here, my dear. When in the world am I going back to school?

GOVERNESS: School?

MILES: Yes. You know, my dear, that for a fellow to be with a lady *always*… Of course, she's a jolly perfect lady. But after all – I am, well, getting on… And you can't say I've not been awfully good, can you?

GOVERNESS: No, I can't say that, Miles.

MILES: Except just that one night, you know, when I went down ... out of the house.

GOVERNESS: Oh, yes. But I forget what you did it for.

MILES: You forget? Why it was just to show you I could. And I can again.

GOVERNESS: Yes, but you won't.

MILES: No, not *that* again.

(THEY RESUME WALKING)

So when *am* I going back, my dear?

GOVERNESS: Were you very happy at school?

MILES: Oh, I'm happy enough anywhere.

GOVERNESS: Well, then, if you're as happy here...

MILES: Ah, but that isn't everything. I want to see more life. I want my own sort! *(pause)* Does my uncle think what you think?

GOVERNESS: How do you know what I think?

MILES: Ah, well, of course I don't, my dear. You never tell me. But I mean does *he* know the way I'm going on?

GOVERNESS: I don't think your uncle much cares.

MILES: Then don't you think he can be made to?

GOVERNESS: How?

MILES: Why, by getting him to come down here.

GOVERNESS: But who'll get him to do that?

MILES: *I will!*

(EDGE OUT. FULL UP)

GOVERNESS: *(as narrator)* I could not follow them into church. I sat on a tombstone, my mind grappling with the implications of what had just transpired. Miles had got out of me that I was afraid – and he'd probably be able to use my fear to gain, for his own purpose, more freedom. My fear was of having to deal with the intolerable question of why he was expelled from his school – since that was really the question of the horrors that lay behind. I ought to have welcomed the idea of his uncle arriving to deal with these things – but I could so little face the ugliness and pain of it, that I simply procrastinated and lived from hand to mouth. Thinking hard, I came out of the churchyard. By the time I reached the house, I'd made up my mind. I would leave Bly – and at once. The house was deserted. This was my opportunity. I made my way up to the schoolroom where there were objects belonging to me that I should have to take. I opened the door – and in a flash I found again my eyes unsealed. Seated at my own table, in the clear noonday light, was my vile predecessor. As I stared, she rose. Dark as midnight in her black dress, her haggard beauty and her unutterable woe, she looked at me – and I had the extraordinary chill of a feeling that it was I who was the intruder. The next minute there was nothing in the room but the sunshine, and the sense that I must stay.

(FADE IN. HOUSEKEEPER'S ROOM)

GOVERNESS: It's all out, Mrs Grose. Between Miles and me – it's all out.

MRS GROSE: What's all out, Miss?

GOVERNESS: It doesn't matter. Do you know why I missed church, my dear? I came home for a talk with Miss Jessel.

MRS GROSE: A talk? Do you mean she spoke?

GOVERNESS: It came to that. I found her in the schoolroom.

MRS GROSE: And what did she say?

GOVERNESS: That she suffers the torments of the damned. And that's why – to share them – she wants Flora. But it doesn't matter. I've made up my mind.

MRS GROSE: To what?

GOVERNESS: To sending for their uncle. If Miles thinks I'm afraid to, he'll find that he's mistaken. I'll show his uncle the headmaster's letter; I'll make it clear that I can't undertake to intervene on behalf of a child who's been expelled…

MRS GROSE: We've never in the least known what for…

GOVERNESS: For wickedness. What else – when he's so clever and beautiful and perfect? There can be no other explanation. And after all, it's their uncle's fault. He left those people here with the children – Quint, Miss Jessel. He carries a burden of guilt for the consequences. I'll write tonight.

(FADE OUT. FADE IN. MILES'S BEDROOM. BEDCLOTHES – HE'S IN BED)

MILES: *(bright and breezy; calls)* I say – you there, outside my door! Come in!

(DOOR OPENS)

GOVERNESS: *(approaching)* How did you know I was there?

MILES: I heard you, of course. You're like a troop of cavalry, my dear.

GOVERNESS: Then you weren't asleep?

MILES: Not much! I lie awake and think. Put your candle down, my dear – and sit down.

GOVERNESS: *(sits on bed)* And what do you think of, Miles?

MILES: What in the world, my dear, but you! *(pause)* And this strange business of ours.

GOVERNESS: What strange business, Miles?

MILES: Why the way you bring me up. *(pause)* And all the rest.

GOVERNESS: You shall certainly go back to school, Miles, if that's what's troubling you. But not to the old place. We must find a better one. *(pause)* Do you know, Miles, you've never said a word to me about your school – never mentioned it in any way?

MILES: Haven't I?

GOVERNESS: Not a word. You've never mentioned even one of your masters or your friends. You've said not a word about the least little thing that ever happened to you at school. Naturally I assumed that you were perfectly content with your present life.

MILES: I'm not – I'm not. I want to get away. My uncle must come down, and you must completely settle things. You'll have to tell him about the way you've let it all drop. You'll have to tell him a tremendous lot.

GOVERNESS: And how much, Miles, will *you* have to tell him? There are things he'll ask you.

MILES: What things?

GOVERNESS: The things you've never told me. Oh, Miles *(hugs him – close)* dear little Miles…

MILES: *(close)* Well, old lady?

GOVERNESS: *(close)* Is there nothing – nothing at all – that you want to tell me?

MILES: I'd like you to leave me alone.

GOVERNESS: Very well. *(stands)* Before I go, Miles, tell me – what happened before?

MILES: Before what?

GOVERNESS: Before you came back to Bly. And before you went away to school in the first place.

MILES: What happened…?

GOVERNESS: *(as narrator)* I caught for the very first time a small faint quaver of consent. It made me drop on my knees beside the bed, and seize once more the chance of possessing him.

GOVERNESS: *(emotional)* Dear little Miles, dear little Miles – if you *knew* how much I want to help you! It's only that! I'd rather die than give you pain or hurt one hair of your head. Dear little Miles – all I want… please – help me to save you!

GOVERNESS: *(as narrator)* A moment later, I knew I'd gone too far. The answer to my appeal was instantaneous.

(ALMIGHTY CRASH OF THUNDER FOLLOWED BY LOUD CONTINUOUS RUMBLING – HOLD UNDER REST OF NARRATION)

(above thunder) A gust of frozen air blasted the room, and the room shook as if a casement had crashed in.

GOVERNESS: *(calls)* Dear heaven! The candle's out!

MILES: I did it! I blew it out, dear!

(EDGE OUT. FADE IN HALL AT BLY)

MRS GROSE: Have you written, Miss?

GOVERNESS: Yes, this is the letter. I'll leave it here on the table. Luke will take it. Isn't Flora with you, Mrs Grose?

MRS GROSE: No, indeed, Miss. I thought she was with you and master Miles in the schoolroom.

GOVERNESS: She was not. Miles has been playing the piano for me... Oh, dear heaven. I see it now. *(calls)* Miles?

MILES: *(distant – calls)* Yes, my dear.

GOVERNESS: *(calls)* Where's Flora?

MILES: *(calls)* I thought she was with Mrs Grose. I've no idea where she is. *(retreating)* Sorry!

MRS GROSE: Oh, she'll be in one of the rooms upstairs. Miss.

GOVERNESS: *(mounting panic and certainty)* No! No! Miles has played his little trick on me – and it's worked. We've been caught! Flora's not in the house! She's gone out!

MRS GROSE: Without a hat!

GOVERNESS: Isn't that woman always without one?

MRS GROSE: She's with *her*?

GOVERNESS: Of course she's with *her!* We must find them. *(retreating)* Quickly!

MRS GROSE: *(calls)* But master Miles. Where…?

GOVERNESS: *(calls – moving)* Oh, *he's* gone to Quint. But we *must* get to Flora before it's too late. Come on!

            (EDGE OUT. FULL UP. OPEN AIR, AUTUMN. GOVERNESS AND MRS GROSE HURRYING THROUGH FALLEN LEAVES)

MRS GROSE: *(breathless, hurrying, calling)* You're making for the lake, Miss? You think she's *in*…

GOVERNESS: *(calling)* She may be – but I don't think so. I think she's returned to the place I told you of – the place where she encountered that vile woman.

MRS GROSE: When she pretended not to see…?

GOVERNESS: With that astounding self-possession! I've always been sure she wanted to go back alone. And now her brother has managed it for her.

MRS GROSE: *(stops walking)* You suppose the children really *talk* of them?

GOVERNESS: *(stops walking)* If we heard the things they say, we'd be simply appalled.

MRS GROSE: And if Flora *is* there…?

GOVERNESS: Then Miss Jessel is. Beyond a doubt. You'll see. Come on!

(EDGE OUT. FULL UP)

GOVERNESS: *(as narrator)* I reached the lake, with my friend close behind me. As at last the greater part of the water came into view and there wasn't a sign of the child, she gave a moan of relief. There was no trace of Flora on either bank, but for about twenty yards on the opposite edge a thick copse came down to the lake.

(FULL UP – OPEN AIR)

GOVERNESS: *(calls)* No, no! Wait! She's taken the boat.

MRS GROSE: Then where is it? I don't see a boat.

GOVERNESS: No, you don't. The strongest proof of all! She's used it to go over — and then she's hidden it.

MRS GROSE: All alone? That child? She's only eight!

GOVERNESS: But she's not alone! And at times like this, she's not a child. She's an old, old woman. Look, there, where the trees come down to the water. The boat could be there.

MRS GROSE: But if it *is* — then where's Flora?

GOVERNESS: That's exactly what we must find out. Come on. *(starting to walk)* We must walk all the way round. It won't take us more than ten minutes. *(retreating)* Come on! Take my arm!

MRS GROSE: *(retreating)* Mercy me!

(FULL UP)

GOVERNESS: *(as narrator)* It took us only eight minutes to find the boat precisely where I had suspected it would be. It had clearly been pulled out of sight of the opposite shore. As I looked at the pair of short thick oars, quite safely drawn up, I realised what a prodigious feat this had been for a little girl. We passed through the trees into the open — and there, a short way off, stood Flora, smiling. She waited for us, not herself taking a step. We approached, and she smiled and smiled…

(FULL UP. OPEN AIR)

MRS GROSE: Oh, my darling! My darling little girl! Thank heaven you're safe! What a terrible fright you've given us. You could have been drowned. Whatever made you do it?

FLORA: Where are your hats and coats?

GOVERNESS: Where yours are, Flora, my dear.

FLORA: And where's Miles?

GOVERNESS: I'll tell you – if you'll tell *me*...

FLORA: Yes? What?

MRS GROSE: Miss! Please!

GOVERNESS: ... where, my pet, is Miss Jessel?

MRS GROSE: *(drawn-out shriek – protective of the child)*

(FULL UP)

GOVERNESS: *(as narrator)* The glare on the child's face, as I broke the silence between us and uttered that name, was like the smash of a pane of glass. A second later I was seizing my colleague's arm.

(FULL UP. OPEN AIR)

GOVERNESS: Look! She's there! She's there!

(FULL UP)

GOVERNESS: *(as narrator)* Before us, on the opposite bank, stood Miss Jessel, exactly as she'd stood the other time. I remember, strangely, that my first feeling was one of joy – my case was proved! She was there, so I was neither cruel nor mad. I was justified! I was more than justified, for the evil that emanated from that black figure could be felt across the water. Mrs Grose's dazed blink across to where I pointed convinced me that she too at last saw. My eyes moved to the child. I was shaken by her reaction. Not even deigning to glance in the direction of the prodigy I announced, she turned instead on me an expression of hard, still gravity – an expression that seemed to read, and accuse, and judge me. I gaped at her coolness, though I was never more sure of anything in my life than that she could see the figure.

(FULL UP. OPEN AIR)

GOVERNESS: *(calls)* She's *there*, you unhappy little thing. There! There! *There!* And you know it as well as you know me!

MRS GROSE: Oh, what a dreadful turn, to be sure, Miss! Where on earth do you see anything?

GOVERNESS: There! As large as life! Hideous – vile. Look! You don't see her as we do? You mean you don't *now*? Look – she's as big as a blazing fire! Only look, dear woman – *look!*

MRS GROSE: Nothing! I see nothing. There's nothing to see!

GOVERNESS: *(to self)* Then I'm lost! Defeated!

MRS GROSE: She isn't there, my little pet. Nobody's there! And you never saw anything, my sweet. How can poor Miss Jessel… when Miss Jessel's dead and buried. We know, don't we, love?

FLORA: Of course we do, Mrs Grose.

MRS GROSE: It's all been a terrible mistake, and a worry, and a joke. Now we'll all go home as fast as we can.

GOVERNESS: A joke? Perhaps – and played on me. For that creature's made herself invisible to your eyes. But there she stands – a monster of evil – and *you* see her, Flora, don't you? As clearly as you see me.

FLORA: I don't know what you mean. I see nobody. I see nothing. I never *have.* I think you're cruel. I don't like you! *(bursts into tears)* Oh, Mrs Grose, take me away, please take me away. Take me away from her!

GOVERNESS: From *me?*

FLORA: From you – from you!

GOVERNESS: Oh, Flora, dear Flora. Darling child. I've lost you – I can see that. I've interfered – and you've been shown, by *her,* the perfect way to counter me. I've done my best, but I've lost you. Goodbye, Flora dear. Now go, Mrs Grose! Go! Take the child away from here!

(EDGE OUT. FULL UP)

GOVERNESS: *(as narrator)* I must have thrown myself to the ground, and given way to a wildness of grief. I must have lain there long, and cried and wailed, for when I raised my head, the day was almost done. I rose, returned to the house and went straight to my room to change what I was wearing. Flora's belongings had all been removed. She spent that night with Mrs Grose.

(FADE IN. GOVERNESS'S BEDROOM)

MRS GROSE: Wake up! Wake up, Miss.

GOVERNESS: What is it? What's happened?

MRS GROSE: It's little Flora. She was very restless in the night – and now she's so … agitated. She won't eat, she'll settle to nothing. She keeps bursting into tears. I'm afraid she's going to make herself ill. And it's all about you Miss.

GOVERNESS: Yes, me, of course. I'm the one who questioned her truthfulness. I certainly put my foot in it, there! She'll never speak to me again.

MRS GROSE: I don't think she ever will, Miss.

GOVERNESS: Has she said a single word to you about Miss Jessel?

MRS GROSE: Not one. And of course you know that when I took her from the lake, there *was* nobody there…

GOVERNESS: Indeed – and nothing in the world could have been cleverer on Miss Jessel's part than to close your eyes to her presence. Flora now has her grievance – and she'll work it to the end.

MRS GROSE: To what end?

GOVERNESS: What Flora wants is to get rid of me. She'll make me out to her uncle to be the lowest creature in the world… She'll say she's unable, she refuses, to live with me.

MRS GROSE: That's what she keeps saying. She never again wants so much as so look at you.

GOVERNESS: And is that what you've come for? To speed me on my way? Oh, no – I've a better way. On Sunday I *was* terribly near leaving. But I've been thinking. It's *you* who must go. You must take Flora away from here. Away from *them*. Away – even most of all, now – from me. Take her straight to her uncle.

MRS GROSE: But what on earth shall I …? *[say to him about all this…]*

GOVERNESS: You must say what your conscience dictates. I have held nothing back from you. I rely on your loyalty.

MRS GROSE: But Miles – do you think he'll…? *[stick by you…]*

GOVERNESS: Not turn on me? I don't think he will. I honestly believe he wants to speak. Last evening he sat with me for two hours in the firelight, as if the words were trembling on his lips. No, take Flora away as soon as possible, and leave me alone with him.

MRS GROSE: *(dubious)* If you say so, Miss…

GOVERNESS: There's one thing, of course. Before she goes they mustn't see each other – not even for a second. That's absolutely vital. *(sudden anxiety)* Mrs Grose – they haven't already…

MRS GROSE: I'm not such a fool as that, Miss. Whenever I've left her, one of the maids has always been with her. She's alone at present, but safely locked in.

GOVERNESS: Then get her things packed, and take her away. I must give Miles some more time before he sees his uncle.

MRS GROSE: Then you'll…? *[be coming up to town yourself with the boy]*

GOVERNESS: Of course. But a day or two may really bring it out. Miles will then be on *my* side – and you can see the importance of that. If nothing happens – if Miles doesn't talk – I'll have failed, but I trust you'll have done what you can with their uncle.

MRS GROSE: Your idea's the right one, Miss. I'll take Flora away this very morning. In any event, I myself…

GOVERNESS: Yes?

MRS GROSE: I can't stay here.

GOVERNESS: You mean that, since yesterday, you've seen…?

MRS GROSE: Not seen, Miss. *Heard…*

GOVERNESS: Heard?

MRS GROSE: From that child. Horrors! *Horrors!* On my honour, Miss, she says such things… *(breaks down)* Dear Lord… Shocking, shocking things – and coming from those innocent lips…

GOVERNESS: About me?

MRS GROSE: About you, Miss – since you must have it. It's beyond everything for a child of eight. I can't think where she must have picked up…

GOVERNESS: I can! Oh, I can! Thank God!

MRS GROSE: Thank God?

GOVERNESS: This so justifies me!

MRS GROSE: It does that, Miss.

GOVERNESS: So, in spite of yesterday, you *believe…*

MRS GROSE: Oh yes! I believe. And that's why I must get her away from this – from *them!*

GOVERNESS: There's one thing, of course. My letter to their uncle – it will have reached town before you.

MRS GROSE: Your letter won't have got there, Miss. Your letter never went.

GOVERNESS: Never went? What became of it?

MRS GROSE: Goodness knows! Master Miles must have...

GOVERNESS: You mean he took it?

MRS GROSE: It's the only explanation. When I came back with Miss Flora yesterday, I saw it wasn't where you'd put it. I asked Luke later, and he said he'd never seen it.

GOVERNESS: Mrs Grose, leave us. Leave us. I'll get it out of him. He'll confess. If he confesses, he's saved. And if he's saved...

MRS GROSE: *(retreating)* ... then you are? Don't worry. I'll save you without him!

(FADE OUT. FULL UP)

GOVERNESS: *(as narrator)* When I came down to breakfast, I learned that the carriage containing Mrs Grose and my younger pupil had already rolled out of the gates. Miles, I gathered, had breakfasted with them, and had then gone out. A sense of unease pervaded the house. The unusual events of the morning had naturally caused the servants some bewilderment. I determined to try to turn the occasion to some good. I let it be known that I was charged with a great deal to do, and assumed a much firmer manner than before. As one indication of the changed circumstances, I decreed that my meals with the boy should be served in the dining room. And so, as the time for luncheon approached, I awaited Miles in the ponderous pomp of the room through whose windows, that first scared Sunday, I'd seen the horrendous vision of the dead Quint.

(HEAVY DOOR OPENS – DINING ROOM. MILES WALKS ON WOODEN FLOOR)

GOVERNESS: Ah, Miles. How do you do?

MILES: *(remote – advancing)* I say, my dear, is she really very ill?

GOVERNESS: Little Flora? She'll soon be better. London will set her up. Bly had ceased to agree with her. Come here, Miles, and take your mutton.

MILES: *(moves)* Thank you. *(sits at table)*

(CHAIR LEGS ON WOOD. CROCKERY. CUTLERY)

Did Bly disagree with her so terribly all at once?

GOVERNESS: Not so suddenly as you might think. You could see it coming on.

MILES: Then why didn't you get her away before?

GOVERNESS: Before what?

MILES: Before she became too ill to travel.

GOVERNESS: She's *not* too ill to travel, Miles. She only might
                have become so if she'd stayed. This was just the
                right moment. The journey will do her the world
                of good.

MILES: I see.

                **(FULL UP GOVERNESS AS NARRATOR –
                NOW, AND FOR THE REST OF THE SCENE, AS
                WE ALTERNATE BETWEEN NARRATION AND
                ACTION)**

GOVERNESS: *(as narrator)* Our meal was of the briefest – mine
                a vain pretence – and I had the things immediately
                removed. While this was done Miles stood with
                his hands in his pockets and his back to me looking
                out of the wide window – the window through
                which, that Sunday, I'd seen... what I had seen.
                We continued silent while the maid was with us
                – as silent, it whimsically occurred to me, as some
                young couple who, at the inn on their wedding
                journey, feel shy in the presence of the waiter. It was
                only when she'd finally left that he turned round.

                **(FULL UP. DRAWING ROOM – NOW AND FOR
                THE REST OF THE SCENE, AS WE ALTERNATE
                BETWEEN ACTION AND NARRATION)**

MILES: So – we're alone!

GOVERNESS: More or less. Not absolutely.

MILES: No. There are … the others.

GOVERNESS: *(as narrator)* He faced the window again, and remained there a while, his forehead against the glass. I had always my hypocrisy of needlework, behind which I now gained the sofa. But as I regarded his back, an extraordinary feeling grew in me – a feeling that at last I wasn't being shut out. On the contrary, it was Miles who seemed to be barred. The frames and squares of the great window seemed to be shutting him out. Was he looking through the panes for something he couldn't see? At last he turned to face me.

MILES: Well, I think I'm glad that Bly agrees with *me*. I've been freer in the last two days than ever before. I've been ever so far – all round about. Now that we're alone together, you'll be more on your own. I hope you don't mind.

GOVERNESS: My dear Miles, though I've renounced all claim to your company, I at least greatly enjoy it. What else should I stay on for?

MILES: You stay on just for *that?*

GOVERNESS: Certainly. I stay on as your friend – and from the tremendous interest I take in you. I'll stay until you're settled into something more worth your while. Don't you remember how I told you, when I came and sat on your bed the night of the storm, that there was nothing in the world I wouldn't do for you?

MILES: Yes, yes! Only that, I think, was to get me to do something for *you!*

GOVERNESS: Yes, it was partly that. But you didn't do it, you know.

MILES: Oh, yes. You wanted me to tell you something.

GOVERNESS: That's it. Out – straight out. What you have on your mind, you know.

MILES: Ah, then is *that* what you've stayed over for?

GOVERNESS: Well, yes. I may as well make a clean breast of it. It was precisely for that.

MILES: Do you mean now? Here?

GOVERNESS: There couldn't be a better place or time.

GOVERNESS: *(as narrator)* He looked round him uneasily, and I had the strange – the rare – impression of the very first approach of fear in him. It was as if he were suddenly afraid – of me!

GOVERNESS: Do you want to go out again very much?

MILES: Awfully! Look, I'll tell you everything – I mean, I'll tell you anything you like. I *will* tell you – I *will*. But not now.

GOVERNESS: Why not now?

MILES: I have to see Luke.

GOVERNESS: Well, then, go to Luke, and I'll wait for what you promise. Only, in return for that, before you leave me please satisfy one very much smaller request.

MILES: Smaller?

GOVERNESS: A mere fraction of the whole. Tell me if yesterday afternoon, from the table in the hall, you took – you know – my letter.

GOVERNESS: *(as narrator)* How he took this I didn't know, for the next minute I sprang straight up and drew him close, instinctively keeping him with his back to the window as I fell for support against the nearest piece of furniture. For the appearance was full upon us – the appearance that I had already had to deal with. Peter Quint had come into view, like a sentinel before a prison. The next instant he'd reached the window. Close to the glass, he glared in, offering once more to the room his white face of damnation.

In an instant my decision was made. Seeing and facing what I saw, I would keep the boy himself unaware. It was like fighting with a demon for a human soul.

MILES: *(anguished, under intense strain)* Yes. I took it.

GOVERNESS: *(hugging him)* Oh, my dear boy. *(close)* My
               dear, dear boy.

GOVERNESS: *(as narrator)* I drew him close. I held him to
               my breast, where I could feel the sudden fever of
               his little body. The tremendous pulse of his little
               heart. And all the while I kept my eyes on the
               thing at the window. I saw it move, and its slow
               wheel was like the prowl of a baffled beast.

GOVERNESS: Why did you take it?

MILES: To see what you said about me.

GOVERNESS: You opened it?

GOVERNESS: *(as narrator)* I held him off a little, and saw how
               completely ravaged he was. But what did this strain
               matter when my eyes went back to the window and
               I saw that the air was clear again? I had quenched
               the influence. It was my personal triumph.

GOVERNESS: And you found nothing?

MILES: No, you said very little. You asked my uncle to
               come down.

GOVERNESS: So what have you done with it?

MILES: I've burnt it.

GOVERNESS: Burnt it? Is that what you did at school. Take
               letters? Or other things?

MILES: Other things? Did I *steal?* Is that what you mean?

GOVERNESS: I don't know what I mean. I don't know why you were expelled from your school.

MILES: Oh, so you knew that I mightn't go back?

GOVERNESS: I knew. Well, *did* you...?

MILES: No, I didn't steal.

GOVERNESS: Well, then, what *did* you do?

MILES: *(draws breath twice as if to speak)* I... I... Well, I said things.

GOVERNESS: Only that?

MILES: They thought it was enough.

GOVERNESS: To turn you out? To forbid you ever to return?

MILES: Well, I suppose I oughtn't to have done it.

GOVERNESS: But to whom did you say these terrible things – these things worthy of the severest punishment?

MILES: Oh... I don't know. I can't remember their names.

GOVERNESS: Was it to so many, then?

MILES: No – only a few. Those I liked.

GOVERNESS: *(as narrator)* "Those I liked?" I seemed to float not into clarity, but a darker obscure. A second later, out of my pity, I was seized with the appalling alarm that he might perhaps be innocent. The thought was, for an instant, confounding and bottomless. For if he *were* innocent, then what on earth was *I*? Paralysed, while it lasted, by the implications of the question, I let him go a little, so that – with a deep-drawn sigh, he turned away from me again and faced the clear window.

GOVERNESS: And did they repeat what you said?

MILES: Oh, yes. They must have repeated them. To those *they* liked.

GOVERNESS: And these things came round…?

MILES: …to the masters. Yes. But I didn't know they'd tell you.

GOVERNESS: But they haven't – they didn't. That's why I'm asking you.

MILES: Yes, I suppose it was too bad to put in writing.

GOVERNESS: Stuff and nonsense! What *were* those things?

GOVERNESS: *(as narrator)* I must have sounded stern, though my sternness was all for his judge, his executioner. Yet it made him avert himself again – and that movement made *me*, with a single bound and an irrepressible cry, spring straight upon him.

For there, against the glass, as if to blight his confession and stay his answer, was the hideous author of our woe – the white face of damnation.

GOVERNESS: *(cry of anguish)* No more! No more! Leave us alone! Come here, my darling. Don't look!

MILES: Is she *here?* Where? Where is she? Outside the window?

GOVERNESS: *She?*

MILES: Miss Jessel! Miss Jessel!

GOVERNESS: It's not Miss Jessel! But it's at the window – straight before us. Look – there! *There! There* – for the last time!

GOVERNESS: *(as narrator)* He was at me in a white rage, bewildered, glaring vainly over the place – and missing the presence wholly, though to my sense it now filled the room – wide, overwhelming, like the taste of poison.

MILES: Who? Who is it? Is it ... *him?*

GOVERNESS: Who do you mean by "him"?

MILES: Peter Quint. You devil! *Where?*

GOVERNESS: *(as narrator)* His words are in my ears still – his supreme surrender of the name, his tribute to my devotion.

GOVERNESS: What does he matter now, my own? What will he *ever* matter? *I* have you – and he has lost you for ever!

MILES: *(pause – long cry of anguish)*

GOVERNESS: *(as narrator – over Miles's cry)* But he'd already jerked straight round, stared, and seen but the quiet day. With the stroke of the loss I was so proud of, he uttered the cry of a creature hurled over an abyss. As if catching him in his fall I grasped him, yes, I held him – it may be imagined with what a passion. But at the end of a minute, I began to feel what it truly was that I held. We were alone with the quiet day, and his little heart, dispossessed, had stopped.

(FULL UP – SINGLE CHURCH BELL, FUNERAL TOLL. DOWN FOR CLOSING ANNOUNCEMENT. UP CHURCH BELL. FADE OUT)

THE GHOST SHIP

A PLAY FOR RADIO
BY NEVILLE TELLER
FROM THE SHORT STORY
"J HABAKUK JEPHSON'S
STATEMENT"BY SIR
ARTHUR CONAN DOYLE

Running time: 30'

FIRST BROADCAST ACROSS THE USA
ON 30 DECEMBER 2015 IN A PRODUCTION BY
SHOESTRING RADIO THEATRE, SAN FRANCISCO

CHARACTERS IN
ORDER OF APPEARANCE

**SIR EDWARD
HARGRAVE** *English, aged about 60*

**CAPTAIN DAVID
MOREHOUSE** *English aged mid-40s*

MR DEVEAU *English First Mate, aged 30*

**DR HABAKUK
JEPHSON** *American, about 50*

MARTHA *Black woman, about 60, once plantation slave*

**SEPTIMIUS
GORING** *African-American, educated, mid-40s*

**CAPTAIN
BRIGGS** *American, about 50*

**JOHN
HARTON** *American, about 25*

MR HYSON   *American, First Mate, mid-40s*

AFRICAN   *Man*

(FULL UP CHATTER. BANG OF GAVEL, CHATTER FADES)

CLERK: Silence! The court is in session.

HARGRAVE: Thank you. Ladies and gentlemen, allow me to introduce myself. I am Sir Edward Hargrave, and I am the Chief Coroner of this British Overseas Territory of Gibraltar. We are gathered here today because the Governor has asked me to conduct a full and searching inquiry into a bizarre occurrence with which you are all doubtless very familiar. He hopes that an open investigation, conducted in accordance with strict judicial procedure, will throw some light on the mysterious events which have baffled the police and, indeed, everyone caught up in them. I intend to question certain naval officers during the course of this inquiry, together with other persons who might be able to assist the court.

(OPENING ANNOUNCEMENT)

HARGRAVE: The Governor has asked this court to perform two functions. One is to establish and put on record the facts concerning this perplexing event. The second is to attempt to reach some explanation of them. I am confident that we can achieve the first. As for the second, I can only hope that we manage to fulfil that as well. Call the first witness.

CLERK: *(calls)* Call Captain David Morehouse.

USHER: *(remote)* Captain David Morehouse.

(STEPS ON WOODEN FLOOR)

CLERK: Take the book in your right hand. Read from the card,

MOREHOUSE: I swear by Almighty God that the evidence I shall give will be the truth, the whole truth and nothing but the truth.

HARGRAVE: You are …?

MOREHOUSE: David Morehouse, captain of the British brigantine *Dei Gratia*.

HARGRAVE: Would you please tell the court, in as much detail as you can recall, the events of Wednesday, December the 4th, 1872.

MOREHOUSE: I will be happy to do so. But with your permission, sir, may I first provide the background to those events by going back a few weeks? Early in November 1872 the *Dei Gratia* lay in harbour in Hoboken, New Jersey, awaiting a cargo of petroleum destined for Gibraltar. Anchored just off Staten Island was a sea-faring friend of mine, Captain Benjamin Briggs, commanding the newly-refitted brigantine *Mary Celeste*. He was fully loaded with a cargo of 1,700 barrels of denatured alcohol, and was about to set sail to Lisbon, Portugal. On Captain Briggs's last night in port, November the 6th, I rowed over to the *Mary Celeste* with two of my officers, and we dined with him, his wife and his three passengers.

HARGRAVE: That is most interesting, Captain Morehouse. Could you tell us a little more about those guests.

MOREHOUSE: Well, I was surprised to see Mrs Briggs at the table, but I learned that my friend had decided that his wife, Sarah, and their small daughter, Sophia, would accompany him on the voyage to Portugal, while his son, Arthur, who was of school age, remained in New York with his grandmother. There were three other passengers – Mr James Harton, a writer employed by the owners of the *Mary Celeste*; Mr Septimius Goring, an African gentleman long resident in America; and the well-known medical specialist on diseases of the lung, Dr Habakuk Jephson.

HARGRAVE: Thank you, Captain Morehouse. Now please proceed.

MOREHOUSE: The *Mary Celeste* set sail on November the 7th. During the next few days we attended to the loading of our own cargo, and the *Dei Gratia* left port on November 15th, bound for Gibraltar. At about 1 pm on Thursday, December the 5th,

(FADE IN SEA SLAPPING AGAINST SHIP'S SIDES, CREAKING OF SHIP'S TIMBERS, CALL OF SEAGULLS. HOLD BENEATH FOLLOWING)

we were midway between the Azores and the coast of Portugal. As I came on deck…

(OPEN AIR)

HELMSMAN: *(calls)* Ship ahoy, sir!

MOREHOUSE: Where?

HELMSMAN: *(calls)* Starboard, sir. About 6 miles. She ain't steady, sir. Veering all over the place.

MOREHOUSE: Let me see! Her sails are set very odd. I think there's something wrong. Steer closer. We'll hail her.

(FADE SEA BACKGROUND FAST. COURTOOM)

MOREHOUSE: As we came closer, I could see that the ship was the *Mary Celeste*, but there was no one on deck. When we hailed them, there was no response. So I ordered Mr Deveau, my first mate, accompanied by Mr Wright, the second mate, to row across and investigate.

(CROSSFADE)

DEVEAU: It took us only a few minutes to ascertain that there was no one on board. No one at all. The vessel was deserted, rocking gently on a dead calm sea. There was no sign of a struggle, no indication that any violence had taken place. In the saloon half-eaten meals lay on the table. In the hold hammocks swung to and fro. Where was the captain? Where was the crew? It was a complete mystery.

HARGRAVE: Mr Deveau, did you and your companion come to any conclusion as to how long the ship had been in this condition?

DEVEAU: Well, sir, from the state of the sails and the rigging, it seemed to us that she'd been deserted for a good few days. This impression was confirmed when we retrieved the ship's log. The last entry was dated 8 am on November the 25th, nine days earlier. There was no mention of rough weather. Nor could there have been any.

HARGRAVE: Why is that, Mr Deveau?

DEVEAU: In one of the cabins, clearly occupied by a woman given the garments we found in there, there was a sewing machine. Standing on it was a bobbin of silk, exactly as though someone was just about to insert it into the machine, but had been called away. If the vessel had rolled more than a few degrees, it would surely have fallen to the floor.

HARGRAVE: So did you conclude that the ship had been becalmed for the whole of that period?

DEVEAU: We did not, sir. Captain Morehouse believed that the vessel must have been abandoned a considerable distance from where we picked her up, for a powerful current runs up in that latitude from the African coast. The ship was pulled along a fair way, but there was little swell, and she remained upright and steady throughout.

HARGRAVE: How strange. Tell me, during your investigation of the vessel, did you discover the lifeboat?

DEVEAU: The lifeboat, sir, was missing.

HARGRAVE: And when you had concluded your inspection?

DEVEAU: Mr Wright and I returned to the *Dei Gratia*, and reported our findings to Captain Morehouse. He ordered us to fix lines to the derelict vessel so that we could tow her the 600 nautical miles into Gibraltar. Our crew of eight was divided and four of us stayed aboard the *Mary Celeste* for the remainder of the voyage. It was on December the 12th that we docked in Gibraltar Harbour…

(CROSSFADE)

HARGRAVE: … that the *Mary Celeste* was abandoned at some point by Captain Briggs, his wife and their small daughter, and the 10 other persons aboard – namely 7 crew members and three passengers – that much is certain. Some of the witnesses have pointed out that the total complement of persons on the ill-fated ship was 13, and have tried to draw some conclusion from the fact, but this, I think, we may safely ignore. We have had a very full account of the state of the deserted vessel, and several witnesses have advanced theories of how and why it came to be so. The court can give credence to none of them. No hypothesis presented to this court can reconcile all the facts of the case. In the utter absence of any sort of evidence as to what may have befallen those aboard the *Mary Celeste*, or how or why the vessel was abandoned, the court is forced to conclude that this case, like many other mysteries of the deep, will never be solved. If crime has been committed — as is much to be suspected — there is little hope of bringing the perpetrators to justice. As for the individuals who have apparently disappeared from the face of the earth, we can only mourn their loss and commiserate with their families and friends. Officers of the United States navy have spoken of the captain of the *Mary Celeste* and how much he will be missed by his colleagues. I must also make special mention of one of the passengers on the ill-fated vessel. Dr Habakuk Jephson was a distinguished physician and also a passionate and effective advocate of the abolition of slavery. The loss of Dr Jephson will be felt in both political and scientific circles...

(FADE. FULL UP)

JEPHSON: It is now ten years since, sitting in the rear of the coroner's court in Gibraltar, I heard Sir Edward Hargrave utter those words. It is not given to many men to learn before their death how much the world appreciates them. Yes, I am Habakuk Jephson – the self-same man who booked passage aboard the *Mary Celeste* back in 1872, and of whom nothing has been heard since the deserted vessel was towed into Gibraltar harbour. Many will doubtless wonder why I have not come forward before, and why I have allowed so much conjecture, so many theories, to pass unchallenged over the past decade. If justice could have been served in any way by revealing the facts in my possession, I should unhesitatingly have done so. But there was no possibility of any such result.

As the years passed I increasingly began to feel that I owed society the duty of revealing all that I know of the ill-fated voyage, but I still hesitated to put pen to paper. Recently, however, I have noted in myself certain symptoms that I am familiar with in others, and I believe that before many months my tongue and hand may be incapable of conveying information. This is why I now take up my pen.

Let me begin by recording that I am Joseph Habakuk Jephson, Doctor of Medicine of the University of Harvard. My father, William K Jephson was a preacher of the sect called Plymouth Brethren. Like most other Puritans of New England he was a determined opponent of slavery, and he inspired the same passion in me.

During the Civil War I accompanied the 113th New York Regiment throughout, and was present at the battle of Gettysburg. Finally I was wounded quite severely at Antietam, and would probably have perished on the battlefield but for the kindness of a gentleman named Murray. He had me carried to his house, a splendid residence set in the midst of his extensive plantation. And there he ensured that I was nursed back to health. He placed my recovery in the hands of Martha, his elderly housekeeper – a woman filled to overflowing with compassion. She had heard of me, and was grateful to me for championing her oppressed people, but she made a wonderful, caring nurse out of the sheer goodness of her heart.

(FADE IN)

MARTHA: *(approaching)* Why, Dr Jephson, what you doing a-sitting out here at this time of the evening? You'll catch your death. Come indoors this very instant.

JEPHSON: Get away with you, Martha. I'm well wrapped, and just look at that sunset. Isn't it wonderful?

MARTHA: It sure is, Dr Jephson. I reckon heaven will look something like that, when I get there.

JEPHSON: You're not going to heaven any time soon, Martha.

MARTHA: Can't be as long as all that. No, sir. And won't I be happy to join the heavenly host!

JEPHSON: Don't talk like that, Martha. The good Lord will grant you many more years. You deserve them. Look how you've nursed me back to life.

MARTHA: And oh, I loved doing it, Dr Jephson. But you be leaving the plantation soon. You be leaving poor old Martha. And after that, who knows how much longer I got on this earth? And when I do go, there's one thing I have – one precious thing – I can't take across the Jordan.

JEPHSON: What are you speaking of, Martha? What thing?

MARTHA: A thing very precious – more precious, more holy than anything else in this world. You ask: why do I have it – a poor old black woman? Because back in the old country my people, they were very great people, leaders, chiefs. My father gave it to me, and his father gave it to him. But now, who shall I give it to?

JEPHSON: Have you no children, Martha? No relatives.

MARTHA: None. I all alone in this world. I trust no one. But Dr Jephson, you I know. I see you week after week. I care for you. I bring you back to life. I know you are a good, good man. I know you write books and fight for coloured folk. And I say to myself – this is a man worthy of it. I give the stone to him, even though he never know what it means or where it come from. This is it. I carry it round my neck. Here, take it. Take it. Keep it safe. Never lose it. Carry it with you always. Remember, it is precious, holy.

(FADE. FULL UP)

JEPHSON: I would never hurt the old woman's feelings, so I took the stone from her and hung it round my neck. Little could I have guessed that in giving me her most precious possession, Martha had saved my life for a second time. When she left me, I took a good look at it.

(FADE IN UNDER THE FOLLOWING THE BEAT OF AFRICAN DRUMS)

The stone was oval, intensely black and extremely hard. It was about three inches long, and an inch and a half broad in the middle. The ends were rounded off. The most curious part about it were several well-marked ridges which ran in semicircles over its surface, giving it exactly the appearance of a human ear. In what might have been the lobe, a small hole had been gouged, and through this Martha had threaded a thin cord.

(FADE OUT DRUMS)

Shortly afterwards I took my leave of the generous-hearted Mr Murray. I returned to Brooklyn, resumed my medical practice, and married. In memory of my old nurse I kept the stone round my neck, and often told the story of how it came into my possession.

Seven or eight years passed, and as my practice grew, so too did the pressure of work, even though I had taken on a partner. My health began to succumb and, when I was clearly in a weakened state, my wife insisted I visit a specialist.

He pronounced me too unwell to continue in my profession, and prescribed a long sea voyage. By this time I was inclined to take his advice. The matter was clinched when I chanced to meet young Russell, of the shipping firm White and Russell, who offered me a passage in one of his father's vessels, the *Mary Celeste*, which was about to set sail from Boston. I first thought that my wife might accompany me, but she has always been a poor sailor and she begged to stay at home. I am not a religious man, but I thank God that she did so and that I concurred.

I arrived in Boston on October the 12th 1872, and proceeded at once to the firm's offices to thank young Russell's father and to collect my ticket. As I sat in the waiting area, a tall, gaunt African gentleman entered from the street, and went across to the counter. I could not help hearing the subsequent conversation.

(OFFICE BACKGROUND – LOW HUM OF CONVERSATION)

CLERK: May I help you, sir?

GORING: I wanted to ask about the *Mary Celeste*. She sails the day after tomorrow, does she not?

CLERK: That is correct, sir.

GORING: Bound for...?

CLERK: Lisbon, Portugal, sir.

GORING: How many in the crew?

CLERK: Seven.

GORING: Any passengers?

CLERK: Yes, sir. Two. An employee of this firm and a doctor from New York.

GORING: Is there room for another passenger?

CLERK: There's accommodation for three more.

GORING: Then I'll go. Please book my passage at once.

CLERK: Certainly sir. And the name...?

GORING: Goring. Mr Septimius Goring. Of New Orleans.

(BACKGROUND OFF)

JEPHSON: The clerk filled up a form and turned it round, indicating where Mr Goring was required to sign. As he stooped over to do so, I was horrified to see that the fingers of his right hand had been lopped off, and that he was holding the pen between his thumb and the palm. He used it skilfully enough, however, for he dashed off his signature, nodded to the clerk and strolled out of the office just as Mr Russell sent word that he was ready to see me. That evening I went down to the *Mary Celeste* to look over my berth. I was met on board by its captain – Benjamin Briggs.

(OPEN AIR. SEAGULLS)

BRIGGS:

(loud, hearty) Welcome on board the *Mary Celeste*, Dr Jephson. She's a spruce little ship, is she not? I'm certain you'll enjoy your voyage with us. I aim to catch the midday tide tomorrow, and I reckon we'll be at sea for about three weeks – and even though my wife, Sarah, and baby daughter will be joining us, I trust we'll have no need of your medical services – what? *(laughs)* Eh? Now I dare say you want to see your cabin. I've no doubt you'll be delighted with it. We do our visitors proud on the *Mary Celeste*. Come along, now, doctor. Just down here...

(CUT BACKGROUND)

JEPHSON:

And indeed my cabin was extremely comfortably furnished, given the small size of the vessel. Mr Septimius Goring was to have the one next to mine. Opposite was the captain's cabin, and next to that a small berth for the young employee of the firm, John Harton, who was the other passenger.

There was one minor mishap before we set sail. At the last moment, and quite inexplicably, two of Captain Briggs's seamen failed to turn up. The missing men, I gathered, were steady reliable fellows who had been with him on several voyages, and he was quite at a loss to understand why they had let him down. When he went on-shore to find replacements, he discovered two black seamen on the quayside seeking work, and he counted himself fortunate in not having to delay his departure.

Our first few days at sea passed pleasantly enough. The weather was all that could be desired, and we were borne along on a fine fresh breeze from the west-sou'-west. Mrs Briggs appeared on deck with her little girl – a dear little thing just able to walk and prattle. It was on our third morning at sea that I witnessed the first of a series of rather odd events.

I had spent the morning on the quarter-deck with our captain, and our conversation had turned to the subject of ocean currents. As there was a small matter in dispute, Briggs invited me down to his cabin to consult the standard work on the subject.

(BACKGROUND SHIP AT SEA)

BRIGGS: Come along, doctor. Here we are.

(DOOR OPENS)

Good heavens! Mr Goring, sir, nobody enters the Captain's cabin without an invitation. May I ask…

GORING: My sincere apologies, Captain Briggs. I have never travelled by sea before. I was walking down the passageway, and I wondered what lay behind this door. Do pray forgive my intrusion into your sanctum.

BRIGGS: *(laughs)* Oh well, Mr Goring, no harm done.

GORING: I have been admiring your splendid set of chronometers.

BRIGGS: My pride and joy, sir. Three of them, each a model of accuracy, and so always in agreement with each other. They have never let me down. Please remain with us.

(BACKGROUND OFF)

JEPHSON: The incident passed off pleasantly enough, and in our subsequent conversation it became apparent that Mr Goring had some practical knowledge of mathematical instruments. He's an intriguing man, who rather improves on acquaintance. It was on our fifth day at sea that I learned a little more about him. Young John Harton came into my cabin for a chat, and we had a cigar together.

(SHIP AT SEA BACKGROUND)

HARTON: Yes, I remember seeing Septimius Goring in Cleveland, Ohio, back in '69. I'd just started working for the shipping line. He was a man of mystery even then – obviously wealthy, though with no visible means of employment. People often speculated about him – where he came from, how he acquired his riches, what sort of business he was engaged in.

(BACKGROUND OFF)

JEPHSON: I noted that as he strolled about, Goring frequently spoke with the black seamen, and I admired him for doing so. They were new on board, and he seemed anxious for them to feel welcome. It was on day six of our voyage that Captain Briggs began grumbling about his chronometers.

(SHIP AT SEA BACKGROUND)

BRIGGS: This is very strange, Dr Jephson. I have had those three chronometers for over twenty-five years now, and this is the very first time that they are failing to register exactly the same time. They are out of sequence with each other, and I'm at a loss to know which of them is recording accurately – if indeed any of them are.

JEPHSON: Does this affect our progress, captain?

BRIGGS: Not significantly – at least not at the moment. I shall work on the instruments, and try to detect what has gone wrong.

JEPHSON: Mr Goring seems to have a good deal of technical knowledge.

BRIGGS: Yes, I had already thought of asking for his help. Thank you, doctor.

(BACKGROUND OFF)

JEPHSON: The next three days turned cold, and produced a persistent drizzle. I remained in my cabin for much of the time, only creeping out for dinner. On the third day, I had a visitor.

(SHIP AT SEA. KNOCK ON DOOR)

JEPHSON: Come in.

(DOOR OPENS. SHUTS UNDER FOLLOWING)

Mr Goring.

GORING: I trust I am not intruding?

JEPHSON: Not at all. It is good of you to look in.

GORING: I trust you are feeling better? We have missed your company. Mind you, I know you are not completely prostrated, for I hear you moving about in here.

JEPHSON: Of course, Mr Goring. And I am not unaware of your presence next door. As you can see, some of the cracks in the partition are so large that I can see you when you are at your table – look through here. Do you see?

GORING: Indeed.

JEPHSON: I note that you are taking a great interest in the progress of our voyage.

GORING: Why do you say so, Dr Jephson?

JEPHSON: Because I see you so often bent over that great chart of yours, hard at work with pencil and compasses.

GORING: Oh, it's a way of passing the time, and I enjoy checking my results with our captain.

JEPHSON: A harmless amusement indeed.

(SHIP INTERIOR BACKGROUND OFF)

JEPHSON: The next day was fine, with scarcely a cloud in the sky, and a fresh breeze pushed us forward. At last I was able to venture up on deck. I was taking a refreshing walk up and down the quarter deck when...

(REVOLVER SHOT)

The shot came from the direction of my cabin. I rushed down to find Mr Goring, revolver in hand, in the passage way,

(SHIP INTERIOR)

GORING: Dr Jephson? Oh, thank heaven you're safe.

JEPHSON: Why, what has happened?

BRIGGS: *(approaching)* I heard a shot. What on earth is going on?

GORING: It was an accident, Captain. I was cleaning this revolver of mine in my cabin. I was absolutely convinced that both barrels were unloaded. Imagine my horror when one of them suddenly discharged – and the bullet went straight through the partition.

JEPHSON: Good grief. Let me see…

(DOOR OPENS)

BRIGGS: There's the bullet hole – just where your head would have been, Dr Jephson. Mr Goring, there's no doubt that if Dr Jephson had been in his bed at the time, he would be a corpse.

GORING: Please accept my profound apologies, doctor. I cannot forgive myself for my lack of care.

JEPHSON: Well, well, no harm actually done, eh Mr Goring? Accidents will happen. Let's forget the whole thing, shall we Captain?

(BACKGROUND OFF)

JEPHSON: The next event to befall us was less easily brushed aside. In fact it haunts me to this very day. Late that night, I had already retired to bed, when there came a loud and persistent knocking at my door.

(BACKGROUND ON. AGITATED KNOCKING ON DOOR)

BRIGGS: *(remote)* Dr Jephson! Dr Jephson!

JEPHSON: Is that Captain Briggs? Come in, captain.

(DOOR OPENS)

BRIGGS: Dr Jephson – my wife. Sarah. She's disappeared. Little Sophia, also. There's not a trace of them anywhere.

JEPHSON: Oh captain, surely not. Your wife has taken the child into some cabin.

BRIGGS: I've looked, doctor. I've searched everywhere. They've disappeared.

JEPHSON: Calm yourself, captain. Come, let's ask Mr Goring and young Mr Harton to join us, and we'll soon run them to ground.

(BACKGROUND OFF)

JEPHSON: It was not to be. We hunted over the ship for an hour and a half without finding any trace of the missing woman or child. Even the seamen, who joined in the search, were affected by the sight of the captain as he roamed bareheaded and dishevelled about the deck, returning again and again to places already searched in vain. Finally we had to conclude that Mrs Briggs and her baby daughter had somehow fallen overboard, unnoticed by the man at the wheel. The mate put the ship about, but of course there was not the slightest hope of picking up the two lost passengers. The captain retired to his cabin in a state of profound shock, where I gave him a powerful dose of opium that rendered him unconscious for a few hours.

What happened next, on this accursed voyage, is almost too appalling to relate. Thoroughly exhausted, we passengers retired to our cabins at about one o'clock in the morning. I fell into a deep sleep. I was awakened by the sound of a gunshot echoing through the ship. I glanced at my carriage clock. It was 3 a.m.

(BACKGROUND ON. KNOCKING ON DOOR)

HARTON: *(remote)* Dr Jephson! John Harton here. Did you hear that shot?

JEPHSON: *(calls)* I did, John. Come in.

(DOOR OPENS)

HARTON: Will you come with me?

JEPHSON: Of course. Give me a moment.

(CLOTHES PUT ON HURRIEDLY)

Come on. Where's Mr Goring?

GORING: *(remote, approaching)* I'm here, gentlemen. I'm afraid I have very bad news. As soon as I heard that shot, I knew it came from the captain's cabin. I've looked in. I'm afraid Captain Briggs has taken his own life.

(BACKGROUND OFF)

JEPHSON: It was a hideous sight. The whole front of his face was blown in, and the cabin was swimming in blood. The pistol was lying beside him on the floor, close to his outstretched arm. Goring and I picked him up and laid him on the bed. By that time the crew had all clustered in the cabin, and the five white hands, who had sailed with Briggs before, were deeply distressed. Young Harton helped us bind the captain in canvas. At midday we committed his body to the deep.

(SHIP AT SEA. GULLS)

GORING: We therefore commit the earthly remains of Benjamin James Briggs to the deep, looking for the general Resurrection in the last day, and the life of the world to come, through our Lord Jesus Christ – at whose second coming in glorious majesty to judge the world, the sea shall give up her dead; and the corruptible bodies of those who sleep in it shall be changed, and made like unto his glorious body; according to the mighty working whereby he is able to subdue all things unto himself. Amen.

(MURMUR OF "AMEN" FROM MEN. HEAVY SPLASH. FADE BACKGROUND)

JEPHSON: Mr Hyson, the First Mate, took over command of the ship, and we continued on our way. But the belief among the seamen was that the vessel was accursed, and the sooner we reached Lisbon, the better. I could not help sharing the feeling.

(SHIP AT SEA BACKGROUND)

HARTON: *(approaching)* May I join you, Dr Jephson?

JEPHSON: By all means, John. With weather as fine as this, I find it very pleasant to sit out here on the deck. I sometimes forget that I am taking this sea voyage for my health – especially after all that has occurred,

HARTON: Our journey has certainly been too full of unexplained incidents for my liking. One mystery still bothers me – we have spoken of this before.

JEPHSON: You refer to our intriguing colleague, Mr Septimius Goring?

HARTON: Precisely. I have tried to draw him out about his profession, and the reason for his voyage to Europe, but he parries all my attempts to do so. I wonder whether he's a private investigator on the track of some criminal who has escaped to Portugal.

JEPHSON: Good gracious. What on earth leads you to that supposition?

HARTON: Well, when we spoke yesterday he rather took offence at my questions and went down to his cabin in something of a temper. After he'd gone I saw that he'd left his book behind. I picked it up, intending to return it to him, and found it was a sort of scrap-book containing a large number of newspaper cuttings. They all related to unsolved murders committed in the United States over the last twenty years or so. In each case the murderer has never been brought to justice.

JEPHSON: Really? How interesting. But rather than supporting your theory that our Mr Goring is a detective, might it not be that he is collecting material for a book he intends to write? In any case, John, it is certainly none of our business.

HARTON: I suppose not...

(FADE OUT. FULL UP)

JEPHSON: Before long this horrifying voyage was to shake my nervous system yet again. I was lying half dozing one night, in the middle watch, trying to drop off into a refreshing sleep. A single ray of moonlight streamed in through the porthole and fell on the cabin door. My drowsy eyes were focused on the silvery circle, but as I lay there I gradually became aware that a small dark object had appeared in the middle of it. I lay quietly watching it as it gradually grew larger and plainer. And then I realized that the cabin door had been cautiously opened, and that a human hand had been inserted – a human hand which, as I observed with nothing short of horror, had no fingers. The door swung cautiously backwards, and Goring's head followed his hand.

In the bright moonlight it seemed to me that I had never seen so utterly fiendish and merciless expression on a human face. I grabbed the gun that I kept under my pillow and sprang out of bed...

(CABIN. SHIP AT SEA BACKGROUND)

JEPHSON: Stay where you are! I have a revolver in my hand.

GORING: Oh, Dr Jephson, I'm so sorry if I startled you. I did not want to waken you suddenly, if you were asleep. It's my teeth. I have the most dreadful toothache, and I was wondering if, as a medical man, you might have some laudanum with you.

JEPHSON: Mr Goring, I do apologize for waving a gun at you, but you did indeed startle me. Of course I'm very pleased to be able to help you. If you take a seat, I'll dispense a dose that I'm sure will be effective in relieving you of all pain. Please...

(FADE OUT. FULL UP DECK. SHIP AT SEA)

HARTON: You have indeed led an interesting life, Dr Jephson. How long did it take you to recover from your wounds in the Civil War?

JEPHSON: A full six months. I was near death's door when I was rescued by Mr Murray.

HARTON: And you spent all that time on his plantation under the care of that black nurse...?

JEPHSON:	Martha. Yes. I can never forget the tender care she lavished on me. Before I left, she gave me the most precious thing in her possession.
HARTON:	Really? What was that?
JEPHSON:	Here, let me show you.

(FADE IN UNDER THE FOLLOWING THE BEAT OF AFRICAN DRUMS)

	I wear it round my neck always, in memory of her.
HARTON:	What a very curious object. I've never seen anything like it.
JEPHSON:	Do you see these ridges marked into the stone?
HARTON:	Indeed. The whole object reminds me of nothing so much as a human ear.
GORING:	*(approaching)* Excuse me, what is that you have there? Show me. Where did you get it?
JEPHSON:	*(offended)* Mr Goring…
GORING:	I apologize, doctor, for my abruptness. Quite inexcusable. But I must confess that the object you are holding quite intrigues me. How did you acquire it?
JEPHSON:	As I have just informed Mr Harton here, it was a gift from a very special lady who nursed me back to health many years ago.

GORING: A lady, let me conjecture, whose ancestors hailed from what is now termed "the dark continent" – namely Africa.

JEPHSON: You are quite correct, sir.

GORING: You see, I recognize this stone as an African artefact. And a rare one, at that. May I examine it a little more closely? Thank you. *(calls)* You men – come and look at this…

(BACKGROUND OFF)

JEPHSON: Our two black seamen happened to be passing, and Goring called them over and handed them the stone. It seemed to fill both of them with great surprise. Goring spoke a few words and pointed at me. As they handed the stone back to him, both bowed in my direction.

(BACKGROUND ON)

GORING: These markings intrigue me, doctor. Most unusual. If I just hold the stone up to the sun…

(CLATTER OF STONE ON WOODEN DECK

HARTON: Look out, sir! You'll have it in the sea in a second. There you are, Dr Jephson. Safe and sound.

JEPHSON: Thank you, John. I wouldn't have lost that stone for the world.

GORING: I do apologize. How clumsy of me. However, no harm done.

(FADE OUT AND LOSE DRUMS)

JEPHSON: I could not help wondering whether Goring had intended to kick the stone overboard. All in all, this strange episode, coupled with the respect shown by Martha about it, convinced me that I had been entrusted by her with some powerful talisman. I determined to make sure that it never left my possession again.

(FADE IN SHIP AT SEA)

Puzzling as that event was, it was nothing compared to what happened the following morning. John Harton and I were walking the deck together, when…

HELMSMAN: *(remote, calling)* Land ahoy! Land ahoy!

JEPHSON: Land? How can that be?

HARTON: We aren't due to reach Portugal for days yet.

JEPHSON: *(calls)* Mr Hyson! Where are we?

HYSON: *(calls)* If only I knew, sir. *(approaching)* I can't make it out, gentlemen. Our chronometers – all three of them are in agreement now – they tell me we are in mid-ocean, some two days off making landfall on the Portuguese coast. Yet plainly we are far off-course.

JEPHSON: Could the instruments have been affected by some magnetic influence?

HYSON: Well, I've never known anything like it doctor, and I've been at sea over thirty years.

(CREEP MUSIC BENEATH THE FOLLOWING)

No, we've veered strongly to the east, and that's not Portugal ahead of us. I recognize that coast line. We're approaching the mainland of Africa. I'd say we're north of Cape Blanco, near the western edge of the Sahara desert.

(UP MUSIC. HOLD A LITTLE. FADE BENEATH FOLLOWING)

JEPHSON: It was that night that the explanation for all the strange incidents I have been recording suddenly became clear. Blind fool that I was, not to have seen it sooner.

I had gone to my cabin about half-past eleven, and was preparing for bed, when there was a tap on my door. I went to open it, and found our two black seamen outside. Without a word they grabbed hold of me, a handkerchief was tied across my mouth, and a coil of rope rapidly and firmly wound round me. Then they dragged me up on deck and lashed me to the davit of one of the boats. I was utterly powerless to do or say anything. As my eyes became accustomed to the gloom, I saw that I was surrounded by the two seamen, our black cook and none other than my fellow passenger, Mr Septimius Goring. Another man was crouching at my feet, but he was in the shadow and I couldn't recognize him – until a moment later when the moon emerged from behind a cloud, and a ray of light fell upon his upturned face. Even though more than twelve years have elapsed, I shudder still as I recall the distorted features and projecting eyes of my cheery young friend, John Harton, lying dead at my feet.

I had scarcely taken in the horror that had been committed on board this ill-fated vessel, nor the fact that I myself clearly stood in the greatest danger, when I perceived the tall, dark shape of Goring standing up in the bulwarks with a lantern in his hand. He waved this to and fro for a moment, and to my inexpressible astonishment I saw it answered immediately from the shore. Powerless, speechless, with the cords cutting into my flesh and the murdered man at my feet, I awaited the next act in the tragedy.

The two black seamen, the black cook and Goring had moved to the other side of the deck and were leaning over the rail. One of them pointed out to sea, and I made out a large dark mass moving towards the ship. As it emerged into moonlight, I saw that it was a great canoe crammed with men. A moment later scores of Africans were clambering aboard. Led by Goring, they swept down the deck in an irresistible torrent. All opposition was overpowered, the unarmed watch were knocked over and bound, and those asleep in their cabins, including our acting captain, Hyson, were dragged out of their bunks and secured.

Goring then assembled the boarding party and the three black members of our crew at the far end of the deck, and held a council to decide our fate. Our black seamen pointed towards me, and I saw a reaction of astonishment from the invaders. One of them, apparently their leader, came across to me.

(FULL UP SHIP AT SEA. OPEN AIR)

AFRICAN: Stone. Stone. Show me. Now. Now.

JEPHSON: Here. Here it is. I wear it round my neck.

AFRICAN: Give. Ohhh! *(exclamation of awe. Calling)* See! See!

(MEN EXCITED, EXCLAIMING)

GORING: *(approaching)* Dr Jephson, speaking personally I have no wish at all to spare your life. If it rested with me you would die, just as the rest of the crew are about to. I've spent my whole life avenging the wrongs done for hundreds of years to my people, by those who invaded our shores and enslaved them. You may thank that stone of yours for the fact that you're still alive. These poor fellows reverence it – and if it is indeed what they believe it to be, they have good cause. However once we are ashore should it prove that they are mistaken, nothing can save your life. Of that I can assure you. In the meantime, we wish to treat you well, so if there are any of your possessions you would like to take with you, you are free to get them.

(BACKGROUND OFF)

JEPHSON: I was led down to my cabin where I put a few valuables in my pockets, together with a pocket compass. They had launched the lifeboat, and I was lowered into it. Then they started rowing towards the shore. When we had travelled about a hundred yards from the ship, our steersman held up his hand, and the rowers paused. There came a sort of dull, moaning sound accompanied by a succession of splashes. That is all I know of the fate of my poor shipmates. Almost immediately the large canoe followed us, and the deserted ship was left to drift – a dreary, spectre-like hulk.

When we reached shore, I was led by a group of our attackers through the sand-hills, treated all the time with the greatest of respect. After a while we reached the outskirts of a town. As we marched through the streets, people began emerging from the houses, beating tom-toms and howling. Soon we were accompanied by a huge crowd of frenzied people. The leader of our group stopped, turned, and shouted some words to them. In an instant the crowd quietened down, and a buzz of wonder succeeded the war-cries of a moment before. Now the whole dense mass proceeded down the broad street, my escort and myself in the very centre.

It was not long before we reached a large building towering high above the surrounding houses. A stockade of beautifully polished ebony rails was planted all round it, and the framework of the tall double doors consisted of two magnificent elephant tusks, sunk in the ground on each side and meeting at the top.

The crowd stopped at the entrance and squatted on the ground. Suddenly Goring was at my side.

(OPEN AIR. MURMURING CROWD)

GORING: The time has come, doctor, to put both your stone, and with it your life, to the test. You will be led into this sacred edifice by the chiefs and elders. But first I must ask you to hand your stone to your escort. You have it round your neck, I believe.

JEPHSON: That I do, sir.

GORING: Be so good as to pass it over.

(BACKGROUND OFF. FADE IN AFRICAN DRUMS BENEATH FOLLOWING)

JEPHSON: I reached round my neck, pulled off the stone and passed it to Goring. I saw him hand it on as my shoes and my hat were taken from me, the huge double doors swung open, and I was led inside by one of the elders who carried my stone in his upturned right hand.

The interior was much larger than could have been imagined from the outside. The walls were hung with mats, shells and other ornaments, but the inside was quite empty except for an enormous statue standing in the very centre of the vast space. We approached it slowly, and as we drew closer I saw that it had been carved from jet-black stone. When we stood before the idol – for such I took it to be – I could see that it was perfect in every respect except that one of its ears had been broken off. Carved into the side of the statue were a series of steps, and my escort now slowly mounted them, one by one, bearing my stone in his hand. Eventually he reached the gigantic head. Stretching up, he placed Martha's black stone on to the jagged surface. There could be no doubt that the one had been broken off from the other. The parts dovetailed together so accurately that when the old man removed his hand, the ear stuck in its place for a few seconds before dropping into his open palm.

(FADE OUT AFRICAN DRUMS)

The group around me prostrated themselves upon the ground. A moment later one of them ran outside and communicated the result to the crowd, which instantly set up a wild whooping and cheering. In a moment I was converted from a prisoner into a demi-god. I was escorted back through the town in triumph, the people pressing forward to touch my clothing and to gather up the dust on which my foot had trod. A large hut was put at my disposal, and a banquet laid before me. It was many hours before finally I was left to retire to a couch made of soft animal skins.

(BACKGROUND – TENT INTERIOR)

GORING: *(remote, approaching)* Doctor Jephson? I trust I do not disturb you.

JEPHSON: I was hoping for a few hours' sleep after all the attention I have received.

GORING: I will not detain you long. Doctor, what do you think of me?

JEPHSON: Think of you? I think you're a bloodthirsty criminal, utterly immoral and without human feelings. You're a mass murderer. When I think of Mrs Briggs and her baby – when I think of our captain – then I think of my poor friend, John Harton…why, I'd strangle you with my bare hands, if I were able.

GORING: Don't speak so loud. I don't want our chat to be cut short. So you'd strangle me, would you? That's rather ironic, for I've come to help you escape.

JEPHSON: You? Why on earth would you?

GORING: Oh, for purely selfish reasons, I assure you. I have long planned to rule these fellows. Indeed I was all set to be acclaimed their king this very day – except for that wretched stone of yours, which has turned their heads. They think you have come down from heaven specifically for the purpose of restoring their idol's ear to them. So the simple fact is that unless you are got out of the way, I'm going to count for nothing. Since I cannot kill you – for that would certainly be the end of me – I'm going to help you get away. Call it simple self-preservation.

JEPHSON: I see. Well, I can understand your reasoning. But as to why this people seem to worship me for restoring the ear of their idol, that I cannot fully understand. Perhaps you would relieve my curiosity about the history of my stone.

GORING: Willingly. A few hundred years ago a group belonging to this tribe quarrelled with the elders, and decided away to move to the south. The elders assured them that without the idol in their midst, they would meet with only ill-fortune. So they decided that they had to carry something of the idol with them to their new home. On the night before the group had planned to set off, a young tribesman managed to get into the temple, and broke off one of the statue's ears. At that time white slavers roamed these lands with no-one and nothing to control them. I have no doubt that soon after he had secured the ear the young man was captured by some slaver, and carried off to America. But ever since the statue was violated there has been a tradition in the tribe that one day the ear would be returned to its rightful place.

No doubt, doctor, you will eventually find your way back to your world. You can carry with you my message of hate. You see this hand of mine? Mutilated beyond use. That was done by a slaver's knife. As for what they did to my mother and my sister – that does not bear thinking about. For twenty years I have wreaked my revenge, murdering until even I became tired of what had once been a joy. You could track my progress by the sudden deaths which have baffled the police. Finally I decided to find some bold, free, black people and to throw in my lot with them. I searched the African continent , and eventually good fortune brought me into contact with this magnificent tribe of desert dwellers. I cannot allow the chance of your stone upsetting my plans.

There is no difficulty about your escape. These adopted children of mine will say that you have gone back to heaven. I have a boat all ready for you, well stocked with provisions and water. Come. Let's be off.

JEPHSON: We passed unchallenged through the town and across the sandy plain.

(FADE UP SEA ON SHORE BENEATH FOLLOWING)

Once more I heard the roar of the sea, and saw the long white line of the surf. Two figures were standing on the shore, arranging the gear of a small boat. They were the two sailors who had been with us on the voyage.

GORING: *(calling)* See him safely through the surf.

JEPHSON: The two men came on either side of me and lifted me into the boat. They sprang in, and pushed the boat off. With mainsail and jib we ran out from land and passed safely over the bar. Then my two companions, without a word of farewell, sprang overboard, and I saw their heads, like black dots on the white foam, as they made their way back to the shore. Meanwhile I scudded away into the night. My last glimpse of Septimius Goring – the last I saw, and the last I shall ever see – was of his gaunt figure cast in sharp relief against a full moon.

On my fifth day at sea I was picked up by the steamship *Monrovia*, and was showed the greatest kindness and consideration by Captain Stornoway and his crew until they landed me in Liverpool, from where I eventually made my way back to New York.

(FADE IN MUSIC BENEATH FOLLOWING)

Turn to a map of Africa. There, above Cape Blanco, where the land trends away to the north and south, there is where Septimius Goring reigned over his subjects. And just beyond the hot yellow sand, onto which the long green ridges of the sea roar and hiss endlessly – there is where Captain Benjamin Briggs, his wife Sarah and their baby daughter lie, together with John Harton and the other poor fellows who were done to death in that ill-fated vessel, the *Mary Celeste*.

(UP MUSIC. DOWN FOR CLOSING ANNOUNCEMENT. UP MUSIC TO END)

THE FOUR JUST MEN

BY EDGAR WALLACE
DRAMATIZED FOR RADIO
BY NEVILLE TELLER

Running time: 60'

FIRST BROADCAST ACROSS THE USA
ON 5 MARCH 2018 IN A PRODUCTION BY
SHOESTRING RADIO THEATRE, SAN FRANCISCO

CHARACTERS IN ORDER OF APPEARANCE

Note: This is a very male-orientated play! In fact, there are no women at all in the Edgar Wallace novel – not one. Consequently, to restore a little balance as well as to deepen the drama, I have invented wives for Sir Philip Ramon and the Prime Minister, as well as a female housekeeper and a secretary.

THERY   *Early 30s. Strong Spanish accent, but weak personality.*

MANFRED   *Mid-40s. The leader. Could be English or have New England accent. Definitely not "foreign". Assured.*

GONZALEZ   *Early 50s. Light Spanish accent. The confidence of wealth.*

POICCART   *Early 50s. Light French accent. The assurance of wealth.*

PRIME MINISTER *Measured, assured. Upper-class English accent*

RAMON   *Sir Philip Ramon, British Foreign Secretary. Mid-40s. Rigid, stubborn, "a man of principle"*

SECRETARY	*Middle aged woman. (2 short speeches only)*
COMMISSIONER	*Head of Britain's police. Early 50s.*
NEWSBOY /MAN #1 NEWSBOY /MAN #2	} } *As newsboys, they shout headlines to passersby to* } *sell papers; as newsmen they urgently recite* } *paragraphs from news reports.*
FALMOUTH	*Mid-40s. A senior and very experienced police officer. Seen it all.*
EDITOR	*Rough, go-getting type. Out for a good story at all costs.*
WELBY	*Late-30s. Senior experienced newspaper reporter.*
JANE RAMON	*Sir Philip's long-suffering wife. She's never been able to shift her husband, so she goes along with him.*
ELIZABETH	*The Prime Minister's wife. A wise and caring woman.*
PINKERTON	*Actually a Pinkerton man. US accent (doesn't matter which). One speech only.*
HOUSEKEEPER	*Middle aged woman, capable type.*
CORONER	*Middle aged. Measured. Judicial.*
CARSON	*Middle aged. One short scene only.*
MP	*Male, 50. One speech only.*

NOTES ON MUSIC, SOUND, ETC

Internet links for the proposed music/effects are set out in the script. Beneath are some working notes about alternatives, and about using the Big Ben recordings.

"THE BOY I LOVE"
HTTPS://WWW.YOUTUBE.COM/WATCH?V=68GCWBY4ELA
(START; 1.03)

"SOLDIERS OF THE QUEEN"
PREFERABLY:
HTTPS://WWW.YOUTUBE.COM/WATCH?V=4ONG65KXPBE
ALTERNATIVE:
HTTPS://WWW.YOUTUBE.COM/WATCH?V=FITUGCTVEEA
(STARTING AT 0.58)

BEETHOVEN'S FIFTH SYMPHONY CONDUCTED BY CHAILLY.
HTTPS://WWW.YOUTUBE.COM/WATCH?V=DBXHTHU55C8

QUARTET PLAYING "ROSES FROM THE SOUTH" WALTZ BY STRAUSS.
HTTPS://WWW.YOUTUBE.COM/WATCH?V=9VQJPMNIZGC

BIG BEN
HTTPS://FREESOUND.ORG/PEOPLE/HYDERPOTTER/PACKS/5227/

Note: for quarter-past, half-past or quarter-to the hour, do NOT use the full hour and simply cut it. All four are different. For full hour, add audio 4 to audio 5. Or for full hour use:

HTTPS://WWW.YOUTUBE.COM/WATCH?V=E9WWBJNAECK

(MUSIC. DOWN FOR OPENING
ANNOUNCEMENT. UP MUSIC A LITTLE.
DOWN UNDER FOLLOWING AND OUT)

ANNOUNCER:
We are in the Spanish port city of Cadiz, way
back in the last years of the nineteenth century.
1898, to be exact. It's a warm afternoon, and four
men are sitting around a café table in the sunshine.
Three of them, well-dressed and obviously
affluent, seem at ease with themselves and the
world. The fourth is shabbier in appearance and
appears somewhat nervous.

(FADE IN OPEN AIR, OCCASIONAL HORSE-
DRAWN CARRIAGE PASSING)

THERY:
But I still don't quite understand why you asked
me...[to come and meet you and what you...]

MANFRED:
My dear Thery – I may call you Thery, senor?

THERY:
Of course.

MANFRED:
Perhaps we should all get better acquainted.
My name, as you know is George Manfred, but
my two friends here... I don't think you've been
introduced. To my right, senor Leon Gonzalez...

GONZALEZ:	Delighted you came, Thery.
MANFRED:	... and to my left, monsieur Raymond Poiccart.
POICCART:	My pleasure, Thery.
THERY:	Senores.
MANFRED:	Of course the name under which we operate was known to you before we made contact – I think it's known to half of Europe. But very few people can put a face to us. You're greatly privileged, Thery. By meeting you like this, we're putting our safety in your hands.
THERY:	I understand, senor Manfred. And it makes me nervous. Why have the most famous criminals in the world entrusted me with this knowledge?
POICCART:	Criminals? No, no you're mistaken, Thery. Dispensers of justice.
GONZALEZ:	justice that corrupt law-enforcers refuse to dispense.
THERY:	Senores, I apologize. I meant no offence.
MANFRED:	And none taken, Thery, I assure you. Look at it this way. Over the past five years a dozen highly-placed individuals – criminals, if you like – who have done terrible things, but who thought themselves beyond the law, have been brought to book. They have paid a just price for their misdeeds.

GONZALEZ: Unfortunately, during the course of our last enterprise we lost one of our number...

POICCART: ...and our new enterprise requires certain skills that we believe you possess.

THERY: I'm honoured beyond belief, monsieur Poiccart, But I have no part in whatever it was that set you all on this path.

GONZALEZ: An injustice so grave, so overwhelming, so deeply embedded in the corrupt system of a certain country...

POICCART: ...so clearly requiring to be remedied...

MANFRED: Thery, you do not need to have shared in the deep injustice that brought us together, an injustice that motivates us to this day. Let our relationship be on a purely business footing.

GONZALEZ: We've been told that you are a patriotic Spaniard.

THERY: I am indeed, senor Gonzalez.

POICCART: And you support the movement for independence? The movement that aims to free the Spanish people from the yoke of this corrupt monarchy that has been foisted upon them?

THERY: Of course. Long live our great leader Manuel Garcia. He's the only man who can lead our movement to victory – the only one.

MANFRED: You're right, Thery. He is. And it's his life that we're trying to save. About six months ago news reached us that the secret police were about to arrest him, put him on trial and have him executed – and so we spirited him away to England. He's safe enough there, for the moment, and he continues his work from London, planning the great revolution that will one day... But enough of that, because now...

GONZALEZ: Now he faces terrible danger. England's foreign secretary is about to bring in a law that is Garcia's death warrant. That law will give the British authorities the power to deport anyone they call an "undesirable alien" back to their country of origin. If that law gets onto the statute book, they will seize Garcia and send him back to Spain, where he will assuredly be silenced forever. This is something we cannot allow. The future of Spain is in our hands.

POICCART: Nor is he the only one. There are at least five other exiled leaders living and working in Britain who are dedicated to freeing their countries from tyranny. We will either succeed in getting the British foreign secretary to stop that law being introduced, or we will kill him. One or the other.

MANFRED: Thery, we need you, and we are all wealthy enough to ensure that you will be generously rewarded if you join us. Are you with us?

THERY: Your cause is just. I am.

MANFRED: Excellent. Now I have here…

(PAPER RUSTLES)

… a document. This, I think, is an exact copy of the description of yourself held in Spanish police headquarters.

THERY: Really?

MANFRED: See here. Is that your trade?

THERY: It certainly is. I know everything about this – everything. If I hadn't made a big mistake a few years ago, I could have earned a very great deal of money. I'd be as wealthy as you are.

MANFRED: We just needed it confirmed. Excellent. Then there's no doubt about it, If that English government minister, Sir Philip Ramon, refuses to give way – and I fear that is exactly what he will do – then he's a dead man.

(BURST OF MUSIC. DOWN FOR FOLLOWING, AND OUT)

PRIME MINISTER: Now, Ramon, what's all this about threatening letters?

RAMON: It's true, Prime Minister. I've received quite a number over the past month or so.

PRIME MINISTER: You informed the police?

RAMON: Of course. They've been of little use. The letters keep arriving. That's why I've advertised a reward of fifty pounds for any information leading to the arrest of the perpetrators.

PRIME MINISTER: The papers are full of it this morning. Have you any idea who they might be, Ramon?

RAMON: Indeed I have, Prime Minister. All the letters are signed "The Four Just Men". You'll have heard of them, I presume?

PRIME MINISTER: A band of vigilantes, killing people they don't approve of.

RAMON: Precisely. And I've been added to their list, it seems.

PRIME MINISTER: I presume it's your Aliens Extradition Bill that excites their disapproval.

RAMON: Unless I abandon the Bill they threaten to assassinate me.

PRIME MINISTER: Good heavens. Her Majesty's government can't give way to threats, Ramon.

RAMON: Indeed we cannot, Prime Minister.

(DISCREET KNOCK ON DOOR FROM OUTSIDE)

PRIME MINISTER: Come!

(DOOR OPENS)

SECRETARY: *(remote, advancing)* A letter, Prime Minister, delivered by hand. It's marked "personal" and "urgent".

PRIME MINISTER: Thank you. Who delivered this?

SECRETARY: I can't say, sir. I did ask, but I was told it was found on the hall table.

(DOOR CLOSES. ENVELOPE TORN OPEN, PAPER RUSTLE)

PRIME MINISTER: Good grief!

RAMON: What is it, Prime Minister?

(FADE IN)

MANFRED: My dear Prime Minister. Your Government is about to pass a law that will remove from Britain a number of patriots who could be the saviours of their nations. One in particular, Manuel Garcia, you would hand over to the most evil government of modern times. We have informed the Minister concerned that unless he withdraws this Bill, we will surely slay him. As proof that we are capable of doing so, we would ask you to look under the side table in your office that stands beneath the portrait of the Duke of Wellington. If that machine contained a detonator or a fuse, which it does not, it could destroy a substantial part of the

Palace of Westminster. Yours sincerely, The Four Just Men.

(FADE OUT)

PRIME MINISTER: Ramon, under that table. No, there. What's that package?

RAMON: *(retreating)* Do you mean this, Prime Minister?

PRIME MINISTER: Careful, be careful! Gently. Bring it here. On the desk.

RAMON: What is it?

(EDGE OUT. EDGE IN)

PRIME MINISTER: What is it, Commissioner? A hoax.

COMMISSIONER: I'm afraid not, Prime Minister. It's just what the letter described, even to the absence of a fuse.

PRIME MINISTER: Was it really...?

COMMISSIONER: Enough to wreck a large chunk of this building.

PRIME MINISTER: But how was it brought into this very office?

COMMISSIONER: Frankly, sir, we've no idea. Of course every single policeman on duty both inside and outside Parliament has been questioned and cross-questioned. Not one of them remembers seeing anyone unauthorised entering or leaving.

PRIME MINISTER: I see. Thank you Commissioner.

(1900 TELEPHONE LIFTED, HANDLE CRANKED)

PRIME MINISTER: Osborne? Have the Press Secretary prepare a statement of what has happened. Issue it as quickly as possible. We can't keep this under wraps.

(TELEPHONE REPLACED)

And Commissioner, you may announce that the government is offering a reward of a thousand pounds for the arrest of whoever gained access to my office and left that machine. Oh, and a free pardon to any accomplice.

(FULL UP "THE BOY I LOVE" (https://www.youtube.com/watch?v=68gCwBy4ElA). BEGIN AT 1'03". DOWN AFTER CHORUS, HOLD SONG BENEATH FOLLOWING)

MANFRED: Well done, Poiccart. The evening papers are full of it.

POICCART: Thanks to you, Manfred. You planned it perfectly.

GONZALEZ: Not a hitch, then?

POICCART: Just one. As the members were all filing out to vote, I saw someone glance at me. He said to the MP beside him: "I thought Bascoe had arranged to be away this evening." But then he shrugged and went on into the voting lobby.

MANFRED: Thank goodness. Of course, it was only because the MPs were voting that you had the chance to slip into the Prime Minister's office.

POICCART: And you were quite right, Manfred – it was the last vote of the night and the staff had all gone. But no one would have questioned me anyway. I was the spit and image of Sir Emanuel Bascoe, MP.

GONZALEZ: Rather you than me, Poiccart. Now this is rather jolly. Nothing like a good old English music hall.

(UP MUSIC FOR END OF SECOND CHORUS. MIX AUDIENCE APPLAUSE TO LONDON STREET, HORSE-DRAWN CARRIAGES, A FEW CARS, CAR HORNS, CROWD)

NEWSBOY/MAN #1: Paper, paper! Read all about it! One thousand pound reward!

NEWSBOY/MAN #2: News! Standard! The Four Just Men! Thousand pound reward!

(CROSSFADE TO INTERIOR)

COMMISSIONER: What progress, Falmouth?

FALMOUTH: None, commissioner. How can you catch people when you haven't the slightest idea of who or what you're looking for?

COMMISSIONER: They've committed crimes is almost every country in the world, and we've still no idea as to who they are?

FALMOUTH: For all we know they could be two women based in the heart of Africa, calling themselves the Four Just Men just to put us off the trail.

COMMISSIONER: What about this letter? The handwriting. Doesn't that give us a clue?

FALMOUTH: It's the sort of hand taught in the Latin countries – France, Spain, Portugal, Italy – and, indeed, Mexico, Brazil and Argentina. But it might be a deliberate fake, and probably is. As you can see. the English itself is impeccable.

COMMISSIONER: So you think they're British?

FALMOUTH: I'm not saying that, sir. Just that whoever wrote that letter has perfect English. It's no help. There's still no clue as to who they are.

COMMISSIONER: So, what *have* you done, Falmouth?

FALMOUTH: Well, we've combed the major cities: London, Birmingham, Manchester, Glasgow. Police holding cells are crammed full of people waiting to be questioned. But it's all a long shot. We don't really think the underworld has anything to do with it.

COMMISSIONER: This is not good enough. Downing Street – the prime minister himself – they're demanding action. Surely there's more we can do.

FALMOUTH: One thing we are doing is to guard Sir Philip Ramon. I'm leading a 6-man protection team. I see Sir Philip daily. He's determined to carry this Bill of his through parliament – says he won't be cowed by idle threats.

COMMISSIONER: The threats may not be idle.

FALMOUTH: So I try to tell him. He takes no notice. So beyond keeping him under our close protection, there's very little more we can do – except wait.

(MUSIC. DOWN FOR FOLLOWING AND HOLD UNDER THROUGHOUT)

NEWSBOY/MAN #1: The Four Just Men – a link to the Mafia. Facts point to a Sicilian connection. Evidence is emerging that the *Cosa Nostra* are directly involved…

(CROSSFADE)

NEWSBOY/MAN #2: A traitor in parliament! Someone who works within the Palace of Westminster is in league with the shadowy organisation that calls itself The Four Just Men…

(CROSSFADE)

NEWSBOY/MAN #1: We have clear proof that the Four Just Men are the infamous Corsican Brothers – the gang that held New York to ransom back in the '60s…

(CROSSFADE TO MUSIC. HOLD A LITTLE. DOWN FOR FOLLOWING AND OUT. HOUSE OF COMMONS)

RAMON: Thank you, Mr Speaker. With your permission, I have a brief statement to make. Honorable members will be aware that a few weeks ago I introduced the Aliens Extradition (Political Offences) Bill on behalf of the government – and that outside interests are threatening my life if it is not withdrawn. It goes without saying that the government has no intention of giving way to blackmail.

(MURMURS OF "HEAR, HEAR")

As for myself, I refuse to be intimidated by common criminals.

(MURMURS OF "HEAR, HEAR")

May I add that this law has been welcomed by a number of governments friendly to this nation. Many have long regretted the fact that individuals and organizations intent on fomenting unrest in their native lands have found sanctuary in this country, and been permitted to continue their nefarious activities. I shall therefore, as previously announced, be moving the second reading of the Bill on Thursday the 27th of this month – that is, in ten days' time.

(FULL UP OPEN AIR, BRASS BAND PLAYING "SOLDIERS OF THE QUEEN" HTTPS://WWW.

YOUTUBE.COM/WATCH?V=4ONG65KXPBE (STARTING AT 0.09) HOLD A LITTLE. DOWN FOR FOLLOWING)

GONZALEZ: A military band. How very English.

MANFRED: I thought it would be a pleasant way to meet, Gonzalez. The park – some music. What's our friend Thery up to today?

GONZALEZ: Poiccart is showing him the sights. Buckingham Palace, the Tower of London…you know. Keeping him occupied.

MANFRED: Very wise.

GONZALEZ: Manfred, are we prepared?

MANFRED: I've taken a place. It's time we came together.

GONZALEZ: Is everything there?

MANFRED: Almost everything. Here's the address. Tell Poiccart, will you? Let's move in, bag and baggage, tomorrow. At noon.

(UP MUSIC, HOLD A LITTLE. FADE OUT. FULL UP)

MANFRED: Well, you see, years ago, when I first came to London, I learned that the easiest way to conceal your identity was to disguise yourself as a public company. That's why I purchased these old printing works, and registered the four of us as the directors of Etherington's Fine Arts Reproduction Limited.

THERY: You've given our names to the authorities?

MANFRED: Good heavens, no, Thery. You're James Leech, artist. I am Arthur W Knight, managing director.

POICCART: And I?

MANFRED: You, Poiccart, can choose. Would you rather be James Selkirk, artist, or Andrew Cohen, financial agent?

POICCART: I'd rather be the money man.

GONZALEZ: Then I'll indulge my artistic temperament.

MANFRED: Excellent. Now we'll live up here on the third floor. You saw that the old printing presses are all on the ground floor. The first floor was the workshop, and the second was a store. Up here, in addition to our living quarters, they kept the cameras and arc lamps. Their equipment was all included in the deal.

THERY: How much longer before anything happens?

MANFRED: Patience my dear Thery. Things are moving ahead.

THERY: No – I'm tired of this life. You won't let me out of doors without a guard.

POICCART: I'm not your guard, Thery.

THERY: You are. You stay with me night and day. I want to go back home to Spain. I was a free man there. I'm sorry I came.

MANFRED: Don't make me sorry – for your own sake, Thery.

THERY: I don't want to kill anybody.

MANFRED: But you don't want Garcia killed either – which he surely will be as soon as he sets foot in Spain again. And that's precisely what Sir Philip Ramon has in mind.

THERY: But to murder the man! Isn't there some other way?

GONZALEZ: Yes, Thery, if he withdraws that Bill. Otherwise, not.

THERY: Who are you? Why are you keeping me prisoner. You don't let me see the newspapers, you don't let me walk alone in the street, I mustn't speak to anybody. You want me to kill, but you won't say how…

MANFRED: Thery, be patient I beg you. We'll lift the restrictions a little. We'll get the daily papers. Let's eat out this evening – a Spanish restaurant . What do you say to that?

THERY: Thank you. But I wish I was more comfortable about what you are asking me to do.

MANFRED:	Listen, Thery. We do not kill for gain. Poiccart here, and Gonzalez, each have fortunes in excess of six million pesetas. I am even wealthier. We kill only in cases where the law of the land is unable to provide a remedy for injustice or corruption.
GONZALEZ:	If we kill you, Thery, it will be the first time we've ever acted in such a way.
THERY:	Me? Kill me?
POICCART:	We've never acted unjustly, not once, but to kill you would be a most unjust thing. Don't make us do it.
GONZALEZ:	Thery, not one hair of your head will be harmed, if you stay faithful to us.
MANFRED:	That I swear, senor. Be patient for just a few days longer. Then we'll all return to Spain, and you will be a wealthy man for the rest of your life. And that young lady in Jerez, awaiting your return – she can have a wedding she'll never forget. Are you with us?

(FULL UP SPANISH MUSIC. HOLD A LITTLE. DOWN FOR FOLLOWING AND OUT)

| MANFRED: | *(reading)* To the Editor, the Megaphone. Dear Sir, we offer you profound apologies for any inconvenience caused to you or your staff this evening. We fear that when you switched on your desk light, the mild explosion must have plunged a section of your press room into darkness. We trust |

you were not too shocked. The detonation was caused by a small plug of magnesium inserted into the light socket. Please believe that it would have been just as simple to use a charge of nitroglycerine, in which case you would have been your own executioner. We arranged this demonstration to prove our firm intention to carry out our promise in respect of the Aliens Extradition Bill. No power on earth can save Sir Philip Ramon if he persists with this measure. We ask you, as editor of a leading newspaper, to oppose the terrible injustice that this law will impose on many innocent people, some of them very distinguished, who are seeking asylum in your country. We beg you to call on your government to withdraw the Bill, and thus also save the life of a Minister of the Crown. Signed. The Four Just Men.

(EDGE OUT. FULL UP)

NEWSBOY/MAN #1: Outrage at the Megaphone!

NEWSBOY/MAN #2: Just Four again!

NEWSBOY/MAN #1: How was it done?

NEWSBOY/MAN #2: Another threatening letter!

NEWSBOY/MAN #1: The Four to keep their promise!

NEWSBOY/MAN #2: Can the police save Sir Philip Ramon?

(EDGE OUT. FADE IN)

EDITOR: Absolutely terrifying, Welby – but it's given us an exclusive. We're upping our print tonight. I guarantee an extra 25,000 at least on the circulation tomorrow.

WELBY: The rest of Fleet Street will be green with envy.

(KNOCK ON DOOR)

EDITOR: *(calls)* Yes!

(DOOR OPENS)

What do you want?

NEWSBOY/MAN: *(remote)* Gen'lman wants to speak to someone. He talks all foreign like – couldn't really make him out. Thought of Mr Welby.

WELBY: Where is he?

NEWSBOY/MAN: Right 'ere behind me, sir.

EDITOR: All right. Be off with you. Hullo, sir. What do you want? Can I help you?

THERY: I want the editor. I must speak with the editor.

EDITOR: I am the editor. Who are you?

THERY: My name is Miguel Thery. I am one of the Four Just Men.

(OPENING CHORDS OF BEETHOVEN'S FIFTH SYMPHONY CONDUCTED BY CHAILLY. HTTPS://WWW.YOUTUBE.COM/WATCH?V=DBXHTHU55C8 HOLD TILL 0.18. DOWN FOR AND HOLD MUSIC UNDER FOLLOWING)

MANFRED: A box is always best in the concert hall. It gives us privacy, and we can talk.

POICCART: Far safer than being followed back to the printing works, if everything had gone wrong. How *did* it go?

MANFRED: Not a hitch. I waited till the editor left the building, then went to reception and asked to see him. Regrets, but not possible. I wander off. Round to the back of the building, slip inside, papers from the briefcase, look purposeful and in a hurry. Up the stairs, down the corridor, to the editor's room. People around, but knock, wait and enter. Fix the desk lamp. Place letter on the desk. Leave. Call a few farewell words as I close the door. Out and away.

POICCART: Full marks, Manfred. But we've some bad news, I'm afraid.

MANFRED: What? What is it?

GONZALEZ: Thery has escaped.

MANFRED: Not good. What's he up to? He doesn't know London. He wouldn't know what to do, where to go.

POICCART: This morning, before you left, you gave him a bundle of newspapers.

MANFRED: That's right. I said I would.

POICCART: The offer of the reward – and the free pardon – was in the Megaphone.

GONZALEZ: I saw he was rather excited this morning, but I put it down to the fact that we told him last night just how we were going to kill Ramon, and the part he was going to play.

MANFRED: How did he get away?

POICCART: We went for a walk this afternoon – to Regent's Street to look at the shops. We stopped to look into a photographer's window, and then suddenly he was gone. There were so many people in the street, it was impossible to locate him. He just – disappeared.

MANFRED: With the full plan in his head.

POICCART: Manfred, listen. My car is quite close. We could get to our launch in Essex in two hours. We could be in France before daybreak.

MANFRED: What do you think, Gonzalez?

GONZALEZ: I say stay and finish the work.

POICCART: Actually, so do I.

MANFRED: I agree. But we must find Thery. Where has he gone?

GONZALEZ: Isn't it obvious? To the newspaper that published the advertisement. Where you were this afternoon. You could have met at the entrance. He's gone to the Megaphone.

(UP MUSIC. HOLD A LITTLE. FADE OUT. FADE IN)

WELBY: Thery? I don't know that name. Where do you come from?

THERY: Jerez in Andalusia.

EDITOR: He doesn't mean that. Where do you come from now? What part of London?

THERY: How should I know? There are houses, streets, people. They want me to kill a man – a Minister. He made a wicked law.

EDITOR: They? Who?

THERY: The other three.

WELBY: Their names. Their names, man!

THERY: You say there is a reward, a free pardon. I want those before I tell…

EDITOR: If you're one of the Four, you'll have your reward. Just a moment.

(TELEPHONE LIFTED. HANDLE CRANKED)

Connect me to the composing room. Hullo. Scargill? Listen to me carefully. Stop the presses. Now. Yes, I do mean it. We may be remaking the front page. Come on, Scargill, we can spare twenty minutes. Now listen, not a man working down there is to leave this building until I give the word. Do you understand? Right.

(TELEPHONE BANGED DOWN)

Now, senor Thery. Tell me all you know.

(KNOCK ON DOOR. DOOR OPENS)

NEWSBOY/MAN: *(remote)* 'Scuse me, sir, I need to let this man… *[in who's got a gun in my back…]*

EDITOR: Not now, boy. I'm busy. Go away. Senor Thery?

THERY: There is a reward and a pardon.

WELBY: For heaven's sake man, you'll get your reward and your pardon. Just tell us – who are the other three men? Where are they to be found?

MANFRED: *(remote, advancing)* Right here, gentlemen. And you, boy. Come on, stand with them. I don't want to waste a bullet on you.

(DOOR SLAMS SHUT)

That's better. A little privacy. You are Mr Manningham, the editor, I take it?

EDITOR: I am, sir. And you…?

MANFRED: One of the three men you were asking after. The other two are waiting outside this building. Oh, and apologies for the minor explosion earlier this afternoon. I'm getting to know this office quite well.

EDITOR: How did you get here…?

WELBY: …and what do you want?

MANFRED: One question at a time, Mr…?

WELBY: Welby.

MANFRED: Ah, the Megaphone's distinguished foreign editor. Well, how I came here your doorkeeper will explain – when he comes to. He's out cold at the moment. And I'm here because I prefer to stay alive – which would be unlikely if our friend Thery here gives you the information you're seeking. That's what I'm about to prevent. I have no quarrel with any of you, but if you try to stop me in any way, I'll have no alternative but to kill you.

WELBY: What exactly do you want?

MANFRED: I want your word – yours and Mr Manningham's – that you will let the two of us leave this building

without raising the alarm. We need three minutes,
no more, from the moment we leave this room.

EDITOR: And if not?

MANFRED: Then you'll leave me with no alternative but to
shoot you and Mr Welby here, and make our
escape. You, boy, you're in no danger.

WELBY: You'd trust our word?

MANFRED: If the alarm goes off before we have left the
building, I'll have to shoot my friend, Thery.

THERY: No. You can't.

MANFRED: Say nothing, Thery. You'd have betrayed your
comrades. You'd have foiled our plans – plans
with a noble purpose. You will come with me, and
be thankful I haven't put a bullet in your head.
Now gentlemen, do I have your word?

EDITOR: I agree – but under protest.

MANFRED: Come on, Thery. On my word as a caballero, I
won't harm you.

(DOOR OPENS)

EDITOR: One moment!

MANFRED: *(remote)* Yes?

EDITOR: Look here, when you get home will you write us an article about yourselves… the Four Just Men… your aspirations, what makes you do – what you do. How about it? I'll publish whatever you write.

MANFRED: Sir, I salute you! The article will be delivered tomorrow.

(EDGE OUT. FULL UP)

NEWSBOY/MAN #1: It is not easy to understand why, having two of the miscreants standing before them, certain journalists connected with a sensational publication allowed them to get away scot free, to continue with their evil work. As a result, the life of a respected statesman is still under threat. This situation is intolerable. These four criminals must be identified and rounded up as soon as possible – and certainly well ahead of the Aliens Extradition Bill passing into law.

(FADE OUT. FULL UP)

JANE RAMON: Philip, I beg you. These men are ruthless. They've succeeded in everything. They penetrated the prime minister's private study, they got into the editor's office at the Megaphone – not once, but twice. Philip, please give way. They are determined to stop this Bill.

RAMON: And I, my love, am equally determined to see it pass through Parliament and become the law of the land.

JANE RAMON: Darling Philip – I admire your firmness of purpose, and I admire your courage. But not at the expense of your life. You've seen what these men can do. Please Philip, give way. Is the Bill so vital?

RAMON: Jane, my dear, let me explain. Foreign agitators are taking advantage of our traditions of freedom, of free speech, of tolerance. We know of several such people intent on inciting revolution, of overthrowing the government, in their own countries. They have fled to Britain so as to escape justice at home, and continue their nefarious activities from here. Those governments are friends of ours. They are requesting – nay demanding – that we return these people so that they can stand trial in their own countries for their crimes. Now do you see why this Bill is so important?

JANE RAMON: I see why it seems politically important to the government. It would reinforce our good relations with a number of states we don't want to annoy – whether or not we agree with how they run their affairs. I do not approve of the Spanish regime, for instance. But I quite see that our government would not wish to break off our relations with Spain. Not for the sake of one man – Manuel Garcia.

RAMON: Good gracious, Jane. I didn't realize you took such an interest in politics.

JANE RAMON: I'm not surprised. I believe this is the first time since we were married that we've ever discussed politics.

RAMON: Then I'm at fault. I take it you have an interest in the British Suffrage movement?

JANE RAMON: I take a keen interest. I favour their call for women to have the vote. I hope that one day you will support it in Parliament.

RAMON: I'm afraid that day is some way off, my darling. Meanwhile, we have more urgent issues to deal with. Like this Aliens Extradition Bill.

JANE RAMON: So you're determined to press ahead?

RAMON: Absolutely.

JANE RAMON: Then I absolutely insist that you follow the security requirements of the police while the Bill passes through Parliament.

RAMON: Oh, Jane...

JANE RAMON: Yes, Philip, I insist. You must do exactly as the police instruct. You simply must.

RAMON: Oh, very well.

(EDGE OUT. FULL UP)

COMMISSIONER: Sir Philip, we're taking the threat very seriously. These men mean what they say, and they've proved they can overcome normal security measures. As a result we've made certain plans...

RAMON: Plans? What plans?

COMMISSIONER: Sir Philip, would you please tell me about your Bill. What is due to take place in two days' time?

RAMON: What we call the Second Reading. Two weeks ago I introduced the Bill to the House of Commons. That's just a formality. We call that the First Reading. On Thursday evening, at exactly nine o'clock, I stand up in the House to present the details. There's a debate, and then the Bill is launched, and we proceed to the next stage.

COMMISSIONER: And these Four Just Men want you to abort the Second Reading, is that right? They threaten that unless you withdraw the Bill – kill it, in fact – they will kill you. In short, they say that you will be dead before 8.30 pm this coming Thursday.

RAMON: So I gather. But I can assure you, Commissioner, I have not the slightest intention of acceding to their demands. It's absolutely monstrous to suppose that a government Minister would allow threats to influence him in carrying out his official duties.

COMMISSIONER: I too have official duties, Sir Ramon, and they are to protect you from harm. Until the Second Reading of this Bill has been successfully concluded, I must insist on certain measures.

RAMON: And these are?

COMMISSIONER: You must take up residence in central London.

RAMON: Our London house is in Portland Place.

COMMISSIONER: So I understand. But I believe you work from offices at number 44 Downing Street.

RAMON: That is so. When I'm in London I drive there every morning. If my Downing Street staff need to contact me at any time, a private telephone line connects my office with Portland Place.

COMMISSIONER: I'm afraid we cannot allow you to drive from Portland Place to Downing Street before the Second Reading is concluded. We must ask you to set up living facilities in your Downing Street office.

RAMON: Good grief, man…

COMMISSIONER: Sir Philip, believe me it is necessary. It's only a matter of a night or two.

RAMON: Oh, very well. I did assure Lady Ramon that I would follow your directions.

(PHONE BELL – ONE LONG RING, NOT DOUBLE. RECEIVER LIFTED. HAMILTON ON DISTORT)

RAMON: Yes, what is it?

HAMILTON: Hamilton here, sir. We have everything ready for you. The bed's made up in the outer office. Oh, and there are sixty men on duty here, with sixty more standing by for when they change rosters. We were wondering when to expect you…

RAMON: Perhaps you've an iron safe to lock me up in, when I do arrive.

HAMILTON: Oh er… er… I – I don't …

RAMON: Goodbye, Hamilton. I'll be along shortly.

            (RECEIVER BANGED DOWN. KNOCK ON DOOR. DOOR OPENS)

JANE RAMON: *(remote, advancing)* I hope I'm not intruding. Good afternoon, Commissioner.

COMMISSIONER: Good afternoon, Lady Ramon. No, not at all. I was just going. I'll leave Sir Philip to explain the security arrangements.

JANE RAMON: Don't go quite yet, Commissioner. I feel you might be interested in this letter. Our footman has just brought it to me. He found it lying just inside the front door.

COMMISSIONER: Oh, good heavens.

JANE RAMON: It's addressed to you, my dear. Here.

            (ENVELOPE RIPPED OPEN. PAPER. FADE IN)

MANFRED: My dear Foreign Secretary. I send you a brief note to remind you that you have until 8.30 p.m. tomorrow to withdraw the Aliens Expulsion Bill. If you have not done so by then, if you persist in trying to obtain a Second Reading for it, then I am afraid we shall be forced to remove you from the parliamentary scene, permanently. In short we shall terminate your life. We seek only justice for those you seek to endanger. The Four Just Men.

(FADE OUT. FULL UP QUARTET PLAYING "ROSES FROM THE SOUTH" WALTZ. HTTPS://WWW.YOUTUBE.COM/WATCH?V=9VQJPMNIZGC BRING UP BACKGROUND – TEAROOM. SMALL CROWD. CHATTER. HOLD MUSIC A LITTLE. DOWN FOR FOLLOWING. CROCKERY AND BOTH WOMEN SIP OCCASIONALLY.)

JANE RAMON: Thank you so much for meeting me, Elizabeth. It doesn't seem quite right to be having tea at the Savoy at a time like this.

ELIZABETH: My dear Jane, you must be desperately worried. When I told Austin that you'd asked to see me, he said I simply had to put anything else to one side. So I did. It doesn't do to disobey the Prime Minister.

JANE RAMON: *(laughs)* Dear Elizabeth. How is Austin taking all this?

ELIZABETH: Well, he's supporting Philip, of course.

JANE RAMON:	Yes, Philip is absolutely determined to go ahead with this wretched Bill.
ELIZABETH:	I know. I'm not so sure that Austin is quite as convinced.
JANE RAMON:	Really?
ELIZABETH:	I think he'd be prepared to postpone the Bill until these Four Just Men, or whatever they call themselves, are caught. He doesn't want to seem to give way to threats, but he's afraid of what this gang can do.
JANE RAMON:	Oh, Elizabeth, if only he could bring Philip round to his way of thinking. If he announced that all efforts were being directed to apprehending these criminals, and that the government would reintroduce the Bill later, surely that would be acceptable to the public?
ELIZABETH:	Well, I would have thought so. The question is: would Philip go along with it?
JANE RAMON:	Elizabeth, would you ask Austin to try? These four vigilantes – nothing seems to stop them. I'm so frightened for Philip. He's stubborn, but surely he'll listen to the PM?

(UP MUSIC. HOLD A LITTLE, FADE OUT)

RAMON:	Austin, you don't want a political crisis on your hands do you? Because if you insist on dropping

this Bill, I'll have no choice but to resign. I've invested too much in it, and I'm damned if I'll let myself be painted as a coward, prepared to give way to blackmail for fear of my life. No, Austin. Unless you positively forbid it, we go ahead tomorrow night, as scheduled, with the Second Reading.

(FULL UP BIG BEN CHIMING HALF-HOUR. HTTPS://FREESOUND.ORG/PEOPLE/ HYDERPOTTER/PACKS/5227/ CROSSFADE TO OFFICE BACKGROUND)

HAMILTON: Half-past eight, Sir Philip.

RAMON: I'm not deaf, Hamilton.

HAMILTON: No, sir. I'm sorry, sir. It's just... er...

RAMON: You don't have to spell it out, Hamilton. By this time tomorrow, unless I've withdrawn the Bill, I'll be dead, according to these Four Just Men.

HAMILTON: Er ... That is what I had in mind...

RAMON: Well, you can put your mind at rest, Hamilton. Neither will occur. I will not withdraw the Bill, and in 24 hours' time I'll still be in perfect health. Don't forget, half the police force in London is guarding us, here in this office. And we *are* in Downing Street, for heaven's sake, hard by the prime minister's official residence. Who do you think could get past all that security?

HAMILTON: Of course you're right, sir.

                **(TELEPHONE RINGS – ONE LONG RING.
                RECEIVER LIFTED. JANE ON DISTORT)**

RAMON: Hello.

JANE RAMON: Hello, Philip. I was wondering if you're settled in
                all right.

RAMON: Thank you, Jane, yes. They've made up what seems
                a very comfortable bed. And we're surrounded by
                police and scores of security guards.

JANE RAMON: Well, that's some comfort – to me, at least.

RAMON: You mustn't worry, my dear. Everything will go
                swimmingly. I'll stay here in the office till eight-
                thirty tomorrow evening. Then I'll be driven
                over to the Commons under heavy guard, for the
                Second Reading. I'll be back here by eleven.

JANE RAMON: This private telephone line of ours is a blessing,
                Philip. You won't mind if I ring you from time to
                time?

RAMON: Of course not, my dear. Whenever you wish.

JANE RAMON: Thank you, Philip. Well, I'll wish you good night.
                Sleep well.

RAMON: I guarantee it. Good night, Jane.

(RECEIVER REPLACED. FADE IN)

MANFRED: I want you to understand, Thery – we bear you no ill-will for what you've done. Senor Gonzalez here, and Senor Poiccart both agree with me – I did the right thing in sparing your life.

THERY: I am grateful, senor Manfred.

MANFRED: Tomorrow night, if it remains necessary, you'll do as you agreed to do. You've had half the promised sum already. We'll pay you the rest, and you'll be free to go…

THERY: But where? Where can I go? Tell me. I've given them my name. They'll have contacted the Spanish police by now, and they'll know all about me. Where can I go? What am I to do?

GONZALEZ: You betrayed yourself, Thery.

POICCART: This is the punishment you've brought on yourself.

MANFRED: But you can stop worrying. We'll find a place for you – a new Spain under other skies. And the girl from Jerez will be there, waiting for you.

THERY: You swear that?

MANFRED: You have my word. And now – you know what's expected of you tomorrow night. You know what's to be done.

THERY: I do, senor.

MANFRED: *(slowly getting worked up)* There must be no mistake. If we have to, we'll kill this unjust man in a way no one will ever guess. It will shock the world. A swift death, a sure death, a death that will defeat all the police, all the security guards... I apologize, gentlemen. I got carried away. For one moment I forgot our cause.

GONZALEZ: Indeed, Manfred, the method we use to achieve justice is less important that our reasons for doing so.

MANFRED: You're right, Gonzalez. Thery, all the equipment you need, every single item you asked for, is laid out for you on the workbench over there. So Thery – to work!

(FULL UP BIG BEN CHIMES QUARTER PAST. FADE IN)

FALMOUTH: Well, Sir Philip, we now know how that non-explosive bomb was smuggled into the Prime Minister's office.

RAMON: Really?

FALMOUTH: Yes. That evening Gerald Bascoe, the MP for North Torrington, was spotted in the House just as members were filing into the voting lobby.

RAMON: And so...?

FALMOUTH: Mr Bascoe was never within a hundred miles of the House on that day. It was one of those so-called Four Just Men in disguise – and what a disguise! It fooled everyone, without exception.

RAMON: Falmouth, I'm so tired of all this, weary with it… Detectives, and disguises, and masked murderers. We seem to be living in a theatrical melodrama…

FALMOUTH: It won't go on, sir, I do assure you. We'll catch them before too long. Please be patient for just a day or two.

RAMON: Will I be able to get to the Commons tonight?

FALMOUTH: Not tonight, sir. That's not part of the security programme. Sir Philip, I need to get back to Scotland Yard for a short while. The Commissioner asked me to look in at about a quarter to ten. I'll be back, sir, within the hour. I promise.

RAMON: *(moving)* Let me see you out.

(DOOR OPENS)

Hamilton, Mr Falmouth is leaving. His coat, if you please.

FALMOUTH: You must excuse these goggles of mine. I had an uncomfortable feeling a few days ago that I was being followed, so I've taken to riding my motor-cycle. These goggles make me pretty indistinguishable from every other motor-cyclist on the road. And I may say, Sir Philip, that this is the only time in my twenty-five years of service that I've ever resorted to a disguise of any sort.

RAMON: This situation is making fools of us all. *(moving)* Well, I'll see you a little later, Falmouth.

FALMOUTH: *(moving, retreating)* Indeed, Sir Philip.

(DOOR CLOSES)

HAMILTON: *(calls)* Do you want me, sir?

RAMON: *(moving)* No, Hamilton. I'll be all right in the study. *(calls)* I think I'll read a little.

(DOOR OPENS IN DISTANCE)

FALMOUTH: *(calls, advancing)* Oh, Sir Philip, I nearly forgot. I'm sorry to bother you, but I wanted to leave this envelope with you until I got back. We can't be too careful. Accidents happen – even to detectives.

RAMON: Why, have you been receiving threats, too?

FALMOUTH: I'm afraid so, sir. And the Commissioner, too. This contains highly confidential information – and it'd be disastrous if anything happened to me and it was found. I'll entrust it to a courier on my return. Till then, may I leave it with you, sir?

RAMON: Of course.

(DRAWER OPENS)

I'll put it in this drawer. Goodnight, Falmouth.

FALMOUTH: *(retreating)* Goodnight, Sir Philip.

(IN DISTANCE BIG BEN STRIKES HALF HOUR. TELEPHONE RINGS. RECEIVER LIFTED. JANE ON DISTORT)

HAMILTON: The Foreign Secretary's office.

JANE RAMON: Is that you, Mr Hamilton?

HAMILTON: Indeed it is, Lady Ramon. How can I help you? Do you wish to speak with Sir Philip? He's in the study, reading, at the moment.

JANE RAMON: I'm not sure I do. I need your advice, Mr Hamilton.

HAMILTON: Of course.

JANE RAMON: We've received a letter, here in Portland Place. We don't know how it was delivered. It was found on the hall mat, not five minutes ago.

HAMILTON: Oh dear. Is it from…?

JANE RAMON: Yes. It's signed The Four Just Men. I don't want to worry Sir Philip even more, but I can't keep it to myself.

HAMILTON: Of course not. Please read it to me.

| JANE RAMON: | "Sir Philip – you will receive one more warning from us. And to ensure that it will not go astray, our next and last message will be delivered into your hands by one of us in person. The Four Just Men."
What do you make of that? |
|---|---|
| HAMILTON: | They're claiming that one of the four of them will penetrate all the security surrounding us, and place a letter into Sir Philip's hands? But that's absolute nonsense, Lady Ramon. Completely impossible… |

(DOOR OPENS)

RAMON:	*(remote)* Did I hear the telephone?
HAMILTON:	Yes, Sir Philip. I took the call in here. I'd switched off the connection to leave you in peace.
RAMON:	*(advancing)* No, Hamilton. Please leave it permanently switched through to my study. I want to receive any calls from Lady Ramon. Is that her on the phone?
HAMILTON:	It is, sir.
RAMON:	Let me have it. Hello. Jane?

(JANE ON DISTORT)

JANE RAMON:	Yes, it is, Philip. I'm sorry to bother you again. We've received a letter. Hamilton will tell you all about it. Please be extra careful, Philip, won't you?

RAMON: Don't worry, my dear. Now, goodnight.

(RECEIVER REPLACED. DOOR OPENS)

Back already, Falmouth? Just in time. There's been a development. Why don't we all go into the study?

(UNDER FOLLOWING BIG BEN STRIKES TEN O'CLOCK IN THE DISTANCE)

FALMOUTH: *(moving)* Something's happened? I've only been away for half an hour.

HAMILTON: Lady Ramon phoned from the house in Portland Place.

FALMOUTH: She's using the telephone?

HAMILTON: Oh, it's quite secure. We're connected by a private line. But they received a letter there – they don't know how it was delivered.

RAMON: From these…

HAMILTON: Yes, sir. The Four Just Men.

RAMON: What did they say?

HAMILTON: Well, it's utter nonsense. They said that one of them would personally deliver their last message directly into your hands, Sir Philip.

FALMOUTH: They've over-reached themselves this time. They're claiming to be able to achieve the impossible. Let's not bother our heads with that. The Commissioner had something of interest to tell me. He's just received a long cable from America. Remember those killings the Four Just Men carried out in the States a few years back? Well, a Pinkerton man has been collecting information about them ever since. Here's the cable he sent our Commissioner.

(EDGE IN)

PINKERTON: Warn Ramon that the Four stick by their promise. If they say they will do something, they will do it. If they mention a certain time, they will keep to it. Warn him against drinking coffee in any form, or opening letters or parcel. Tell him to be accompanied at all times by an armed police officer. Examine his bedroom to ensure no gases can be introduced, and make sure an armed guard is stationed outside. These men mean what they say.

(EDGE OUT)

HAMILTON: Mr Falmouth, is that this evening's Megaphone you have there?

FALMOUTH: Yes, I got it just outside Scotland Yard. Why?

HAMILTON: Look at the headline. "The Four Just Men explain their creed".

(RUSTLE OF NEWSPAPER)

FALMOUTH: Let's see what they have to say for themselves.

(EDGE IN)

MANFRED: Our purpose is to dispense justice when corrupt politicians or judges fail to do so, to deliver their just deserts to those responsible for committing evil who would otherwise escape justice. So we ourselves are careful to be just and meticulous at every stage. We leave nothing to chance, but if the slightest hitch occurs, then we would acknowledge defeat, and abort our mission. For example, Sir Philip Ramon must receive a final warning, and by our code it is essential that it is handed to him by one of us in person. Unless this is done before ten o'clock tonight, our arrangements fall to the ground, and the execution we have planned must be forgone...

(EDGE OUT. BIG BEN CHIMES THE QUARTER IN THE DISTANCE)

HAMILTON: But it's a quarter *past* ten. That's Big Ben just striking. Don't you see? It's all over. There's no longer any need to guard Sir Philip.

RAMON: It's a ruse. A trick. Surely. To put us off our guard.

FALMOUTH: I don't think so. I believe that these men, ruthless as they are, really mean what they say. It's what that Pinkerton man from the States believes. It's what they themselves call their creed. In twenty-five years I've never put an ounce of faith in anything any criminal says, but with this lot – somehow I can't disbelieve them. If they've failed to deliver their message, they won't trouble us again.

RAMON: I wish I could believe that.

NEWSBOY/MAN #2: *(remote – calls)* Mr Hamilton, sir. Telegram.

HAMILTON: *(calls)* Right. Bring it here. Thanks. It's addressed to you, Sir Philip.

FALMOUTH: I'll take it.

(ENVELOPE RIPPED OPEN)

From the editor of the Megaphone. Listen to this: "Received a phone call from one of the Four. He says they've just delivered their last message to you. Is this true?"

RAMON: Good grief.

FALMOUTH: But what does it mean?

RAMON: It means, my dear Mr Falmouth, that your noble Four are liars and braggarts as well as murderers. And it also means, I hope, an end to your ridiculous faith in their honesty.

FALMOUTH: Tell me, did anybody come here after I left?

HAMILTON: Not a soul. I can vouch for that, Mr Falmouth.

FALMOUTH: Sir Philip, you've seen no-one this evening except your secretary and myself?

RAMON: No-one. Absolutely nobody.

FALMOUTH: *(retreating)* Well, I'm afraid I'll have to go back to the Yard and try to…[*sort out this mess once and for…*]

RAMON: *(calls)* Don't forget your package.

FALMOUTH: *(remote)* What package?

(DESK DRAWER OPENS)

RAMON: The envelope you left me for safe keeping. This.

FALMOUTH: *(advancing)* What is this?

RAMON: You seem bemused, Mr Falmouth. Perhaps it's because your touching faith in the honesty of these criminals has been shattered. I really must ask the Commissioner to send me a detective with a better appreciation of the criminal mind.

FALMOUTH: Sir Ramon, would you please explain what you mean by saying that I handed you this envelope for safe keeping.

RAMON: Has the shock affected your memory as well? A moment after you left, you remembered this package and returned to leave it in my care.

FALMOUTH: Sir Ramon, I assure you that I did not return. Nor did I leave any envelope with you. Please hand it to me.

(ENVELOPE RIPPED)

This, Sir Ramon, is your final warning from the Four Just Men.

HAMILTON: But you delivered it.

FALMOUTH: I most certainly did not, Mr Hamilton. That was one of them. Dressed in long-coat like mine and with goggles on. Sir Philip, the Four have done precisely what they said they would do. Their final message has been handed to you in person.

(FADE IN)

MANFRED: We allow you until tomorrow evening to reconsider your decision regarding the Aliens Extradition Bill. If by six o'clock no announcement has appeared in the afternoon papers that you have withdrawn this measure, we shall, with reluctance, fulfil our promise. You will be dead by 8.30. Beneath this note I set out in brief the secret police arrangements for your safety. Farewell. The Four Just Men.

(FULL UP. BIG BEN STRIKES THE HALF. EDGE IN)

ELIZABETH: Austin, this has gone far enough. Can you imagine what dear Jane is going through? You must put a stop to this.

PRIME MINISTER: If only I could, Elizabeth.

ELIZABETH: But these men mean what they say – and they seem capable of doing anything they put their mind to. If that Bill isn't withdrawn, I do honestly believe that Philip will lose his life. It simply isn't worth it.

PRIME MINISTER: I agree with you, my dear – I do. But you know Philip. He's as stubborn as a mule. He is absolutely determined not to be shifted, especially by threats.

ELIZABETH: But you're the prime minister. You lead the government. You could simply order the Bill to be postponed until these criminals are caught.

PRIME MINISTER: Elizabeth, let me explain. If he's not allowed to proceed with this legislation, Philip has threatened to resign. The party simply can't face a political upheaval at this time. The government would fall; we'd have to call a General Election. And if I'm any judge of the public mood, there's every chance we'd lose it. I can't risk all that. Nor can I really be seen to have given way to the threats and blackmail of a gang of international criminals. I have to keep the broader picture in mind.

ELIZABETH: I do understand, Austin. Indeed I do. With my head. My heart urges me in quite a different direction. Is there no room for the heart in politics, Austin?

PRIME MINISTER: It's a question of balancing one course of action against another – and judging what the consequences of each are likely to be. We've placed an unprecedented cordon around Philip. The police and security services of the nation are intent on safeguarding him – at no little cost, I may say. The likelihood of anything happening to him has been reduced to a minimum. Whereas, if he resigns, the political consequences are only too clear. As PM it's this sort of difficult decision I'm called on to make all the time,

ELIZABETH: You had your weekly audience with the Queen yesterday evening. What did Her Majesty have to say?

PRIME MINISTER: She began as you did, my dear. She enquired whether the Bill could be postponed. And I explained the full situation, just as I've explained it to you. She accepted that my decision was logical and reasonable.

ELIZABETH: I know that you're doing your best, Austin. I do trust you to make the right decisions. All we can do now is to wait – and hope.

(FADE IN HOUSE OF COMMONS, LIGHT CROWD)

MP:	May I ask the Prime Minister whether it is the intention of Her Majesty's government to proceed with the Aliens Extradition Bill? In view of the extraordinary circumstances that have arisen, has he considered postponing the measure?
PRIME MINISTER:	I know of no circumstance likely to prevent my right honourable friend, who is unfortunately not in his place tonight, from moving the second reading of the Bill tomorrow.

(MURMURS OF "HEAR. HEAR". CROSSFADE TO OFFICE AT SCOTLAND YARD)

COMMISSIONER:	Have you seen the morning papers, Falmouth?
FALMOUTH:	Haven't had time, sir. I didn't sleep very well in Downing Street, and I came straight here.
COMMISSIONER:	Well they're unanimous that the Bill should be dropped. Not one of them thinks Sir Philip is doing the right thing. One way or another they're all saying that the Bill is not important enough to risk a life for.
FALMOUTH:	But public opinion is pretty divided about the Bill itself.
COMMISSIONER:	That's true. They're split very nearly fifty-fifty. But whatever they think about the measure, everyone seems to believe that Sir Philip would be foolhardy to go ahead regardless. And I must say I agree with them.

FALMOUTH: And so do I. Killing Sir Philip would seem to be an impossible task, given the degree of security we've laid on. We're going to keep him isolated until it's time to get him to the Commons this evening. No one will be allowed to approach him. And yet... and yet...

COMMISSIONER: You think these Four Just Men can achieve even the impossible?

FALMOUTH: What seems impossible to us may be achievable by them. Perhaps we haven't thought out every possible way they could get at him.

COMMISSIONER: That's your job, Falmouth. Think away. As for me, I'm going round to see Sir Philip.

(EDGE OUT. BIG BEN STRIKES QUARTER . EDGE IN)

COMMISSIONER: I tell you, sir, we can do no more than we've done, and I'm still afraid. If you look out of the window, you can see a small section of Whitehall. I assure you that it is packed end to end with police. We've banned all traffic in the area covered by Charles Street, Birdcage Walk and the Mall. We've men up on the roofs. We've searched every house.

RAMON: It sounds like martial law.

COMMISSIONER: Close. In fact, two Guards regiments will be under arms for the rest of today and tonight, ready for any emergency.

RAMON: Overkill, wouldn't you say?

COMMISSIONER: Let me be quite honest with you, Sir Philip. These four criminals frighten me. I'll admit this to no-one else, but I have a horrible dread that, despite all our precautions, we've left something out of our reckoning – that we've failed to see some way in which they could get at you; that despite all our security you are still vulnerable. Sir Philip, for God's sake, I beg of you, think well before you reject their terms. Is the timetable for this Bill so absolutely necessary? Is it worth your life?

RAMON: Commissioner, I will not withdraw, not under any circumstances. I have gone too far. I have got beyond fear. To me, it's now a question of right and wrong. Is it wrong to remove from this country scores of dangerous criminals who enjoy immunity from arrest while encouraging others to commit acts of violence and treason? I firmly believe that I am right to do so – and if that's the case, then the Four Just Men are in the wrong. I trust my own judgement in this matter. That is why I must proceed with the Bill.

COMMISSIONER: Thank you, Sir Philip. I understand.

RAMON: You were quite right to take the precautions you have, Commissioner. I've been foolish to resent them.

COMMISSIONER: We must tighten them further, sir. Between six and half-past eight this evening we wish you to remain here, in your study, to lock the door, and under no circumstances to open it to anyone – anyone at all. Not even to myself or Mr Falmouth. During that time you must keep the door locked. Will you do that, sir?

RAMON: I'll follow your instructions to the letter.

COMMISSIONER: This room cannot be breached in any way. During the night it's been subject to a thorough inspection. The floor, the walls, the ceiling, the fixed steel shutters. Nothing can get through. I'll leave you now, Sir Philip. but Mr Falmouth and I will be back at six o'clock this evening.

RAMON: And at half-past eight…?

COMMISSIONER: We leave for Parliament under heavy guard. That's the plan. Please God we're able to carry it out.

(BIG BEN STRIKES THE HALF-HOUR. FADE IN. RAMON ON DISTORT)

JANE RAMON: Hello. Hello. Philip?

RAMON: Hello, my dear. Yes it's me.

JANE RAMON: Are you all right? Is everything going to plan?

RAMON: I'm afraid it is. I've been locked in this study all alone for half an hour already. They intend keeping me locked up in here till eight-thirty.

JANE RAMON: Thank heaven for that! It's only two hours, my love. It's already half past six.

RAMON: I've told them I'll grin and bear it. I've given up complaining. I suppose it's all for the best.

JANE RAMON: I'm sure it is. I take it you won't be coming back to Portland Place after the debate?

RAMON: No, they intend to keep me under close guard until tomorrow. I'll sleep here in Downing Street tonight.

JANE RAMON: Then I'll see you later tomorrow. I wish you well in the debate.

RAMON: Thank you, Jane. Well, goodnight.

JANE RAMON: Goodnight, Philip.

(RECEIVER REPLACED. FADE IN)

MANFRED: It's nearly time.

THERY: But why are we standing in the dark? I can't see a thing.

MANFRED: It's necessary. Believe me.

THERY: Let me at least strike a match.

POICCART: No. We must remain invisible. Silent and invisible.

THERY:	But I can see nothing.
GONZALEZ:	I'll help you. Just a moment. Here's one of the wires. Hold out your hand. You have it?
THERY:	I have it.
GONZALEZ:	Now, where…? Here we are. Here's the second.
THERY:	That's all I need. Give me a minute. There. Is it time now?
MANFRED:	No, no, not yet. Hold on. Wait… wait… *Now!*
THERY:	*(roar of agony, followed by a convincing death from electric shock, gasping for breath as his heart gives out).*

(BODY FALLS TO GROUND)

POICCART:	For God's sake – what's happened?
MANFRED:	Let me get at him. Help me Gonzalez . *(pause)* It's no good. He's gone.
GONZALEZ:	But why? What happened?
MANFRED:	Thery bungled the job. It's as simple as that. Thery bungled, and he's paid the price.
POICCART:	But Ramon? What of Ramon?
MANFRED:	We shall see. We shall see.

(FADE OUT. BIG BEN STRIKES THE QUARTER. FADE IN OUTER OFFICE)

COMMISSIONER: A quarter past eight.

FALMOUTH: Another fifteen minutes.

HAMILTON: Just let me…

(KNOCK ON DOOR)

(calls) Sir Philip? Are you all right, sir?

RAMON: *(muffled)* Perfectly, thank you, Hamilton.

HAMILTON: *(calls)* Excellent, sir. We'll soon have you out of there.

COMMISSIONER: Yes, it really does look as though this nightmare will soon be over.

FALMOUTH: Please, Commissioner, don't let's count our chickens before they're hatched. You know what I think about these gangsters – what they're capable of achieving.

COMMISSIONER: But even you must admit, Falmouth – it looks as though this time they've bitten off more than they can chew.

FALMOUTH: I do admit, Commissioner, that I can't think of what might happen. I don't see how it's possible for those fellows to keep their promise. But all the same, nagging at the back of my mind…

COMMISSIONER: Yes, Falmouth. I know what you mean.

FALMOUTH: I'll just listen at the door. Nothing. Wait – was that the telephone?

(IN DISTANCE BIG BEN STRIKES THE HALF-HOUR)

HAMILTON: It's half-past eight. It's all over. *(calls)*. Sir Philip! You can unlock the door.

RAMON: *(muffled, remote. Replicate Thery's death – roar of pain, gasping as heart gives out)*

(DISTANT CRASH OF BODY FALLING TO THE GROUND)

FALMOUTH: Quick – get this door open. *(calls)* You two out there – lend a hand. Right – One. Two. Three.

(CRASH AS DOOR BURSTS OPEN)

My God!

HAMILTON: Sir Philip! Sir Philip!

COMMISSIONER: *(short pause)* He's dead. I must get straight over to the Prime Minister. Falmouth, keep everyone out of this room. Come on, all of you. Out.

HAMILTON: Does that include the outer office?

COMMISSIONER: Yes. See to it Falmouth, will you? Get the outer door locked. Make this building secure. Then you can join me in Number 10.

FALMOUTH: What about Lady Ramon, sir? Somebody will have to break the news.

COMMISSIONER: I'll do that – as soon as I've informed the Prime Minister. Get moving, everyone.

(FADE OUT. FADE IN. SMALL CROWD CHATTING. GAVEL BANGS ON DESK. CHATTING STOPS)

CORONER: May I remind everyone present that this is in no sense a trial. An inquest is a formal method of attempting to reach the truth about a certain circumstance – often a death. You, gentlemen of the jury, are asked to listen carefully to the evidence placed before you, and then, on my guidance as coroner, to reach a verdict. You have listened to a great deal of evidence, but I must tell you that so far I do not believe you can decide the exact cause of Sir Philip Ramon's death. Or rather, to put it another way, we have no means of determining exactly how Sir Philip was murdered. For, gentlemen of the jury, I believe you can go this far – namely that Sir Philip did not die of natural causes. His death was caused by person or persons unknown, and by means which so far remain equally mysterious. Before I call Detective Superintendent Falmouth to give evidence, I would like to record that I have received a great many letters from all kinds of people containing a great many theories as to the cause of Sir Philip's death, some of them fantastic beyond belief. I have passed them all on to the police, who inform me that they are eager to receive suggestions, no matter how bizarre. And now, call Detective Superintendent Falmouth.

(CROSSFADE)

FALMOUTH: Yes, sir. The windows were fastened, and were covered with tightly-closed wooden shutters sheathed with steel. I examined them carefully. There was absolutely no indication that they had been tampered with.

CORONER: Did you institute a search of the room?

FALMOUTH: I did, sir. A thorough search.

CORONER: The foreman of the jury has his hand up. You have a question, Mr Foreman?

MANFRED: Yes, sir. Some members of the jury would like to know when the room was examined. How soon after the discovery of the body.

FALMOUTH: As soon as the forensic team had completed their work and the body was removed. Every article of furniture was taken out of the room, the carpets were taken up, and the walls and ceiling stripped.

CORONER: And nothing was found?

FALMOUTH: Nothing.

CORONER: Is there a fireplace in the room?

FALMOUTH: There is, sir, and it was subject to a thorough search. It had not been disturbed, there was no soot on the ground. There was no possibility at all of anyone gaining entry to the room by that means.

CORONER: Yes, Mr Foreman?

MANFRED: Excuse me, sir, but may I ask the witness if there was any indication of gas when he entered the room. A smell, perhaps?

FALMOUTH: Nothing of any sort.

MANFRED: But there are gases that are poisonous but without any odor.

FALMOUTH: Indeed there are, but I was inside the room within seconds of hearing Sir Philip fall to the ground. No gas could dissipate as quickly as that. I would certainly have detected it, if it had been present.

CORONER: Did you find *anything* unusual?

FALMOUTH: Well, sir. In falling to the floor Sir Philip swept a number of items from his desk, including a small bowl of roses. He was found to be clutching one of the roses.

CORONER: This was included in the Commissioner's report to me. There was something odd about Sir Philip's hand, was there not?

FALMOUTH: Yes, sir. Beneath the flower, there was a round black stain.

CORONER: Can you account for that?

FALMOUTH: No, sir. I have no explanation for it.

(FADE OUT. FADE IN)

JANE RAMON: I had those roses sent over to Downing Street about mid-morning. They were picked in our own gardens in the country, and sent up to London by the milk train. I included a little note, with my love.

COMMISSIONER: Then I can well understand why Sir Philip may have clutched at one in his dying moments.

JANE RAMON: Thank you for that, Commissioner. But I'm absolutely certain they could not have caused his death. Look, over there on the grand piano. Those are some of precisely the same roses. In any case, you must have examined the ones in Philip's room.

COMMISSIONER: Indeed we did, Lady Ramon. They were sent to the Home Office for analysis. And of course, we found nothing out of the way.

(FADE OUT. FADE IN COURTROOM)

CORONER: Detective Superintendent Falmouth, I believe you know of a man called Thery.

FALMOUTH: I do, sir. He was one of the gang calling themselves The Four Just Men. We believe he was involved in the plot to murder Sir Philip Ramon.

CORONER: Has he been found?

FALMOUTH: Yes, sir. His body was discovered this morning on the Romney Marshes.

CORONER: Was there anything particularly significant about it?

FALMOUTH: Yes sir. On his right palm was a stain similar to the one found on Sir Philip Ramon's hand.

CORONER: Yes, Mr Foreman?

MANFRED: Was a rose also found in his hand?

FALMOUTH: No. His hands were empty.

MANFRED: Did the forensic report on these stains suggest how they might have been caused?

FALMOUTH: Not really. Carbolic acid was suggested. But other than that, they remain a mystery.

CORONER: Before you stand down, Detective Superintendent, is there any other circumstance that you wish to bring to the attention of the court – any matter that I may have failed to ask you about.

FALMOUTH:	Well, something that can have no possible bearing on the case – but in examining the exterior of 44 Downing Street soon after Sir Philip's death…
CORONER:	Yes?
FALMOUTH:	I hesitate to mention it – but I found two dead sparrows on the window sill outside Sir Philip's study.
CORONER:	Two dead sparrows?
FALMOUTH:	Yes, sir.
CORONER:	Did you send them away for examination and analysis?
FALMOUTH:	I did. sir. The forensic surgeon who examined them found no trace of poison in either the stomach or the lungs. In his report he suggested they'd died of exposure, and fallen from the parapet above. He did not believe that the birds had any connection to Sir Philip's murder.

(CROSSFADE)

CORONER:	Gentlemen of the jury, are you agreed upon your verdict?
MANFRED:	We are, sir. Although our verdict is unprecedented, we find that Sir Philip Ramon died from an unknown cause, but that he was wilfully murdered by a person or persons unknown.

(FULL UP. LIGHT CROWD)

CORONER: Hello, Carson. Wouldn't have expected to find you here. Don't your bankruptcies keep you busy enough? Plenty of businesses seem to be going bust just now.

CARSON: Oh, I took time off. Fascinating affair.

CORONER: Isn't it? Extraordinary. Were you in court all the time?

CARSON: I was.

CORONER: Did you notice what a bright foreman we had?

CARSON: Indeed. He'd make a smarter lawyer than he is a businessman.

CORONER: Why, do you know him?

CARSON: I do, poor devil. Took Etherington's the printers off our hands – thought he was going to set the Thames on fire. Now we've got it back. Said he made a mistake. Can't make a go of it. He says he doesn't like the English weather, either. He's off to sunnier climes. What's his name, now?

CORONER: His name? Oh yes, Manfred.

(BURST OF MUSIC. QUICKLY DOWN FOR)

COMMISSIONER: They beat us, Falmouth. There's no denying it.

FALMOUTH: But how did they do it? That's the question.

COMMISSIONER: And this letter doesn't help.

FALMOUTH: Letter, commissioner?

COMMISSIONER: This arrived here just before you did,

FALMOUTH: How did it get here? Who delivered it?

COMMISSIONER: No, no. it came in the mail, with Her Majesty's portrait in the top right hand corner of the envelope. Listen. "When you receive this…"

(CROSSFADE TO MANFRED)

MANFRED: "When you receive this we, who for want of a better title, call ourselves The Four Just Men will be scattered throughout Europe. Don't bother trying to catch us. You are most unlikely to succeed. I write to tell you that though we did what we said we would, it was with the utmost regret. Sir Philip Ramon's death could have been avoided. One thing did go wrong with our carefully laid plans. They died through an accident. We depended too much on his technical knowledge. He bungled – and paid the price. Perhaps, after the most careful investigation, you will manage to solve the mystery of how Sir Philip Ramon met his death alone, in a locked room, sealed from the outside world. Then you will understand also how it was that our colleague, Thery, met his end.

Farewell. The Four Just Men.

(CROSSFADE)

COMMISSIONER: Farewell. The Four Just Men." This tells us nothing.

FALMOUTH: Careful investigation! We've torn the house in Downing Street apart! We searched it from end to end.

COMMISSIONER: Then let's widen the search. Have you examined the Ramon house in Portland Place?

FALMOUTH: No. Lady Ramon is in residence.

COMMISSIONER: No, no – she's gone back to the country. It's unoccupied at the moment, except for their housekeeper. Go over there now, Falmouth. Search the place.

(EDGE OUT. EDGE IN)

HOUSEKEEPER: Everything is just as Sir Philip left it, sir. The lawyers are due to make an inventory tomorrow. I believe Lady Ramon is going to sell up.

FALMOUTH: I'd like to start with the study.

HOUSEKEEPER: *(moving)* I'll lead the way, sir. It's up on the first floor. No, sir, this staircase. It leads straight to the study door. It's locked. Lady Ramon locked it before she left for the country. Here we are.

(DOOR UNLOCKED. DOOR OPENED)

Please come in. I'll just pull back the curtains. Let in some light.

(HEAVY CURTAINS PULLED APART)

That's better. Oh, good heavens. What's happened to that table? The wood's all blistered.

FALMOUTH: Never mind the table. Just look at that telephone. It's as though it's been struck by lightning. Is this Sir Philip's private line to Downing Street?

HOUSEKEEPER: That's right, sir.

FALMOUTH: Touch nothing. Lock this door again as soon as I leave. Let no-one into this room. Do you understand? No one at all.

(FADE OUT. FADE IN)

FALMOUTH: Sir Philip was electrocuted. They tapped into the wire that led direct from the Portland Place house to Sir Philip's study in Downing Street.

COMMISSIONER: But Lady Ramon was living in Portland Place.

FALMOUTH: They didn't need to get into the house. Once they'd identified the private line, they could tap into it at any point. They planned to use that wire to convey a killing current of electricity from end to end. But something went wrong. At the crucial moment Thery bungled. The surge of current that reached Portland Place was way in excess of what he intended – and it killed him outright. In Downing Street I thought I heard the telephone ring briefly. Sir Philip must have picked up the receiver, and the shock he received was enough to stop his heart and kill him. That scorch mark on his hand had nothing to do with the rose he clutched at.

COMMISSIONER: And the two dead sparrows?

FALMOUTH: They may well have been roosting on the wire itself when the charge went through.

COMMISSIONER: The Four Just Men indeed.

(FULL UP. HOUSE OF COMMONS)

PRIME MINISTER: My right honourable friend was a man of principle. He believed that giving sanctuary to men intent on disruption and revolution in their own countries was wrong. He believed that criminals and anarchists were taking advantage of our traditional tolerance, and that when friendly governments asked us to repatriate them to their own countries, we should comply. For that reason, and to honour the memory of a very brave man that I was proud to call friend, I have decided to take the Aliens Extradition Bill through to its Second Reading myself.

(CRIES OF "HEAR, HEAR")

The debate will take place tomorrow evening at eight-thirty.

(FULL UP BIG BEN STRIKES THE HALF HOUR.
CROSSFADE FINAL CHIME WITH MUSIC.
DOWN FOR CLOSING ANNOUNCEMENT. UP
MUSIC TO END)

THE DAMNED THING

BY AMBROSE BIERCE
DRAMATIZED FOR RADIO
BY NEVILLE TELLER

Running time: 30 minutes

SCHEDULED FOR TRANSMISSION ACROSS
THE USA DURING 2019 IN A PRODUCTION BY
SHOESTRING RADIO THEATRE, SAN FRANCISCO

CHARACTERS IN
ORDER OF APPEARANCE

NARRATOR   *One introductory speech only*

SCHOO   *Around 60. Coroner. Upright, leading citizen of a rather rural and impoverished county. Folksy much of the time, but aware of his formal duties also. Quite shrewd. (Incidentally, Schoo is a real historical character, and was the Coroner of Fremont County in 1910)*

CAMPBELL   *Rugged backwoodsman type, heavy rural dialect*

BILLY   *Bright young lad, an apprentice journalist. Just a few speeches.*

HARKER   *Around 30. Well educated. A seasoned journalist.*

MORGAN   *Around 35-40. Well educated, Much of the time bewildered, distracted, beset by fears of the unknown. Must be able to act out being mauled to death by some huge creature, including some good screaming.*

ROWLAND   *Woman doctor around 40-45. A real historical character – Dr Mary Canaga Rowland was a pioneer woman medical student, and among the first of America's qualified women doctors.*

MRS SCHOO   *Aged around 60, gentle but with some real character. She stands up to Schoo on occasion.*

(SPOOKY MUSIC. DOWN FOR OPENING
ANNOUNCEMENT. MUSIC UP BRIEFLY THEN
FADE BENEATH FOLLOWING)

NARRATOR: Wyoming in 1910 – remote and rural. Cattle ranchers, farmers and homesteaders scratched a livelihood from the vast territory in which the Rocky Mountains meet the Great Plains. In 1910 Wyoming had been one of the United States of America for only 20 years. Administration, law and order were still feeling their way forward. But already well established was the system of county coroners, set in place to investigate unexplained or unnatural deaths – which, sadly, were not uncommon in those rough times.

(FADE IN MURMUR OF MALE VOICES. GAVEL
BANGS ON WOOD. VOICES HUSH)

SCHOO: I guess I don't have to introduce myself to you fellers, but since these proceedings are being taken down in shorthand by young Billy Miller here – you got a great career ahead of you Billy on the Hudson Journal – I'd better get it on the record. I'm Jim Schoo – that's "school" without the "L" – and I'm the coroner in this here Fremont County. Served my first term back in 1897 for seven years, then took up the reins again three years ago. That's enough about me. Now you fellers are my jury, you've all been sworn in, and we're here to decide just how that poor corpse some of you discovered a few days ago met his death.

CAMPBELL: *(calls)* Hey Jim, that wasn't just some corpse. That was Hughie Morgan. We all knew him.

SCHOO: You aren't wrong, Bob. I'll either call him by his name from now on, or refer to him as "the deceased". Now. I'm looking round for our chief witness, but I don't see him in the room. Does anyone know what's become of Mr Harker?

BILLY: Mr Schoo, sir…

SCHOO: Yes, Billy?

BILLY: Mr Harker went down to the telegraph office to post his account to the Journal.

SCHOO: Did he now? I'm not sure I approve of a journalist getting his account into his paper before he's given sworn evidence. How long do you reckon he'll be?

BILLY: The office closes at 6, and it's already past that. He can't be…*[more than a few minutes…]*

(DOOR OPENS)

That's him, now.

HARKER:	*(calls, remote, advancing)* My profound apologies to the court, and to you Mr Coroner.
SCHOO:	We've been waiting for you, Mr Harker. This business must be finished and done with tonight.
HARKER:	Of course. I quite understand, and I'm sorry to have kept you. I wasn't evading your summons. I went to send the Journal an account of what you want me to relate here.
SCHOO:	Well, since this court will have your account direct from you, and ahead of your newspaper, I suppose I can't complain. Though I do hope what you tell this court will be more credible than the sort of beefed up garbage you usually dish up to your readers. I want the plain unvarnished truth, Mr Harker. Not incredible, unbelievable, nonsense.
HARKER:	That goes without saying – even though I'm afraid the facts are indeed incredible. I have a copy of what I sent. It wasn't written as news – I didn't think readers would believe it. So I wrote it as fiction. I'll pass it to you before I leave the court. You may certainly include this copy in the record as part of my testimony under oath.
SCHOO:	Speaking of which, take that Bible in your right hand and read what's on that card there.
HARKER:	I swear to tell the truth, the whole truth, and nothing but the truth, so help me God.

SCHOO: Right. Your full name for the record.

HARKER: William Harker.

SCHOO: How old are you?

HARKER: Twenty-seven.

SCHOO: Your profession?

HARKER: Journalist on the Hudson Journal.

SCHOO: You knew the deceased, Hugh Morgan?

HARKER: I did. Very well.

SCHOO: You were with him when he died?

HARKER: Near him. I was near him.

SCHOO: How did that come about? Your presence, I mean?

HARKER: Well, he was a friend from way back. We'd rather
             lost touch, and then I suddenly had a message
             from him. He wanted me to visit, It so happened
             I had a couple of week's leave due from the paper,
             and we arranged for me to come and stay at
             his place and enjoy some shooting and fishing
             together.

SCHOO: I see. Well that seems reasonable enough.

HARKER: I must admit I had an ulterior motive.

SCHOO: Indeed? What was that?

HARKER: Well, I write fiction from time to time – stories, novels. I have three novels published.

SCHOO: I've read one of them.

(LAUGHTER FROM JURY)

HARKER: I'm flattered. Anyway, a part of my purpose in visiting with him was to study his odd, solitary way of life. I have a new novel in mind, and I had an idea for a character rather on his lines.

CAMPBELL: *(calls)* Hughie Morgan was a right nice guy.

HARKER: Indeed he was. But even his best friends would admit he was a bit of a loner.

CAMPBELL: *(calls)* Fair enough. All of us on the jury would agree with that.

SCHOO: Quite right, Bob. And thank you, Mr Harker. Now if you don't mind, would you please relate the exact circumstances of Hugh Morgan's death. You may use any notes or memoranda that you please.

HARKER: In that case, Mr Coroner, I'll refer to the copy of the account that I have sent to the Journal.

SCHOO: As you please.

(PAPER RUSTLES)

HARKER: *(clears his throat)* Well, four days ago Morgan and I left the house just as dawn was breaking. We each carried a shotgun. We were looking for quail. Morgan said that the best ground was just beyond a certain ridge, so we crossed it by way of a narrow trail that led through the chaparral. Each side of us was a dense thicket of shrubs. We were just emerging from the chaparral to reasonably level ground covered with wild oats, when a little way off to the right, we heard a strange noise.

SCHOO: What sort of noise, Mr Harker? Please be more explicit.

HARKER: Well, at first I thought it was a deer. I actually said to Morgan: "I wish we'd brought a rifle." But he was gazing at the shrubs and bushes waving about, and he suddenly cocked both barrels of his shotgun and raised it, ready to aim.

(FULL UP OPEN AIR. LEAFY BRANCHES WAVED ABOUT VIOLENTLY)

HARKER: *(calls)* Oh come on, Hughie. You're not going to fill up a deer with quail shot, are you?

MORGAN: *(calls)* That ain't no deer, Bill.

HARKER: What you reckon it is, then? Oh God, you don't think it's a grizzly, do you? Come on, we'll tackle this together.

MORGAN: It'll outdo the both of us, Bill. You take my word
            for it.

HARKER: How d'you know that?

MORGAN: We ain't no match for it.

(BRANCHES STOP)

HARKER: It's gone quiet. What is it, Hughie? What the
            devil is it?

MORGAN: *(husky, fearful)* That's it. I don't rightly know. I
            call it – that Damned Thing.

(FADE IN CORONER'S ROOM)

SCHOO: Could you repeat that, Mr Harker?

HARKER: "That Damned Thing". That's what he called it.

SCHOO: That Damned Thing? That suggests that he knew
            what it was, and that he had encountered it before.

HARKER: You may be right. But I wasn't thinking all that
            clearly at the time, because I could see that the
            disturbance had moved in a most inexplicable
            way. It was no long the shrubs, bushes and small
            trees in the chaparral that were waving about, but
            the great field of wild oats in front of us. It looked
            as if it was being stirred by a great wind – but not
            as you'd expect.

SCHOO: Very vividly put, Mr Harker. You follow the best traditions of your profession. But I think you'll have to explain yourself a bit further. What precisely do you mean?

HARKER: Well, when a wind passes over a great plain of oats, the plants bend and recover. But what I saw was quite different. The oats were not merely bent, but they seemed to be pressed down. Crushed. They didn't rise up again. But the terrifying thing was that this crushing motion was advancing towards us.

SCHOO: *(calls)* Yes, Bob?

CAMPBELL: *(calls)* Me and the rest of us here on the jury can't quite get a handle on this.

SCHOO: Not sure I can, either. Mr Harker, what is it exactly that you could see?

HARKER: But I've told you. There was nothing to see, except the oats being crushed, bit by bit, and the crushing getting closer and closer. I'd never seen anything like it in my life. I could see no reason for what was happening. It was like the plants were being trampled under foot, but there was nothing trampling them. And it was advancing towards us, slowly but surely.

SCHOO: Were you frightened?

HARKER: Frightened? No, not really. Disturbed, puzzled.

SCHOO: How about Hugh Morgan?

HARKER: Oh, now, Hughie – he *was* scared. I could scarcely believe it when I saw him suddenly lift his gun to his shoulder and fire both barrels towards the oats. But he was shooting at empty air.

(DOUBLE GUNSHOT, WILD ANIMAL CRY – AS TERRIFYING AS POSSIBLE. IT DIES AWAY. PAUSE. FULL UP CORONER'S ROOM)

SCHOO: A cry you say? Like an animal in pain?

HARKER: That is so, Mr Coroner.

SCHOO: But you saw no animal?

HARKER: No, sir.

CAMPBELL: *(calls)* Mr Schoo, sir.

SCHOO: Yes, Bob.

CAMPBELL: The jury here would like to know if Hughie could have hit an animal when he fired his gun.

SCHOO: Mr Harker?

HARKER: Well, it was a shotgun – and shot goes all over the place, as you know. I suppose it's possible. All I can say is that, to my eyes, he was aiming just above the oats at nothing at all, and he fired into the open air. But then…

SCHOO: Yes, Mr Harker?

HARKER: Then – the next thing – something hit me full in the chest, and I was flung backwards on to the ground.

SCHOO: Something?

HARKER: Some soft, heavy substance. There was so much smoke about because of Hugh Morgan's two shots that I couldn't see what had struck me.

SCHOO: And then?

MORGAN: *(screaming in agony, as if being mauled by a wild beast)*

           (FULL UP SNARLING OF WILD BEAST LIKE A LION MAULING A PREY. FADE EFFECTS AND MORGAN'S SCREAMING RATHER SLOWLY BENEATH FOLLOWING)

HARKER: Well, before I could get back on my feet and recover my gun, I heard Hughie Morgan crying out as if in mortal agony. Terrified I struggled to my feet and looked towards my friend. May heaven in mercy spare me from such a sight again. Less than thirty yards away from me, he was down on one knee, his head thrown back at a frightful angle, and his whole body in violent movement, shaken backward and forward, backward and forward. And horror of horrors, his right arm was flung up pouring with blood, but I could see no hand.

SCHOO: Gentlemen of the jury, the body I examined in the mortuary earlier today has no right hand. What's more, it lacks a left arm altogether.

HARKER: His left arm was invisible to me.

SCHOO: Can you provide the jury over there with a few more details? You've painted a vivid picture of our friend, Hugh Morgan. He seems to have suffered some sort of terrible accident, which may have brought on an epileptic fit. But what else can you recall of the scene?

HARKER: Well, when I try to remember what it was I was seeing, it comes to me that different parts of Hughie's body kept disappearing – as if they were being blotted out. Then a shifting of his position would bring it all into view again.

SCHOO: You mean, what with the terrifying events taking place before you, and the smoke from the shotgun, your eyesight began playing tricks on you?

HARKER: *(hesitant, uncertain)* Ye-es. I suppose so. It's certainly possible.

SCHOO: What did you do? Please tell the court precisely what happened next.

HARKER: Well, it took me only a few seconds to recover. I threw down my gun and ran the thirty yards to my friend. Before I could reach him he was down on the ground and lying still. But horror-struck as I was, I couldn't attend to him directly, because my eyes were fixed on that same mysterious movement of the wild oats. But this time the crushed plants were retreating from the trampled area around me toward the edge of a wood. It was only when they reached the first trees that I was able to look down at my companion. He was quite dead.

SCHOO: Thank you, Mr Harker. You may stand down. Now ladies and gentlemen, and gentlemen of the jury, yesterday morning I had a long discussion about this most extraordinary case with our State Governor. Mr Brooks was insistent that the most experienced and best qualified doctor available should be contacted to assist us in determining the cause of Hugh Morgan's death. He used his good offices in obtaining the services of the highly distinguished physician who has been good enough to join us for this inquest. I call Doctor Mary Canaga Rowland.

CAMPBELL: *(calls)* But she's a woman!

ROWLAND: *(remote, advancing)* I most certainly am. Do you have any objection to that, Mr Foreman?

CAMPBELL: I guess not, Ma'am. 'Cept I ain't never seen a woman doctor before.

ROWLAND: Mr Coroner, before I take the oath, would you object if I made a short statement?

SCHOO: Please go ahead, Dr Rowland.

ROWLAND: Thank you. Firstly, folk are sometimes surprised to learn that the first woman to receive a medical degree did so more than 60 years ago, back in 1849 – and that was Dr Elizabeth Blackwell. Nor is it generally known that, though most doctors in the United States are men of course, no less than 6 per cent are women. I am privileged to count myself among their number – which, I may say, is bound to grow very greatly in the future.

SCHOO: The Governor is sure of it. It was the Governor who told me of you – indeed he recommended you most highly. He also said there's a female surgeon in the US army.

ROWLAND: Perfectly true. That's Dr Mary Edwards Walker. A great friend of mine. Well, having got that out of the way, I trust the jury is satisfied that I'm perfectly qualified to provide the medical evidence you're seeking?

CAMPBELL: *(calls)* I guess so, Ma'am.

SCHOO: Thank you, Bob. Now, Dr Rowland, if you'd take the good book in your right hand and read what's on the card.

ROWLAND: I swear to tell the truth, the whole truth, and nothing but the truth, so help me God.

SCHOO: Would you please provide the jury with a brief summary of your findings?

ROWLAND: I conducted an autopsy on the late Hugh Morgan yesterday, three full days after his death.

SCHOO: The delay being due to…?

ROWLAND: The time taken for the request for an inquest to be conveyed to the Governor, for the Governor's commission to reach me, and for me to travel all the way from Cheyenne.

CAMPBELL: *(calls)* It's a fair old way from Laramie county, ma'am.

SCHOO: It sure is, Bob. Well, you're here now, Dr Rowland. Please continue,

ROWLAND: Mr Morgan was a healthy man of about thirty, in excellent physical condition. But even the fittest individual could not have survived the traumas inflicted on the deceased. I've rarely seen a body more damaged – there were contusions everywhere.

SCHOO: Contusions?

ROWLAND: The body was extensively and very severely bruised. The man seemed to have been crushed or beaten to a pulp. His left arm seems to have been ripped from his body, and his right hand was missing. Moreover the entire skin surface, front and back, was lacerated. In places the skin was hanging off the corpse in strips. The lacerations were particularly severe around the throat. The wounds in that area were akin to those sustained when a wild animal – a lion, or tiger – attacks its prey.

SCHOO: So which do you judge the cause of death, doctor – the contusions or the lacerations?

ROWLAND: In my opinion he was dead before his body was torn to shreds.

SCHOO: I can testify that Hugh Morgan's left arm was with the body when I saw it. His right hand was not. Has it yet been recovered?

ROWLAND: I checked with the morgue earlier today. It has not.

SCHOO: I see. What, in your professional opinion, caused these extensive wounds?

ROWLAND: Some sort of wild animal is my best guess. The country round here is pretty rugged. You know better than I do what creatures roam these parts.

SCHOO: We sure do. Thank you Dr Rowland. You have been extremely helpful. Now, gentlemen of the jury, we have no more evidence to lay before you. Your duty has already been explained to you. If there's nothing you wish to ask, you may go outside and consider your verdict. Yes, Bob?

CAMPBELL: Before we do that, Jim – er, Mr Coroner – as foreman I'd like to ask Mr Harker something.

SCHOO: You may certainly do so. Yes?

CAMPBELL: I'm speaking for all of us. Mr Harker, what asylum did you escape from?

SCHOO: Mr Harker, the gentlemen of the jury are enquiring what asylum you last escaped from? *(pause)* I have put the question, Mr Foreman, but the witness declines to answer.

HARKER: I do, Mr Coroner. But if the court has done insulting me, sir, I do have a request.

SCHOO: Indeed, Mr Harker. And what might that be?

HARKER: That book you have there. I recognize it as Hugh Morgan's diary. I noticed you reading parts of it while I was giving my testimony.

SCHOO: I was glancing through it.

HARKER: I should like very much to see it. May I? I'm sure the public would be extremely interested in whatever Mr Morgan...*[might have said in the] days before his...]*.

SCHOO: This book. Mr Harker, will not figure in the inquest. Obviously all the entries in it were made while Mr Morgan was still alive, and therefore have no relevance to the issue we are considering today – which is precisely how our friend met his death.

HARKER: As you wish.

SCHOO: Well now, gentlemen of the jury, you may retire to consider your verdict.

CAMPBELL: There's not much need for that. Just give us a minute, will you Mr Coroner?

SCHOO: Take all the time you want.

(COURTROOM BACKGROUND. WHISPERING)

SCHOO: *(pause)* Ah, I see you've finished your deliberations. Bob – Mr Foreman – have you reached a verdict?

CAMPBELL: We sure have, Mr Coroner. *(slow, as if writing)* Just – give – me – a – minute to finish writing it out… There.

SCHOO: Is this a verdict you're all agreed on?

CAMPBELL: It is.

SCHOO: Then what have you agreed?

CAMPBELL: *(reading)* We, the jury, find that the late Hughie Morgan came to his death by way of an encounter with a mountain lion.

(CHORDS OF MUSIC LIKE A FINALE, FOLLOWED BY MELODY. HOLD A LITTLE. DOWN FOR FOLLOWING, AND FADE OUT UNDERNEATH. HOTEL BEDROOM. KNOCKING ON DOOR FROM OUTSIDE)

ROWLAND: *(calling)* Yes? Who is it? I'm just coming. A minute.

(UNLOCKING. DOOR OPENS)

Oh, it's you. Mr Harker, isn't it? I'm giving no interviews to the Press.

HARKER: No, no, Dr Rowland. I'm not here professionally. Not at all. May I come in?

ROWLAND: I suppose so.

(DOOR CLOSES)

Make yourself comfortable – well, as comfortable as a hotel bedroom allows. Use that easy chair. I'll sit here. Yes, Mr Harker. What can I do for you?

HARKER: I find this a little awkward. I do hope you'll forgive me, Dr Rowland…

ROWLAND: Oh, do stop beating about the bush, man. Out with it. What is it you want of me?

HARKER: Dr Rowland, whatever you thought of the account I gave of how my friend met his death, I want to assure you that it's God's own truth. I know the jury didn't believe me – well, they showed that by their verdict – and I dare say you don't either.

ROWLAND: I'll tell you what I believe, Mr Harker. It's perfectly clear to me that your friend was attacked by a vicious wild animal – an animal that crushed and mauled him to death. It probably severed his right hand with one snap of its jaws, and almost certainly consumed it. The jury believe it was a mountain lion. I suppose it could have been.

HARKER: If it was a mountain lion, then I didn't see it. Dr Rowland I saw no wild animal at all – and I'll swear that Hugh Morgan didn't either. Hugh saw what I saw – but the difference was that he knew what it was he was seeing. He'd seen it before. He recognized it.

ROWLAND: That Damned Thing?

HARKER: Precisely. Which is why it's vitally important that I get to see that diary of his which Mr Schoo refused to hand over. You see, if Hugh had come across this Thing before, then he must have recorded those encounters.

ROWLAND: Are you saying that Mr Schoo read those accounts, and decided for reasons of his own to suppress them?

HARKER: I suppose I am.

ROWLAND: But what reason could he possibly have for doing so?

HARKER: I don't know. Nor can anyone know till whatever Hugh Morgan wrote is revealed.

ROWLAND: But why on earth have you come to me, Mr Harker? What do you think I can do about it?

HARKER: As you can tell from what passed in court a few hours ago, I am not in good standing with Mr Schoo. He believes I sensationalize the truth in order to gratify my readers. He certainly gave little credence to my account of my friend's death – all that about me escaping from an asylum. I know I'd be wasting my time if I went and asked him to hand over that diary.

ROWLAND: But you think that if I did...?

HARKER: Precisely. You are in extremely good standing with him, Dr Rowland. What is even more to the point, you will be leaving Fremont County tomorrow. Letting you view the diary would have little if any repercussions on the local community. If you were to suggest a professional interest in identifying "That Damned Thing" that Hugh Morgan referred to...

ROWLAND: Well, you've certainly aroused my curiosity, Mr Harker.

HARKER: So you'll do it?

ROWLAND:	What's the time?

| HARKER: | Nine-thirty. Ideal. He'll have finished dinner, and be relaxing with a glass of something. Just in the mood to be generous. Look, Dr Rowland, you must ask to borrow the diary overnight, and swear to return it to him before you leave for Cheyenne tomorrow. I'll wait for you here, and we can go over it together. What do you say? |

(VERY SLOW FADE ON FOLLOWING SPEECH)

| ROWLAND: | Oh, why not? I'll get my hat and coat. Do you happen to know where the Schoos live? |

(FADE IN)

| ROWLAND: | It's very good of you to see me, Mrs Schoo. I'm afraid it's rather late. |

| MRS SCHOO: | Not at all, Dr Rowland. I know you leave us tomorrow morning. |

| SCHOO: | Tell me, Dr Rowland, how do you find our one hostelry here in Lander? |

| ROWLAND: | Oh, it's comfortable enough, Mr Schoo. |

| MRS SCHOO: | I must say I feel terribly guilty for not being able to offer you our hospitality. But as you can see the house has been virtually given over to the builders. We have one living room and our bedroom at the |

moment. Even our domestics have had to lodge out overnight.

ROWLAND: I'm sure the house will be quite splendid when all the work is completed.

MRS SCHOO: Well, I certainly hope so. I suppose you have come to see my husband?

SCHOO: Don't try to excuse yourself, my dear. You know there's nowhere for you to retire to.

MRS SCHOO: That's true enough.

ROWLAND: I have nothing confidential to say, Mr Schoo, though I do come as a result of the inquest.

MRS SCHOO: That poor Mr Morgan.

ROWLAND: Indeed. And the verdict has been preying on my mind somewhat.

SCHOO: Really? In what way, Dr Rowland?

ROWLAND: Well, I am most certainly of the opinion that Mr Morgan was attacked by some form of ferocious wild beast, Excuse me, Mrs Schoo, if I don't go into the details – they are too horrible to contemplate. What stays in my mind is one detail in Mr Harker's evidence.

SCHOO: I'm afraid that I rather discounted much of what he said.

ROWLAND: And I can understand why. But what struck me as possibly true was his insistence that Mr Morgan had encountered this creature before. The phrase "That Damned Thing" sticks in my mind. I can't see why Mr Harker would have invented that.

MRS SCHOO: That poor Mr Morgan. He took the death of his wife very badly.

SCHOO: A good few years ago now. He closed in on himself. Became almost a hermit. I suppose it says something for young Mr Harker that he remained a friend.

ROWLAND: That's what bothers me, I suppose. Granted that Mr Harker is a somewhat sensational journalist, is his whole account of his friend's death an invention? Or are parts of it true – for example that Hugh Morgan had actually encountered this creature before? Tell me, Mr Schoo – did Mr Morgan mention earlier encounters in his diary?

SCHOO: Dr Rowland, let me be frank with you. I've looked through that diary kept by Mr Morgan, and I'm very anxious that its contents should not be made public.

MRS SCHOO: John!

SCHOO: I have very good reasons, Elizabeth. It would do our community no good at all to know what it contains.

ROWLAND: Mr Schoo, as you know I'm leaving Fremont County tomorrow morning, probably never to return. May I ask you to let me borrow that diary overnight? I give you my word that I'll return it to you first thing in the morning – and I guarantee that nothing in it will ever reach the public.

MRS SCHOO: John?

SCHOO: Dr Rowland, I'm the appointed coroner for this county. I am one of its leading citizens. I feel a sense of responsibility for this place and for everyone who lives here. It's far from a prosperous part of these United States. The people here are industrious and hard-working, but many are poor and ill-educated. Old superstitions like belief in evil spirits, belief in the devil, die hard. I don't want to see this community riven by mass panic. They have enough of a struggle making a decent living.

MRS SCHOO: Are you saying mass panic is what's likely to happen, John, if the contents of that book get known?

SCHOO: I fear it may, Elizabeth. All the same, Dr Rowland, I of course accept your word. In the spirit of professional cooperation I am quite content to loan you Hugh Morgan's diary. This I can tell you – nothing in it will challenge what you testified in court as to the cause of his death.

ROWLAND: Well, that is good to know, Mr Schoo.

SCHOO: I have the volume here, by me. I entrust it to your safekeeping.

ROWLAND: It'll be back in your hands by nine o'clock tomorrow.morning. I can assure you of that.

(CROSSFADE TO MUSIC. DOWN FOR FOLLOWING AND LOSE UNDERNEATH)

MORGAN: *(as narrator)* September the 1st. Out in the chaparral with the shot gun. Mid-afternoon I noticed Scratch behaving very oddly. He'd run in a half-circle, keeping his head turned always toward the centre. Then he'd stand still, barking furiously. He did this several times. Finally he ran away into the brush as fast as he could. I thought at first that he'd gone mad, but returning to the house I found no alteration in his manner. He was as normal as ever. We know a dog's sense of smell is ten times more powerful than our own. Can a dog actually see with his nose, I wonder? Do odours produce some picture in his brain?

September the 2nd. Never mind Scratch – is it me that's going mad? Looking at the stars last night as they rose above the ridge that lies east of the house, I saw them successively disappear – from left to right. Each was eclipsed for an instant, and only a few at the same time, but all were blotted out right along the ridge. It was as if something had passed along between me and them. But I could not see it. And there weren't enough stars to define its outline. Ugh! I don't like this. Not at all.

(FULL UP. HOTEL BEDROOM)

HARKER: But Dr Rowland, this is precisely the sort of thing I saw, the day he died. It's what I was trying to tell the court this afternoon.

ROWLAND: And this was the first time Hugh Morgan encountered it? Only – what – two months ago?

HARKER: It would seem so. What's next?

ROWLAND: This doesn't seem to follow. Oh look, several pages have been torn out. I do hope Mr Schoo won't think I did that.

HARKER: I wouldn't worry about that, Dr Rowland. I should think he has examined this book very closely. I'd wager anything that he knows all about the missing pages.

MORGAN: *(as narrator)* September the 27th. It has been about here again. I find evidence of its presence every day. I watched again all of last night in the same cover, gun in hand, double-charged with buckshot. In the morning the fresh footprints were there, as before. Yet I would have sworn that I didn't sleep – indeed, these days I hardly sleep at all. It is all terrible, insupportable. If these amazing experiences are real, I shall go mad. If they aren't really happening, then I'm mad already.

HARKER: What do *you* think, Dr Rowland? Had he lost his mind? Was he imagining impossible things?

ROWLAND: I don't know what to think, Mr Harker. He seems rational enough. Oh, my goodness. Look at these next entries.

MORGAN: *(as narrator)* October the 3rd. I won't go. It won't drive me away. No – this is my house. This is my land. I won't go! God hates a coward.

October the 5th. I can stand it no longer. If I stay here alone, I will indeed go mad. No, I've invited William Harker to spend a few weeks with me. He has a level head. If I'm going mad, he'll tell me. He'll help me.

ROWLAND: And was that what happened, Mr Harker?

HARKER: Not exactly. I certainly found him very stressed when I arrived. The next day we went out shooting together, and he was on edge all the time. But he never told me why, nor did he ask me to help him. In fact, he seemed to calm down in the next few days.

ROWLAND: So nothing untoward happened?

HARKER: Not till that last terrible day, no. One evening we were sitting on the front porch, drinking together. We'd spent more than a week in each others' company, out on the savanah most of the day fishing and shooting together, and we were enjoying the last of another peaceful day. It seemed to me at one moment as though he was on the verge of asking me something. Or perhaps telling me something. But the moment passed. Next day...

ROWLAND: Well, let's look at his next entries.

MORGAN: *(as narrator)* October the 7th. Now I understand. At last I understand. It came to me suddenly last night – a flash of inspiration. How simple – how terribly simple. There are sounds that the human ear cannot hear. At the top and the bottom of the scale, there are sounds that we cannot detect, although some animals can hear and respond to them. How can thousands of birds all take off suddenly together, unless there's some sort of signal that no human ear could catch? How can bats fly and hunt in complete darkness? It's known that a school of whales, basking on the ocean, miles apart, will sometimes dive at the same instant – all gone out of sight in a moment. A signal has been sounded – a signal too deep for the ear of a sailor up the mast, or for his comrades on deck, to discern. But what they do experience are its vibrations in the ship – and they talk of it as being like a cathedral whose very foundations are stirred by the bass notes of the organ.

And as with sounds, so it is with colours. At each end of the spectrum, scientists can detect the presence of what are known as "actinic" rays. They represent colours which our human eyes are unable to discern. The colours of the rainbow extend in both directions well beyond what we think of as the normal seven, although we cannot see them. Perhaps other creatures can. Who knows? The important thing is that I'm not mad. I'm not mad. There are certainly colours that we can't see. And, God help me, that Damned Thing is a creature of such a colour.

ROWLAND: That poor man believed that some freak of nature was haunting him. We now know much more about the science of genetics than Mr Charles Darwin. Your poor friend came to believe that some massive animal which, through a genetic mishap, had been born with a coat of a color beyond the normal spectrum...

HARKER: ...thus rendering it invisible!

ROWLAND: ...precisely – that such an animal was stalking him It's beyond the bounds of belief,

HARKER: Maybe. But it's consistent with what I saw that terrible day, when my poor friend was mauled to death by a creature that I certainly couldn't see – perhaps indeed a mountain lion.

(REPEAT EARLIER SOUND EFFECT)

MORGAN: *(screaming in agony, as if being mauled by a wild beast)*

(FULL UP SNARLING OF WILD BEAST LIKE A LION MAULING A PREY. FADE EFFECTS AND MORGAN'S SCREAMING RATHER SLOWLY UNDER FOLLOWING)

ROWLAND: You believe whatever you wish, Mr Harker. There are certainly other explanations of how poor Mr Morgan met his death. But I can understand perfectly why Mr Schoo would wish to prevent this diary from becoming generally known. There

505

have been no other unexplained incidents since Mr Morgan met his death. Why terrify people with tales of a ferocious, but totally invisible, animal roaming the countryside? A tale dreamed up in the brain of a man who feared he was going mad? I shall return this book to Mr Schoo first thing in the morning, and try to forget that I ever read it. And I trust you will keep your word to me, Mr Harker, and also expunge this from your mind.

(FADE IN MUSIC UNDER THE FOLLOWING, PRE-SET TO END JUST AFTER CLOSING ANNOUNCEMENT)

HARKER: I will certainly honour my promise, Dr Rowland. But as a journalist, I must make one tiny reservation. If by any chance further mysterious deaths started to occur in this county, I reserve the right to go back to Mr Schoo and seek his permission to reveal what my friend, Hugh Morgan, has set down. If nothing further occurs, my lips are sealed.

ROWLAND: Then I'm pretty sure your lips are sealed for ever. For if that creature did exist, I reckon it was mortally wounded by Hugh Morgan.

HARKER: We shall see, Dr Rowland. We shall see.

(UP MUSIC. DOWN FOR CLOSING ANNOUNCEMENT. UP MUSIC TO END)